D0990017

'MAY 2018

Gilgamesh among Us

Frontispiece. *Statue of a Hero (Gilgamesh?) Taming a Lion.*
From the Palace of Sargon II, King of Assur in Khorsabad. Louvre,
Paris. Photo Erich Lessing. Permission of Art Resource, NY.

Gilgamesh among Us

Modern Encounters with the Ancient Epic

Theodore Ziolkowski

Cornell University Press

Ithaca and London

First published 2011 by Cornell University Press
Printed in the United States of America

Library of Congress Cataloging-in-Publication Data

Ziolkowski, Theodore.
    Gilgamesh among us : modern encounters with the ancient epic / Theodore Ziolkowski.
        p. cm.
    Includes bibliographical references and index.
    ISBN 978-0-8014-5035-8 (cloth : alk. paper)
    1. Gilgamesh.   2. Gilgamesh—Adaptations.   3. Gilgamesh—Influence.   I. Title.
    PJ3771.G6Z56 2012
    892'.1—dc23   2011027253

Cornell University Press strives to use environmentally responsible suppliers and materials to the fullest extent possible in the publishing of its books. Such materials include vegetable-based, low-VOC inks and acid-free papers that are recycled, totally chlorine-free, or partly composed of nonwood fibers. For further information, visit our website at www .cornellpress.cornell.edu.

Cloth printing   10   9   8   7   6   5   4   3   2   1

For our oldest friend
Arthur Fort Harman III
Who shares our Montevallo memories

Contents

Preface

Why is a scholar of modern European literature writing about Gilgamesh? This book began as chapter 2 of a work tentatively entitled "The Road to Hell," in which I planned to explore modern literary variations of such mortuary journeys as those depicted in the myths and literatures of the ancient Near East, Greece, and Rome and in the Christian tradition. But when I had finished the introduction and turned to the epic of Gilgamesh as the earliest ancient example, my material rapidly reached a point at which I realized that the topic deserved more extensive scrutiny—treatment perhaps analogous to that of my earlier books *Virgil and the Moderns, Ovid and the Moderns,* and *Minos and the Moderns.* So I abandoned the initial project and devoted myself instead to the modern reception of Gilgamesh.

I can no longer recall when I first encountered Gilgamesh or in which translation I first read the epic. By the time I was a graduate student of German literature at Yale University in the early 1950s, I was familiar with the epic because it figured in the thought and works of so many of the modern writers with whom I was concerned: notably Rainer Maria Rilke, Hermann Hesse, and Thomas Mann, but also Hans Henny Jahnn, Carl Gustav Jung, and others. For many years that great foundation stone of world literature remained little more than that for me: a touchstone in my reading of various modern writers. Gradually, as the occurrence of such cases—translations, retellings, adaptations, musical and visual versions—became more frequent, I began noting them sporadically. The first opportunity to discuss the epic, if only briefly, presented itself in the opening pages of *The Sin of Knowledge: Ancient Themes and Modern Variations*.

It was only when I had committed myself to a book on "Gilgamesh and the Moderns" that I began to look systematically for modernizations of the theme in Western literature and culture and to acquaint myself with the fascinating story of the rediscovery of the epic, its early decipherment and study by professional scholars of the Near East, and its initial transmission and reception by a broader public. I should emphasize at the outset that I am by no stretch of the imagination an Assyriologist: I can neither decipher the cuneiform script nor translate the transliterated text. I have studied extensively and appreciatively many works by the scholars of Mesopotamian literature of the past century and a half and made grateful use of their findings. However, I was reassured that my enterprise would not be utterly pretentious by the fact that, almost without exception, the modern Western writers with whom I deal also knew no Akkadian and relied solely on translations in their various languages. Indeed, even many "translations" of the epic are not based on the original but have been adapted from other translations. (I have tried to indicate these distinctions consistently.)

Unlike classical antiquity, where one can usually take for granted at least a modest acquaintance with Latin and Greek on the part of writers who take their subjects from that realm, Mesopotamian culture offers a wholly different set of problems. That realm, whose glories have been exposed to our eyes by first-rate scholars of the Near East, has in the past half-century caught the imagination not only of novelists, poets, dramatists, composers, and graphic artists but also of the general public in the Western world. Their vivid response, I believe, now deserves at least a preliminary assessment. (I leave it to the appropriately qualified scholars to explore the resonance of the epic in modern Arabic literatures and in the Far East.)

Apart from a few articles comparing Gilgamesh with individual works from the twentieth century, which I have cited in the notes, I know of only two general studies. Christine Hopps's innovative dissertation "My-thotextuality and the Evolution of Ideologies: The Reuse of the 'Epic of Gilgamesh' in North American Texts" (Université de Sherbrooke, 2001) discusses several, though by no means all, novels, adaptations, television programs, and children's books published in Québécois and English in Canada and the United States. In her feminist analysis, Hopps organizes her twelve writers into three categories of four each: "Goddess Rising," or the effort in the 1960s and 1970s, based on newly discovered Sumerian texts, to reinstate Ishtar and the other goddesses in the matriarchal roles from which, according to her theory, they were dethroned by the later Akkadi-ans; "Mythic Authority" of the next two decades, which sought to devalue the positive role of women; and "Mythotextual Dialogues," which enter into discourse with the ancient epic. While I do not follow or in every case agree with Hopps's categorizations, I have referred in several instances to her insightful discussion of individual works. Jürgen Joachimsthaler's suc-cinct survey "Die Rezeption des Gilgamesch-Epos in der deutschsprachi-gen Literatur" (in *Literatur und Geschichte: Festschrift für Erwin Leibfried,* ed. Sascha Feuchert, Joanna Jablkowska, and Jörg Riecke (Frankfurt am Main: Peter Lang, 2007], 147–61) restricts itself, as the title indicates, to German literature and organizes the material, more bibliographically than analytically, into three rather loose categories: (1) works that see the epic as an "Ur-Text" representing primordial values; (2) those that regard it as an occasion for "fabulizing narration"; and (3) those that use it for "the deconstruction of all cultural security." My own comparative analysis of the reception proceeds in a wholly different manner. Gianna Zocco's *Sag an, mein Freund, die Ordnung der Unterwelt: Das Gilgamesch-Epos in Hans Henny Jahnns "Fluß ohne Ufer,"* Wiener Beiträge zu Komparatistik und Romanistik 17 (Frankfurt am Main: Peter Lang, 2010), reached me only after my book was in production. It includes a brief look at the reception in Germany and internationally and cites, without further discussion, a few of the works treated in my book.

Of course no study of reception can reasonably aspire to absolute com-pleteness: a new novel or opera or graphical work may appear today or tomorrow. It was only in the course of writing that I became aware of Anna Ghadaban's gouaches and Jenny Lewis's verse drama, both from 2009. Moreover, I have made no effort to include, apart from representative and influential examples, all the translations, versions, and audio recordings listed in John Maier's extensive bibliography *Gilgamesh: A Reader* or cited more recently on the Internet.

What one can hope to achieve, however, is at least a representative coverage: a selection that indicates the variety of forms in which a theme has manifested itself in Western culture and—of equal significance—an analysis that suggests some of the reasons for its appeal to different generations and to readers in different countries. That is what I have tried to accomplish for the Gilgamesh epic in its general cultural—not scholarly and Assyriological—reception since its rediscovery almost a century and a half ago. The introduction and first chapter sketch the background: the rediscovery of the twelve tablets in 1872; the first translations and earliest literary treatments; the reasons for the epic's initial appeal in the last decades of the nineteenth century to a broader public, notably in Germany, England, and the United States; and its sporadic literary reception in the first half of the twentieth century. Chapters 2 through 5 then survey chronologically the spread of the epic across various countries and in different artistic genres in the years since the Second World War and consider some of the most conspicuous factors that account for its popularity. I was surprised and gratified, as I began to summarize and consolidate my findings for the conclusion, to realize how neatly Gilgamesh could be slotted into the matrix of my other books and articles going back some forty years, many of which stem from a concern with the role of religion and myth in the modern world.

A word about the title. Initially, I had planned, following the model of several earlier books of mine, to call this one "Gilgamesh and the Moderns." But it soon became clear that the astonishing popularity of Gilgamesh was not due to the classic modern writers and artists, who were drawn to such themes of Greek antiquity as Homer's *Odyssey* or the Minoan legends of Europa and the Bull or of the Minotaur and were attracted to such Roman poets as Virgil and Ovid, Horace and Catullus. Indeed, the epic of Gilgamesh was just barely beginning to become known when those modernists flourished in the first half of the twentieth century, and apart from brief mentions in Germany, I am aware of only a few works dealing with Gilgamesh by writers or artists considered typically "modern." Instead, for reasons yet to be considered, that Sumerian hero rose to his new glory among later generations of readers and writers in the second half of the twentieth century and the first decade of the twenty-first: our contemporaries. Indeed, unlike most other figures from myth, literature, and history, "Gilgamesh" has established himself as an autonomous entity or simply a name, often independent of the epic context in which he originally became known. (As analogous examples, one might think, for instance, of the Minotaur or Frankenstein's monster.) For this reason his name is italicized in the text only when it occurs within a specific title, and not when it refers to the hero or to the epic generally.

The hero's name as well as other personal and place names are spelled variously in the different languages and texts: Utnapishtim, for instance, occurs with and without the final "m" or a hyphen after "Ut" and in other variants. While I have tended (except in titles) to standardize "Gilgamesh," in other cases—for local color or for precision when the authors intentionally reverted to the older Sumerian names ("Ziusudra" for "Utnapishtim," for instance)—I have normally retained the original spelling or form, to the extent that the references are absolutely clear. I have often recapitulated the plots of novels and plays—in part because several are not available in English but, more importantly, because the thematic interests of the individual authors emerge essentially from their varying treatments of the basic story: their additions, deletions, and thematic emphases. All translations, unless otherwise noted, are my own.

With this book more than any other I have relied heavily and gratefully on the good will and expertise of the Interlibrary Loan Services of Princeton University and on the rich resources of the Princeton Theological Seminary Library and the Staatsbibliothek in Berlin. John Larson, archivist of the Oriental Institute of the University of Chicago, provided me with otherwise unavailable biographical information on Alexander Heidel. Lisa J. Radcliff, Sylvie Brière, Robert Desmarais, and Charles Bernstein all offered useful assistance by pointing me in the right direction in the matter of copyrights. Thanks to Peter Potter of Cornell University Press, who provided constant encouraging support, I benefited from the careful and sympathetic reading of a knowledgeable specialist in ancient Near Eastern studies. I am grateful to Martin Schneider for his incisive copyediting of my manuscript. Again it has been a pleasure to work with Susan Barnett, Karen M. Laun, and the other gratifyingly responsive colleagues of the professional staff at Cornell University Press. It goes without saying that any mistakes are my own responsibility.

This project was encouraged from the start by my son Eric Ziolkowski, Dana Professor of Religious Studies at Lafayette College, who first read

Gilgamesh as a freshman in college and for the past twenty years has regularly treated the epic in his course on world religions. Himself the author of a provocative piece on the epic's reception ("An Ancient Newcomer to Modern Culture," *World Literature Today* 81 (2007): 55–57), he generously lent me his extensive collection of recordings of Gilgamesh music, to which I frequently refer. Finally, no one can attest better than my wife Yetta, who patiently shared our life with him day in and day out for many months, that Gilgamesh is still among us.

ACKNOWLEDGMENTS

For their assistance in obtaining copies of the illustrations for this volume, and the authorization to use them, I would like to thank the following individuals and institutions: Melissa Acosta and Steven Ferguson of Special Collections, Princeton University Library; Tricia Smith of Art Resource; Andrea Fisher of Artist Rights Society; and Dr. Corinna Höper and Ilona Lütken of Staatsgalerie Stuttgart.

It is a special pleasure to express my appreciation to Hillary Major, Michel Garneau and Derrek Hines for their generous permission to use lines from their copyrighted poetry. I am also indebted to the following individuals and publishers for permission to reprint:

Lines from Rudolf Pannwitz, *Das namenlose Werk*. Munich: Hans Carl, 1920. Reprinted with permission of Fachverlag Hans Carl GmbH, Nuremberg.

Lines from F. L. Lucas, *Gilgamesh: King of Erech*. London: Golden Cockerel Press, 1948. Reprinted courtesy of Andrew Lindesay of Golden Cockerel Press Ltd.

Lines from D. G. Bridson, *The Quest of Gilgamesh.* © 1972 by D. G. Bridson. Reprinted courtesy of Sebastian Carter of Rampant Lions Press.

Lines from Charles Olson, *The Maximus Poems.* Berkeley: University of California Press, 1985. Works by Charles Olson published during his lifetime are copyright © the Estate of Charles Olson. Used with permission and courtesy of Archives and Special Collections, Thomas J. Dodd Research Center, University of Connecticut Libraries.

Lines from Michel Garneau, *Gilgamesh: Théâtre.* Montréal-Nord: VLB, 1976. Reprinted courtesy of Michel Garneau.

All Louis Zukofsky material © Paul Zukofsky; the material may not be reproduced, quoted, or used in any manner whatsoever without the explicit and specific permission of the copyright holder.

Lines from Peter Huchel, "Die Neunte Stunde," from *Gesammelte Werke.* © 1984 by Suhrkamp Verlag. Reprinted with permission of Suhrkamp Verlag GmbH & Co.

Lines from Stephen Mitchell, *Gilgamesh: A New English Translation.* © 2000 by Stephen Mitchell. Reprinted with permission of Free Press, a Division of Simon and Schuster, Inc. All rights reserved.

Lines from Edwin Morgan, *The Play of Gilgamesh.* © 2005 by Edwin Morgan. Reprinted with permission of Carcanet Press.

Lines from Hillary Major, *Gilgamesh Remembers a Dream.* Hollins University *Album,* spring 2000; rpt. in Benjamin R. Foster, ed., *The Epic of Gilgamesh* (New York: Norton, 2001). Reprinted courtesy of Hillary Major.

Lines from Anne-Marie Beeckman, *Gilgameš.* © 2008 by Pierre Mainard. Reprinted by courtesy of Pierre Mainard.

Excerpt from GILGAMESH, translated by Herbert Mason. Copyright © 1970, renewed 1998 by Herbert Mason. Reprinted by permission of Houghton Mifflin Harcourt Publishing Company. All rights reserved.

Lines from Raoul Schrott, *Gilgamesch. Epos.* Nachdichtung und Neuübersetzung von Raoul Schrott. Mit einem wissenschaftlichen Anhang von Robert Rollinger und Wolfgang Schretter. © 2001 Carl Hanser Verlag München. Reprinted by courtesy of Carl Hanser Verlag.

Lines from Derrek Hines, *Gilgamesh.* London: Chatto and Windus, 2002; and from Derrek Hines, *Gilgamesh: The Play.* London: Oberon, 2007. Reprinted courtesy of Derrek Hines.

GILGAMESH AMONG US

INTRODUCTION

Can there still, in the early twenty-first century, be any educated person who has not been exposed, at least casually, to the tale of Gilgamesh? In the mid-twentieth century a Swiss scholar could lament that Gilgamesh was but a "remote topic" that had not become, like *The Iliad* and *The Odyssey,* part of the Western cultural tradition.[1] That same year, 1952, as though to exemplify his point, it did not occur to Robert Hutchins and Mortimer Adler to include the epic of Gilgamesh in the fifty-four volumes of their *Great Books of the Western World* nor, thirty-five years later, to the editors of the *Norton Anthology of World Masterpieces* (1987).

Today the situation has changed dramatically, sometimes even reaching comic extremes. Gilgamesh opens the Prentice-Hall *World of Literature* (1999), the *Norton Anthology of World Literature* (2003), the *Bedford Anthology of World Literature* (2004), and the *Columbia Anthology of Gay Literature* (1998). Heralded as "the world's first novel" (Steven Moore, *The Novel: An Alternative History,* 2010), it is available in well over a dozen recent English translations and, according to the UNESCO *Index Translationum,* some seventy-four versions worldwide. It has been widely adopted in college courses on comparative literature, the history of religion, and world mythologies. In 2009 the story was featured online in "Kidipede—History and Science for Middle School Kids," as a video created by American students for their high school mythology class, and in "Unsucky English Lectures" by the education editor and writer Clay Burell. In addition to a 26-episode Japanese *anime* television series, youthful devotees can enjoy Gilgamesh in illustrated versions, comic books, and video games. The myth is known to music lovers in the operas created by Bohuslav Martinů and Per Nørgård and to fans of musical theater in other manifestations. The aficionado can wear a Gilgamesh T-shirt; dine at Gilgamesh, a London restaurant featuring "Babylonian-style space" and Pan-Asian cuisine; and drink tea from a Gilgamesh mug while perusing books about Assyrians published by the Gilgamesh Press and waiting to attend performances by the Gilgamesh Theatre Group of New York or by jazz-rock bands from Great Britain and Japan styling themselves "Gilgamesh."

By what process did this hero of a Mesopotamian epic from the third millennium B.C.E. become a twenty-first-century cultural icon?

The Story

The basic storyline in its most familiar form (the so-called Standard Version) goes as follows.[2] Gilgamesh, the king of Uruk, is two-thirds god (from his mother Ninsun), one-third human (from his father, the former King Lugalbanda), and "heroic in stature." Increasingly tyrannical, he harries the young men of the city and pursues the young women to such an extent that the citizens complain to the deities. The goddess Aruru from a lump of clay creates Enkidu, a wild man of the steppes who grazes with the gazelles and drinks at the watering hole with the other beasts. When he destroys a hunter's traps and snares, the man's father instructs him to notify Gilgamesh and to seek out a harlot to entrap the creature. He does so and brings back Shamhat, who strips off her clothes and seduces Enkidu in a sexually explicit manner. When, sated from coupling with her for six days and seven nights, he seeks to return to his herds, the beasts of the field shy away from his defiled body. So he stays with Shamhat, who intrigues him with stories about Uruk and Gilgamesh, telling him that Gilgamesh has already foreseen his appearance in two dreams: one in which a great rock from the heavens falls at his feet, and another in which he finds an axe in the streets of Uruk. At a shepherds' camp, Enkidu learns the ways of humankind: to eat and drink prepared foods (bread and ale), groom himself, and dress in woven garments. In appreciation Enkidu protects their flocks at night from wolves and lions. At length, a stranger passing through the camp on his way to attend a wedding banquet in Uruk relates that Gilgamesh, who enjoys the *jus primae noctis*,[3] will be the first to couple with the wife-to-be. Enkidu is outraged at this news and goes straight to Uruk, where the people recognize in him a fitting rival for mighty Gilgamesh. When the king arrives at the wedding house, Enkidu blocks his way and they fight furiously to a draw. (Some translators give the match to Gilgamesh, some to Enkidu; the text is ambiguous.) Recognizing themselves as equals, they embrace in friendship, and Gilgamesh introduces him to his mother Ninsun as his brother.

Gilgamesh proposes an adventure to his new friend: to slay the monster Humbaba in the sacred Forest of Cedar. Enkidu, who while roaming with his herd learned of the terrible Humbaba, whose very breath is death, warns against the enterprise, but Gilgamesh shames him into agreement. Despite the warnings of the city's elders and Ninsun's worried prayers, they set out for the distant Forest of Cedar on Mount Lebanon. During the journey Gilgamesh has a number of frightening dreams, which Enkidu interprets in a reassuring manner. When they reach the forest and creep up the mountain, Humbaba hears them and reproaches Enkidu, the man of nature, for betraying his kind. Gilgamesh is frightened by the giant's appearance, but, roused by the sun god Shamash, the Thirteen Winds come to their aid and blind Humbaba, who pleads for his life. Enkidu urges Gilgamesh to kill the ogre before the gods hear of their sacrilegious actions. As Humbaba curses them, Gilgamesh cuts off his head and Enkidu pulls out his lungs. Felling a lofty cedar, they float the timber down the Euphrates with Humbaba's head in tow.

When they get back to Uruk, the goddess Ishtar, enflamed by Gilgamesh's glory, urges him to wed her, but Gilgamesh insults her by recounting the many earlier lovers whom she has betrayed. Enraged, Ishtar appeals to her father Anu to send down the Bull of Heaven to kill Gilgamesh. Despite his grave reservations, Anu accedes, and the Bull of Heaven arrives at Uruk, causing vast desolation across the land. However, the two heroes succeed in slaying the beast: in a scene often depicted in Mesopotamian images, Enkidu seizes it by the tail while Gilgamesh plunges his knife into its neck. As Ishtar rages on the walls of Uruk, Enkidu tears off a haunch of the Bull and hurls it at her scornfully. That night he dreams that the gods, deciding that one of them must die to atone for their sacrileges—slaying the guardian of the sacred Forest of Cedar as well as the Bull of Heaven—have settled on Enkidu. Enkidu relates his dream to Gilgamesh and, in the delirium that now besets him, curses the door made of cedar from the sacred Forest as well as the hunter and Shamhat, who lured him away from his natural habitat into civilization. But when the god Shamash points out to him all the good he has experienced in the city and describes the fine funeral he shall have, Enkidu repents and blesses them all. In a final vision he is bound and taken down to the House of Dust, the Underworld, which he describes to Gilgamesh before falling ill for twelve days and dying.

Gilgamesh mourns for Enkidu and makes sacrifices in his memory. The fact of his friend's death brings home to Gilgamesh the reality of human mortality: "I shall die, and shall I not then be as Enkidu? Sorrow has entered my heart" (70). In the hope of understanding, he wanders the earth in search of Uta-napishti, the human being who enjoys the immortality of the gods—and along the way kills a herd of lions and clads himself in their skins (see the frontispiece). Passing the scorpion-men guarding the entrance to the twin mountains of Mashu, which support heaven and reach down to the netherworld, Gilgamesh makes his way for twelve double-hours through the interior of the mountain (the route of the sun between setting and rising) and through a garden whose trees are adorned with jewels in place of fruits. He reaches the seaside tavern of the innkeeper Siduri, who warns him of the dangers of his quest, which leads across the Waters of Death, and tells him that he should forsake his unrealistic wish for immortality and instead cling happily to life itself. Nevertheless, she directs him to Ur-shanabi, the boatman of Uta-napishti. When Gilgamesh finds the boat, he shatters the Stone Ones. (The meaning is disputed: depending on the translator, the Stone Ones are the boat's crew or its stone oars or anchors. In either case the stone is impervious to the Waters of Death, which wither human flesh.) Ur-shanabi orders him to go into the forest and cut a large number of long punting poles. When after three days of sailing they reach the still Waters of Death, Gilgamesh propels the boat using one oar at a time. When the oars have been all been used, he holds up his garment as a sail, enabling them to cover the final furlongs.

For Uta-napishti, who meets them at the shore, Gilgamesh rehearses yet again the story of his adventures and grief at the loss of Enkidu and pleads that now finally "the gate of sorrow be barred" (85). The sage reminds him of the inevitability of death: the gods have established both life and death, declining only to disclose its time. When Gilgamesh asks how it happened that Uta-napishti was granted eternal life, he hears the legend of the great deluge that the gods sent to extinguish early mankind. Uta-napishti and his family, forewarned by one of the gods, built a great boat and survived. Rewarded with eternal life, they were required to live apart from the gods and other mortals. If Gilgamesh desires immortality, he must demonstrate his suitability by staying awake for six days and seven nights. (Death and sleep are related in many mythologies.) When he fails the test, Gilgamesh finally accepts his mortality, is clothed in splendid new royal garments, and sent away again with Ur-shanabi with no reward but information about a plant that will renew his youthfulness. Gilgamesh recovers the plant, but while he bathes, it is eaten by a snake, which—as a demonstration of the plant's effectiveness—immediately sloughs off its old skin. Realizing that all his hopes have been in vain, Gilgamesh returns to Uruk, where he proudly displays to Ur-shanabi the handsome walls of the city, which he now recognizes as his great human achievement.

The text as it has come down to us has so many lacunae that it has inevitably tempted not only scholars but also poets, novelists, and dramatists to fill in the gaps. Yet even as it stands, the epic clearly involves so many themes of universal validity and appeal that its attraction for modern readers is easy to understand: the criticism of tyranny, the drive to achieve glory, the lure of sex, man's alienation from nature, the power of friendship, the fear of death, the satisfactions of human achievement. Moreover, Gilgamesh emerges as something like a "Kulturhero" who brings exotic timber to the land of the steppes, digs wells in desert places, invents sails and deep-sea diving, and initiates cultic rituals and civic order.[4] Moreover, the epic presents those themes through exciting adventures within a narrative frame that anticipates the modern bildungsroman or quest novel. At the same time, its ambivalences have exposed it to many different theoretical approaches: from the religious, mythic-archetypal, and political down to its cooptation by ecological-environmental interests, gender and gay studies, science fiction, and other contemporary theoretical slants.[5] It will be our undertaking in the following pages to survey the variety of these modern Gilgameshes and to locate them within the context of twentieth-century cultural history.

The Text

The evolution of the Gilgamesh material, from the earliest Sumerian poems through the Old Babylonian version down to the Akkadian "Standard Form" and beyond to later copies, has been capably surveyed by Jeffrey H. Tigay.[6] It is widely accepted that the original Gilgamesh was a historical figure—according to official Sumerian King Lists[7], the fifth king of Uruk in the early part of the third millennium B.C.E. (flourished c. 2750)—and that he was famous in antiquity for building the great ten-kilometer wall surrounding and protecting that first urban metropolis. His fame was so great that various adventures, real and invented, soon accrued to his name. As is often the case with renowned figures in world culture, other legendary or folkloristic motifs gravitated toward his irresistible pull: notably, the set of stories, common in myth, surrounding a wild man who lives among the animals as well as the story of the deluge and the sexual adventures of a vengeful queen.

By 2500 the historical Gilgamesh had come to be deified, known as king of the netherworld, and worshipped in cults. Around 2100—during the "Sumerian Renaissance," when Sumerian enjoyed the cultural cachet that later surrounded Greek in Augustan Rome, Latin in the Middle Ages, or French at eighteenth-century European courts—the tales, which presumably for several centuries also circulated orally, began to be written down in the cuneiform script of Sumerian and perhaps recited on certain festive occasions. Five such separate compositions are known, four of which, mythical in character, were used in the creation of the Akkadian epic, which took shape originally in the Old Babylonian period of the early second millennium: *Bilgames and Huwawa, Bilgames and the Bull of Heaven, Bilgames and the Netherworld,* and *The Death of Bilgames.*[8] (In non-Semitic Sumerian many of the names, such as Bilgames, occur in different forms, while other figures—e.g., Ziusudra rather than Uta-napishti—have different names altogether.) It is also noteworthy that Enkidu functions in these early poems more as Bilgames' servant than as his friend.[9]

Around the time of Hammurabi (fl. 1770) the various stories and legends that had previously existed independently were shaped by an unknown author into an aesthetically integral whole. This early form of the epic, written in the Semitic Akkadian language and still only partially known, was characterized by Enkidu's promotion to the role of Gilgamesh's friend and unified by the pervasive theme of death and Gilgamesh's search for immortality. Ishtar is treated contemptuously by Gilgamesh and Enkidu, and Aruru, earlier revered as the great Mother Goddess, is reduced to her role as the creator of Enkidu.[10] That this Akkadian version was widely known in the Middle Babylonian Period (1600–1000 B.C.E.) is attested by its many copies as well as translations into such other languages as Hittite and Hurrian. By about 1200 the epic had achieved the form of some 3000 to 3500 lines that is now known as the Standard Version and traditionally attributed to an exorcist and scholar named Sin-leqi-unninni: essentially the story as recapitulated above, to which three ingredients have been added.

First, a substantial prologue anticipates the conclusion, giving the epic a satisfyingly rounded form: it hails Gilgamesh as the ruler "who saw the Deep, the country's foundation," who was wise in all matters—that is, who had achieved wisdom in the course of his wanderings—and who brought back from his journeys the tale of the deluge and its prehistory. It praises the great wall of Uruk and states that the wall contains a cedar box with a bronze clasp that holds an account of Gilgamesh's adventures, implying that the following narrative is in fact Gilgamesh's own third-person autobiographical record of his life and achievements. Second, the Uta-napishti episode was expanded by a full account of the deluge—taken from an earlier Old Babylonian version known as the epic of Atrahasis ("Surpassing Wise"), an epithet applied to Uta-napishti—which originally had no connection with the Gilgamesh story. Finally, an episode was tacked on that lies completely outside the integral unity of the tale completed by Gilgamesh's return to Uruk and for this reason is often omitted in modern translations or adaptations of the epic: namely, a translation of the second half of the Sumerian poem *Bilgames and the Netherworld* telling of Gilgamesh's own descent to and return from the underworld. In addition, the poetry was enriched by the addition of various familiar formulaic passages: temple-city hymns, wisdom sayings, blessings, curses, and threats.

This final version was traditionally inscribed on twelve cuneiform tablets, at least four copies of which were preserved in the great seventh-century library of Ashurbanipal at Nineveh.

The epic was widely known in pre-Christian times: in 2003, fragments from as many as seventy-three different copies were recorded, and still more have been discovered since then.[11] Various claims have been made concerning its impact: that it influenced such ancient texts as the Hebrew Bible (notably the story of the deluge, but also the divine creation of Enkidu from clay) as well as Homer's *Iliad* (the friendship of Achilles and Patroclus) and *Odyssey* (notably the quest structure as well as the descent to and return from the underworld).[12] Its influence has also been maintained in later Near Eastern works such as *The Arabian Nights*.[13] But for various reasons, its popularity declined: the last known cuneiform copies were made around 130 B.C.E., and it was never translated into such dominant Western languages as Greek and Latin. With surprising rapidity, the great epic was totally forgotten for over two thousand years.

The Rediscovery

In 612 B.C.E. the city of Nineveh, known for its great palaces and library, was sacked and razed and its population either massacred or deported. It lay buried and largely forgotten near Mosul in present-day Iraq for some twenty-five hundred years. In the 1840s the young British adventurer Austen Henry Layard (1817–94) and his assistant, Hormuzd Rassam (1826–1910), began to excavate the huge mound that had accumulated upon the former city over the centuries. In 1849 Layard's workers uncovered the palace built by Ashurbanipal's grandfather Sennacherib.[14] Then in 1853 Rassam returned to the site on his own and, in further excavations on the other side of the vast mound, discovered the remains of Ashurbanipal's palace containing the great library with its thousands of fired clay tablets collected by Ashurbanipal. Layard and Hormuzd were unable to read the cuneiform script of the tablets they uncovered but, soon appreciating their immense interest and value for the emerging study of Assyriology, sent thousands of them back to the British Museum.

It was during these same years that Sir Henry Rawlinson (1810–95) and others succeeded in deciphering the cuneiform inscriptions. Rawlinson had been sent to Persia in the 1830s as a British officer to train the shah's army. While there, he learned Persian and became fascinated by the inscriptions that he saw everywhere, and notably the great trilingual (Old Persian, Akkadian, Elamitic Susian) inscription of Darius the Great on the lofty Behistun Rock. In 1835, in daring climbs up the sheer face of the cliff, he made casts and transcriptions of the monumental inscription—a Mesopotamian analogue of the Egyptian Rosetta Stone, which had been deciphered only a decade earlier. Using his knowledge of Old Persian and drawing on the work of the German classicist Georg Friedrich Grotefend (1775–1853), who as early as 1802 had made the first fruitful attempts to decipher Old Persian cuneiform inscriptions, Rawlinson succeeded in decoding the Akkadian portions. Following his retirement from the military, Rawlinson returned to London, where he became a Member of Parliament and director of the East India Company. At the same time, he worked extensively with the thousands of tablets that had accumulated in the British Museum with an eye toward publishing a series of large volumes titled *Cuneiform Inscriptions*. In 1867 he arranged to have a young museum intern named George Smith appointed as his assistant.

George Smith (1840–76) was a self-taught Assyriologist. A banknote engraver by profession and with little formal education, he was initially drawn to the Near Eastern collection of the British Museum because of his interest in biblical studies. Gradually he became obsessed with the cuneiform inscriptions in the collections and began to read everything he could find on Mesopotamia. He soon turned to the tablets themselves, stored in disorder in a dark room, and eventually learned to decipher some of the signs—more skillfully, indeed, than the director of the department and his assistant. Moreover, his trained engraver's eye and skilled craftsman's hands enabled him to piece together the disparate and often scattered fragments of shattered tablets. Soon he was making discoveries of his own and, in 1866, published his first article. In 1867, when Rawlinson needed an assistant to help with his work on *Cuneiform Inscriptions,* Smith was the obvious candidate.

In November 1872, while at work on volume 4 of the inscriptions, Smith discovered a fragmentary tablet that referred to a flood and a ship that settled on a mountaintop—details that immediately caught the notice of a young man who had grown up with the Bible. On December 3, before what the *London Times* described as "a large and distinguished company assembled in the rooms of the Society of Biblical Archaeology," Smith presented a paper describing "the Chaldean History of the Flood." (The implications were exciting enough for the entire account to be reprinted on page 2 of the *New York Times* on December 20, 1872.) As noted there by his patron, Sir Henry Rawlinson, who presided and introduced his protégé generously as "the first of the day" among Assyrian scholars, "the crowded state of the meeting evinced the great public interest which was taken in the subject."

Smith described the process by which he had stumbled upon the account. For convenience he was organizing the collection of tablets by subject matter into six divisions, and among those comprising mythological topics he found half of a tablet providing a history of the flood. Sorting through thousands of smaller pieces, he was able to ascertain that the description of the flood was actually the eleventh tablet in a set of twelve forming a continuous legend about a king named Izdubar— Smith's preliminary reading of the name Gilgamesh. (He also found fragments of three duplicate copies of the same text, all belonging to the library of Ashurbanipal at Nineveh.) After Smith had read his translation of the flood story, comparing it in detail with the biblical record, "an interesting and learned discussion followed," in which not only Rawlinson but also such a personage as Prime Minister William Gladstone participated. On the basis of his electrifying discovery, the London *Daily Telegraph* sponsored an expedition to Nineveh, in the course of which Smith almost immediately and fortuitously discovered a fragment with a missing piece of the flood story and identified further tablets of the Izdubar legend.

He first recounted his journey and findings in his book *Assyrian Discoveries* (January 1875).[15] Following a detailed account of his excavations, in chapter 11 (165–222) he discusses the twelve tablets of "The Izdubar and Flood Series of Legends."

> Independently of the fact that these tablets give the Chaldean account of the flood, they form one of the most remarkable series of inscriptions yet discovered. These tablets record primarily the adventures of an hero whose name I have provisionally called Izdubar. Izdubar is, however, nothing more than a makeshift, and I am of opinion that this hero is the same as the Nimrod of the Bible. (166)

On the basis of the relatively few lines that he had managed thus far to decipher, Smith provided a rather rambling account of the legend. Izdubar is a hunter or giant who drives off a tyrant who rules over Erech. Then

> a seer or astrologer named Heabani came to his court at Erech, becoming his close friend. Together Izdubar and Heabani destroy other wild animals, and conquer a chief named Humbaba, who ruled in a mountainous region full of pine-trees. Another chief named Belesu was next subdued, and then an animal called "the divine bull" was killed. (166–67)

Just when Izdubar is at the height of his power, misfortunes set in.

> First Heabani was killed by a wild animal called a "tamabukku" [. . .]. Next Izdubar was struck with a disease, apparently, from the description, a kind of leprosy. Izdubar went on a wandering excursion to the sea-coast to be cured of his malady, and is supposed there to have met the deified hero who escaped the flood. [. . .] Hasisadra is supposed to have told Izdubar how to obtain his cure, and then the king returned to Erech, and again mourned over his friend Heabani. (167)

After citing the fragmentary lines from the earlier tablets on which he bases his sketch of the legend, Smith quotes at length the account of the flood on the relatively intact Tablet XI (184–98). Following brief citations from Tablet XII, he provides a lengthy exegesis of the flood story, which he regards as "the principal incident in these legends, and the most important one in relation to the Bible" (207). He concludes the chapter with a discussion of Tablet XII, which is presented as "in some respect the most remarkable and important of the legends, for it clearly shows that the early Babylonians believed in the existence of the soul, of a future life, and of heaven and hell" (219). In the second half of the volume (chs. 12–23) Smith surveys and translates early Babylonian cuneiforms, Assyrian inscriptions (from 1320 to c. 250 B.C.E.), miscellaneous texts (prayers, laws, syllabaries) and foreign inscriptions and briefly describes a few objects illustrating the arts and customs. In his conclusion Smith comments generally on the many remaining questions concerning Babylonian history, culture, and mythology and on the importance of future excavations: "The light already thrown by the Assyrian inscriptions on Biblical history forms one of the most interesting features in cuneiform inquiry, and there can be no question that further researches will settle many of the questions still in doubt, and give us new information in this field, of an important character" (448–49).

However, the publication that stirred the most widespread public excitement was Smith's bestselling *The Chaldean Account of Genesis,* which appeared later that same year (1875) and was respectfully dedicated to Sir Henry Rawlinson.[16] Although it repeated some of the material from *Assyrian Discoveries,* its title suggests the new focus of interest in this second account, which is no longer archaeological but literary. The author states emphatically that the Izdubar legends "are principally of interest from their containing the Chaldean account of the Deluge" (166). (Although he cites the same lines from Tablet XII, correcting errors from his earlier translation, he no longer attributes to this tablet any significance as proof for Babylonian belief in a soul and a future life in heaven or hell.)

The much fuller account of the twelve Izdubar tablets occurs in chapters 11 through 16, after the author has related the story of his discovery of the Genesis legends, sketched a brief history of Babylonian literature, reviewed Chaldean legends and Babylonian mythology and fables, and cited various Babylonian accounts of the Creation. Smith's version of the Izdubar story, when he finally reaches that point, is not a connected narrative, although the chapters reflect a natural progression: "The Izdubar Legends" (general introduction), "Meeting of Heabani and Izdubar," "Destruction of the Tyrant Humbaba," "The Adventures of Ishtar," "Illness and Wanderings of Izdubar," and "The Story of the Flood and Conclusion." Again he proceeds from tablet to tablet, describing each one, providing background information as needed, and then citing in considerably fuller translation the badly broken and largely incomplete lines of the narrative.

His translation is colored throughout by his identification of Izdubar with the biblical Nimrod and Humbaba with an Elamite ruler who tyrannizes Babylonia—not a monster. He discreetly omits in two places the details of Heabani's (Enkidu's) seduction by the temple harlot "because they were on the one side obscure, and on the other hand appeared hardly adapted for general reading" (205). He continues to believe that Heabani comes to the biblical Erech (Uruk) in order to interpret Izdubar's dream and that the great fight is not with Heabani himself but with a tiger that Heabani brings to test Izdubar's strength. He is unclear about the circumstances of Heabani's death—it is Izdubar who is struck down by a loathsome disease—and attributes his vision of the netherworld to Ishtar, inserting into Tablet VII (from another source altogether) the legend of Ishtar's descent to the netherworld. And he does not mention the magical plant of rejuvenation and its loss to the snake.

It is difficult to recognize from his account the epic of Gilgamesh as we know it today—a work that Smith regarded as noteworthy solely because it included the story of the deluge. He acknowledged, to be sure, "some differences between the account in Genesis and the Inscriptions" but attributed them principally to the differences between the countries of Palestine and Babylonia and the religious ideas of the monotheistic Hebrews and the polytheistic Babylonians (285). To support his argument he provides a table showing twenty-three points of similarity between the two accounts of the flood: a table absent from his earlier book and showing how intensively Smith had thought about the legend and its implications during the intervening months. Smith modestly denies his competence to pronounce an independent opinion in matters of biblical criticism. Moreover, "the views of Biblical scholars on the matter are so widely at variance, and some of the them so unmistakably coloured by prejudice, that I feel I could not take up any of the prevailing views without being a party to the controversy" (284)—an allusion no doubt to the raging theological debates triggered by Darwin's theory of evolution as well as recent geological findings on the age of the earth.[17] Smith insists only on one point: the agreement of many scholars that "a connection of some sort" must exist between the biblical narrative and the cuneiform texts, a connection whose clarification must await further researches in Babylonia and Palestine.

The foregoing characterization is not in the least intended to belittle George Smith's pathbreaking accomplishment and enormous contribution to the fledgling field of Assyriology but simply to indicate that major developments necessary for the world to become acquainted with the epic of Gilgamesh as we know it today had not happened yet. The contemporary impact of Smith's work can be judged by the enthusiasm of the reviewer of his *Assyrian Discoveries* in *The New York Times* (Feb. 27, 1875, p. 10), who begins by stating that "the narrative of [Smith's] progress and results has been too eagerly looked for to need other commendation to the attention of the public than the simple announcement of publication." The reviewer attributes proportionately more interest to the epic itself and less to the flood narrative than does Smith. Among the translations and discussions of inscriptions, he notes, "the first in order and in interest is the cycle of Izdubar legends, in which the account of the deluge forms an episode." (The review goes on to summarize the plot of the "epos—for such it may properly be called.") But the reviewer, apparently a follower of the new Higher Criticism of the Bible, attributes the current popular fascination with the account of the deluge to a misunderstanding. Rather than affording testimony to the historical fact of the flood, it "proves only that the unity of tradition was not wholly broken by the separation of one part of the family from the rest." While Smith's work is "not a book that can be read lightly," he concludes, "it ought not to be passed over by anyone who would estimate aright the religious tendencies of the age. The letters and fragments are mainly historical in bearing, but the preface and the discourses are full of topics of a doctrinal and ecclesiastical character which will interest all, quite irrespective of any opinions that individuals may themselves entertain."

The review of the *Chaldean Account of Genesis* in the London *Times* (Dec. 4, 1875, p. 4) is more restrained in its enthusiasm. The reviewer finds that "the Bible narratives wear an air of truth and simplicity which does not appear in the meretricious ornamentation and studied improbability of the mythology of Babylon." He rehearses at some length the adventures and misfortunes of Izdubar, accepting the identification of the hero with the biblical Nimrod, of Heabani as a mystical hermit, and of Humbaba as his Elamite rival. But he focuses primarily on the "most remarkable" account of the deluge, which, he finds, "differs essentially" from "the simpler and consequently older version" of the Scriptural narrative. Anticipating subsequent trends in comparative mythology, the reviewer suggests that the epic resembles in style the Norse sagas and Indic vedas "in its elevated diction and deep pathos" and notes the resemblances between Izdubar and the exploits of Hercules as well as Ishtar and the descent of Orpheus. In the last analysis, however, the Babylonian myths "differ so considerably from the Mosaic books that they cannot be claimed for more than incidental illustrations and examples of value for comparative profane mythology."

In sum, George Smith's epoch-making discovery and translation of the twelve tablets represented only the first, albeit major, step in the gradual appreciation of the great epic of Gilgamesh and its eventual popular appeal. The "new edition" published by A. H. Sayce (New York: Scribner's,

1880) amounted to an extensive revision of the original, changing Smith's first-person narrative to the third person, making a number of corrections as well as extensive additions based on newly discovered tablets, filling in some of the gaps in the translation, and correcting certain of Smith's misunderstandings. However, the new edition did not modify in any significant way Smith's account of the Izdubar legend or its cultural impact.

The Early Translations

Eight years after Smith's *Chaldean Account,* Paul Haupt (1858–1926), a brilliant young German Assyriologist who spent most of his academic career at Johns Hopkins University, established the basis for all future treatments of the epic with his edition of the complete cuneiform text of the "the Babylonian Nimrod Epic" (*Das Babylonische Nimrodepos,* 1884), made from his own autograph copies in the British Museum but not including a translation.[18]

In 1891 the German-reading nonspecialist audience got access to the epic when Alfred Jeremias published his translation of "the Old Babylonian heroic saga" (*Izdubar-Nimrod: Eine altbabylonische Heldensage*), the first complete modern translation of the epic in any language. Jeremias (1864–1935), a Lutheran minister in Leipzig who was also a historian of religion and professional Semiticist, realized that the saga of Izdubar-Nimrod had greatly stirred the interest of the cultivated world. To satisfy that curiosity, he presented "for the first time a scholarly based translation and explanation that faithfully follows the cuneiform text" (v).[19] Because it was meant for a more general audience, he omitted any comprehensive transcription of the original text and provided notes only to the extent necessary to justify his translation of especially difficult passages. A brief introduction discussed Izdubar's name and his religious significance; rehearsed the discovery of the tablets by Hormuzd Rassam and their deciphering by Smith; sketched the historical and mythological background; and characterized the poetic form of the work, which ranges from simple narrative to hymnic tones. His appendix comprises brief notes on the role of Ishtar in the epic, disputes any connection of the twelve tables with the stages of the zodiac (as had been widely held ever since Rawlinson), recommends caution regarding any identification of Ishtar with Semiramis, and notes parallels between the legends of Izdubar and Herakles.

The translation itself (14–44) is a straightforward prose rendition of Haupt's edition, introduced tablet by tablet with a brief account of the state of the cuneiform text. The quoted passages are introduced by interspersed transitions, which make a readable text of the whole, as is evident from the following example:

Tablet II

(according to Haupt, I) is rather completely preserved with the exception of column I. Column II (p. 8) shows us *Izdubar* as the famed hero of *Uruk*. Parents complain that their sons and daughters turn to the hero in mindless enthusiasm. "*Izdubar* did not leave any son to his father, any daughter to a hero, any wife to a hero. . . ." The parents protest to the ears of the city goddess: "'He has no rival [. . .] your inhabitants are led [to battle], *Izdubar* does not leave any child to its father, by day and night [they cry]: He the shepherd of *Uruk-[Supuri]*, . . . he their shepherd and . . . , the mighty one, the praised one, the wise one [. . .] *Izdubar* does not leave any maiden [to her mother], any daughter to a hero, any wife to her master.'" (15)

Only in one place, the seduction scene, does the translator depart from the available text, remarking simply that "a scene follows that depicts in epic breadth and in a straightforward manner the seduction of *Eabani,* closing with the words: 6 days and 7 nights *Eabani* approached *Uhat,* the beloved. After he had sated himself on her *lalû,* he turned his face back to his cattle. . . ." Following his translation of the largely intact Tablet XI, he notes that "the connection with the biblical reports is a burning question of Old Testament scholarship." Citing a contemporary authority, he maintains that the content of the story in the Bible and in cuneiform represents "an old and common possession of the Semitic tribes from the lands of the Tigris and Euphrates" (36–37).[20]

Following his translation of Tablet XII, Jeremias expresses his hope that "the literary, religious-historical and especially mythological significance of the *Izdubar*-epic should emerge clearly from what has been provided" (44). He concludes with the fervent exclamation, emphasized by italics, that "the renewal of the excavations in Nineveh is in the interest of international scholarship" (44).

It is worth noting, as a further sign of the international fascination with the topic, that Jeremias's translation received an extensive review in *The New York Times* (May 10, 1891, p. 18, by "S.S.M."), which states that "the main interest of the work centres in the account of the flood" and reminds readers that "Hebrews and Babylonians were branches of the same great Semitic family." The writer briefly recapitulates the story of Izdubar before observing that "we have now arrived at the most interesting portion of the whole poem": namely the depiction of the deluge on Tablet XI, which is quoted in full (in English translation). "Here is a powerful poetry," S.S.M. concludes, "imbued with popular native vigor, in which the deeper problems of national life and the longings for deliverance are presented in an unaffected, childlike way, in pictures and parables. . . . It is the eternally old song of the suffering of the human soul which in its own strength seeks but never finds deliverance," even though the moral problem as such is never comprehended.

At this point, in October 1890—and too late for Jeremias—it was finally established that the proper rendition of the hero's name was not Izdubar or any of the other provisional readings but, rather, Gilgameš/Gilgamesh—the version used henceforth by most scholars and translators.[21] The first partial translation of the epic into English, by Morris Jastrow (1861–1921), the distinguished Polish-American and German-trained professor of Semitic languages at the University of Pennsylvania, appeared in his book *The Religion of Babylonia and Assyria* (1898), which in turn constituted the second volume in a series of "Handbooks on the History of Religions."[22] Jastrow's treatment of Gilgamesh comes after chapters on magical texts, prayers and hymns, penitential psalms, oracles and omens, and the cosmology and zodiacal system of the Babylonians. The sequence is necessary, according to Jastrow's scheme, because—even though he rejects earlier readings of the tale by Rawlinson and others as a solar myth reflected astrologically in its twelve tablets (515)—he believes that Gilgamesh becomes a solar deity, who in that capacity defeats the Heavenly Bull, which in Babylonian mythology is a symbol of the storm (486). Moreover, he regards Gilgamesh as the model for the biblical hero Samson, whose name he believes to be identical with Shamash, the god of the sun (515).

Jastrow accepts the epic essentially as related by Smith and Jeremias, but rather than providing a straightforward English translation, he retells it in prose with his own running commentary on the episodes and with his own translation of occasional key passages directly from the original texts as known from Haupt's edition. Unlike the earlier translators, he is quite explicit about the sexual scenes:

> The hunter follows the instructions of Gilgamesh.
> Eabani falls a victim to Ukhat's attractions.
> Ukhat exposed her breast, revealed her nakedness, took off her clothing.
> Unabashed she enticed him.

The details of the meeting are described with a frank simplicity that points again to the antiquity of the legend.

> For six days and seven nights Eabanis enjoyed the love of Uhkat.
> After he had satiated himself with her charms,
> He turned his countenance to his cattle.
> The reposing gazelles saw Eabani,
> The cattle of the field turned away from him.
> Eabani was startled and grew faint,
> His limbs grew stiff as his cattle ran off.
> But Uhkat has gained control of him.
> He gives up the thought of gazelles and cattle and returns to enjoy the love
>   of Ukhat. (477)

In keeping with the thesis of his magisterial work, Jastrow devotes almost half of his lengthy chapter to Gilgamesh's visit to Parnapshtim (= Uta-napishti) and the account of the flood, again related as a prose narrative with interpolated translated lines. "It will be proper before leaving the subject," he concludes, "to dwell briefly upon the points of contact between this Babylonian tale and the Biblical narrative of the Deluge" (506). The source of the tradition, he believes, must be sought in the Euphrates Valley: "The ark of Noah can only be understood in the light of methods of navigation prevailing in Babylonia; and it is in Babylonia, and not Palestine, that the phenomenon was annually seen of large portions of land disappearing from view." However, the myth of the flood has nothing to do originally with the Gilgamesh epic, which he terms "a composite production" and "a medium for the perpetuation of various popular traditions and myths" (513). Only four of his deeds—the conquest of Erech, the victory over Khumbaba, the killing of the divine bull, and the strangling of the lion—belong to Gilgamesh; all the other incidents, including Heabani and Parnapshtim, are extraneous to his legend. Yet despite the felicity of his translated lines, Jastrow's presentation could hardly become the basis for any broader popularity of the epic of Gilgamesh. First, it does not provide a complete translation of the story; and second, his account occurs in a volume intended for a scholarly audience and as a guide to students—as he puts it in his preface, "gathering the *disjecta membra* of Assyriological science [for] future progress" (vii).

The translation that Haupt did not include was provided by Peter Jensen's monumental edition and translation of 1900, which has been called "the milestone in the philological understanding of the epic."[23] But his treatment of "Das Gilgamíš (Nimrod) Epos," which appeared in an esoteric scholarly source, could hardly provide the basis for any popular appeal.[24] The same restriction applies to the first French translation by Édouard Dhorme, which appeared, along with a transcription of the cuneiform (according to Jensen) and a detailed scholarly apparatus, in a volume intended for Assyriologists.[25] Any broader reception by the interested reading public had to await the twentieth century.

1

The Initial Reception (1884–1935)

In what follows we shall leave aside, for the most part, the steadily increasing and often fascinating scholarly studies of the Assyriologists and concentrate instead on the popular reception of the epic of Gilgamesh.[1] Sometimes, of course, the scholarly conclusions of the Assyriologists have influenced popular conceptions. But other non-academic factors are often involved, as we shall see in the chapters to come.

The First Literarization

The first literary adaptation of the Gilgamesh legend for a modern—that is to say, Victorian—audience was undertaken by an unlikely author: a young American lawyer and businessman who later worked in Boston as an advertising agent, reporter, and executive secretary of the National Business Men's League.[2] When Leonidas Le Cenci Hamilton (1850–1906) published his *Ishtar and Izdubar* (1884), he had already written "a general sketch of the Republic of Mexico" called *Border States of Mexico* (1881) as well as *Hamilton's Mexican Laws* (1882) and *Hamilton's Mexican Hand-Book* (1883) in the hope of promoting business and mining interests with that country. Hamilton, who was educated in the Greek and Roman classics, had at least a rudimentary knowledge of Akkadian (based on A. H. Sayce's *Assyrian Grammar for Comparative Purposes* [1872]) and had studied the principal works of the major English, French, and German scholars.[3] He tells us that he began writing his work in 1881 in San Francisco, continued it in New York and Boston in 1882–83, and rewrote it in London in the winter of 1883–84: "The difficulties to be encountered in the reproduction of the great Epic of Babylon, the Iliad of Babylonia, are such as have never existed heretofore in the restoration of any work of literature" (xxii). Some of these difficulties are outlined in the proemium to his work, which begins with a paean to the harmony that distinguishes true poetry; speaks of the problems concerning accentuation in Assyrian; waxes elegiac over lost civilizations; praises Mesopotamia, the home of the biblical Abraham; mentions early visitors to the site of Nineveh while crediting England with the recovery of its past; and cites the leading contemporary scholars in the field of Assyriology, including Paul Haupt, who was just publishing his magisterial edition of the cuneiform script of the epic of Gilgamesh. Hamilton reports that he "availed [himself] of the results of the labours of these great Assyriologists," including Sayce's revision of Smith's *Chaldean Account of Genesis* (xx). It was his aim "as far as possible to reproduce in our poem all the fragments of the great Epic of Babylon, and fill the blanks, guided by the suggestions and allusions to be found in the text, in the Accâdian and Assyrian hymns, sculptures, seals, bas-reliefs, and every available data."

Ishtar and Izdubar is heavily indebted to Smith's translation and to various works that Hamilton cites in his notes, but his concerns are quite different from Smith's. He does not even include the story of the deluge in his version, which focuses primarily on the love interests. (He planned to include the stories of the creation and fall, the flood, and the tower of Babel along with other myths in a second volume, as advertised at the back of volume 1, but he never completed it.) Hamilton's poem is not so much a translation as an extremely free adaptation "constructed from translations of the great Accadian epic and the legends of Assyria and Babylon, found in cuneiform inscriptions of tablets lately discovered on the site of the ruins of Nineveh, and now deposited in the British Museum [. . .] restored in modern verse" (title page). It expands the three thousand fragmentary verses of the original to some six thousand lines of often clumsy rhymed couplets in forty-eight cantos, which through their very form change the tone of the work from a heroic epic to a poetic romance—influenced no doubt by the current popularity of Edward FitzGerald's *Rubáiyát of Omar Khayyám* (the first four editions of which appeared from 1859 to 1879) and by Edwin Arnold's recently published life of Buddha entitled *Light of Asia, or the Great Renunciation* (1879), whose "sweet and tender lines" Hamilton praises glowingly in his proemium (xi). He invented a number of new episodes (arranged by "Tablet" and "Column" but with no relation to the original) and altered the character of the participants. Thus Heabani becomes an aged "hermit seer," a voluntary exile from Erech who dresses more like a Turkish pasha than an ancient Babylonian:

> Before a cave within the Gâb-ri wild,
> A seer is resting on a rock; exiled
> By his own will from all the haunts of men,
> Beside a pool within a rocky glen
> He sits; a turban rests upon his brow,
> And meets the lengthened beard of whitest snow. (45)[4]

As the poem begins, Erech has for many years been under the brutal control of Khumbaba's Elamite forces, but Izdubar comes out of the desert with his troops, rescues the city, and is crowned. He falls in love with Ishtar until, "with hot and balmy breath, and trembling form aglow" and "burning for a kiss," she seeks to seduce him. The noble Izdubar rejects her advances indignantly: "What meanest thou, thou wanton brazen thing? / Wouldst thou on me the direst curses bring?" (31).

When Izdubar has two troubling dreams that his seers cannot interpret, they send a messenger and then two maidens to entice Heabani to return to Erech, where he declares Izdubar to be a god. They are victorious in their expedition against Khumbaba and the fight with "the Winged Bull of Anu," but the angered Ishtar casts a spell on Heabani so that he sees a vision of the gods' decision to punish them both for their sacrilegious deeds. So they set out together to consult the seer Khâsisâdrâ (Hasisadra: that is, Uta-napishti). Meanwhile, several further columns (based on the Sumerian

"Descent of Inanna") recount Ishtar's descent to Hades and the restoration and escape of her beloved Tammuz from Hades, whereupon Ishtar returns, bringing light and love back to earth. Then Heabani is killed in a contest with dragons in the mountains, and Izdubar is afflicted with a disfiguring disease. Izdubar—after a stay in the Happy Halls with two maidens named Sîdurî and Sâbîtu—makes his way to Khâsisâdrâ, who cures him and makes him immortal. He falls in love with the seer's daughter Muâ and offers marriage. (Hamilton appears to have taken the name from Smith's *Assyrian Discoveries* [132], where "a female named Mua" welcomes Izdubar to Hasisadra's island; in *The Chaldean Account,* in contrast, she is called Ragmu-seri-ina-namari and is identified as Hasisadra's wife.) When she refuses to leave the kingdom of the immortals, he returns to his responsibilities as king of Erech but promises to come back to her.

> O Muâ, Muâ! how my heart now sings!
> Thy love is sweeter than all earthly things!
> I would I were not crowned a king!—away
> From this bright land—here would I ever stay!
> As thou hast said, I soon will here return;
> The earth cannot withhold me from this bourne,
> And soon my time allotted there will end,
> And hitherward how happy I will wend! (200)

In his extremely free "restoration" of Smith's version, Hamilton has wholly altered the tone of the epic: from ironic tragedy to the sweet strains of love and harmony, from grim realism to cheery optimism. Ishtar brings light and love back to the world, and Izdubar will enjoy eternal bliss among the immortals in the arms of his Muâ. The planned second volume was to end with "Izdubar's return to Heaven, and final reconciliation with Ishtar."

Babel and Bible

We have already seen that the initial interest in the epic stemmed from its inclusion of the flood story. Tablet XI excited George Smith in 1872 so greatly that he reputedly tore off his clothes in the cuneiform storage room of the British Museum. His introductory lecture in December of that year focused on the deluge and only incidentally mentioned the epic, which he still knew only in fragmentary form. Even his translation of the more completely restored work in 1875 was simply part of a larger volume on what he took to be Chaldean parallels to, and sources for, the biblical book of Genesis. It was his account of the flood as a source for Genesis that initially attracted public attention and stirred theological controversy, as witness the reports in the London *Times* and *The New York Times*. At the same time in Germany, Friedrich Delitzsch (1850–1922), who had earlier provided notes and addenda to the German translation of Smith's *Chaldean Genesis*,[5] compiled and published the cuneiform fragments of Tablet XI in his *Assyrian Reader* (*Assyrische Lesestücke*, 1876, 2d ed. 1878), which was almost immediately translated by Paul Haupt for his professorial habilitation lecture (1881) and reprinted in the second edition of Eberhard Schrader's volume on cuneiform inscriptions and the Old Testament (1883).[6] Peter Jensen provided yet another early translation in his *Cosmology of the Babylonians* (*Die Kosmologie der Babylonier*, 1890).[7] And both Jeremias (1891) and Jastrow (1898) highlighted the flood account in their renditions.

It was against this background that on January 13, 1902, Delitzsch, professor of Assyriology at the University of Berlin, summarizing conclusions from twenty years of teaching, delivered before the august audience of the recently founded Deutsche Orient-Gesellschaft in the grand auditorium of the Sing-Akademie (a choral society) the first of three lectures on "Babel und Bibel," which gave the name to the fierce controversy that arose in these years and in which the Gilgamesch-Epos played a significant role. Delitzsch, who cites Gilgamesh only in passing and among many other texts and images, states his thesis quite clearly toward the end: that "a considerable Babylonian element adheres to our religious thought through the medium of the Bible" (44).[8] It is Delitzsch's belief that only the elimination of those elements, purely human—indeed, anthropomorphic—will allow the "true religiosity" of the Old Testament and of Jesus' message to emerge through the process of "purification more truly and spiritualized than ever." Delitzsch's lecture, the first major blow in the battle that undermined the textual and historical authority of the Bible, much as Charles Darwin's work had indirectly discredited its account of human genesis, was repeated, at the personal request of Kaiser Wilhelm II, on February 1 at the Royal Palace in Berlin.

While the first lecture focused primarily on the flood story, in a second lecture a year later, again in the Sing-Akademie and in the presence of the Kaiser and his wife, Delitzsch turned his attention to parallels between Hammurabi's code and Moses' table of laws.[9] The two lectures aroused such a controversy and so much public interest and indignation that by September 1903 Delitzsch had collected some 1,350 smaller and over 300 longer newspaper and journal articles as well as twenty-eight mostly negative brochures. Both lectures were immediately translated into several languages, including English.[10] After Delitzsch published a third lecture—this one delivered not in Berlin, where the Kaiser had distanced himself from his radical views, but in Cologne and Frankfurt am Main in the fall of 1904—he felt challenged to respond to his critics in yet a fourth work, a "Look Back and Forward" in which he defended not only his views but also his facts.[11] It was his conviction that the Hebrew Bible was hopelessly contaminated by the Babylonian elements that led him, many years later in his book *The Great Deception* (*Die große Täuschung,* 1920/1921), to propose that the Old Testament be removed altogether from the Christian canon and even to suspect that Jesus was of Aryan descent.[12]

A typical example of the responses to Delitzsch's polemic was published in 1902 after the first lecture by Chr. Dieckmann, a self-proclaimed "country parson" ("Landpfarrer") with no training in Assyriology. But using Jensen's translation, which purported to make it possible for interested parties to study and carry out research in the field without knowing Assyrian or the other relevant languages, Dieckmann set out to prove that the Bible loses nothing through such study but "remains what it should be for a Christian: the book of truth" (6).[13] Indeed, the opposition of Babel and Bible exposes the splendor and power of the Bible even more than before (7). After his presentation of the epic, its historical background, its country of origin, and its divine mythology, the author concludes that "Babylonia doomed itself through its mythological chaos" and that it is inconceivable that "from such a mythological brew the Bible should have baked the bread of life" (173). To be sure, the Bible knows Babel, better indeed than the finest Assyriologists. And for that reason the Bible fights a holy battle against Babel. At this point he sketches the Bible's polemic in the stories of the fall of man, of the deluge, and of the tower of Babel. "The Bible has nothing from Babel," he concludes. "Babel has nothing from the Bible. Babel argues against the Bible, the Bible argues against Babel. Who has the truth? Who will be victorious? The Bible rests in the truth and offers the truth. The Bible will retain the victory" (197).

A more restrained view than Delitzsch's was offered by Alfred Jeremias in his handbook on the Old Testament in the light of the ancient Orient (*Das Alte Testament im Lichte des Alten Orients,* 1904).[14] Apart from a chapter on nonbiblical traditions regarding the flood, which considers at some length the account in the epic, he equates Humbaba's cedar mountain and forest with the biblical paradise, identifies Nimrod with Gilgamesh, and finds that Gilgamesh shares with Samson such qualities as his strength-giving hair and his twelve deeds.

The most outspoken advocate of the epic as the Bible's source was, beyond any doubt, Peter Jensen in the first volume of his monumental monograph on Gilgamesh in world literature (*Das Gilgamesch-Epos in der Weltliteratur,* 1906). The Assyriologist concedes at the outset that his topic has led him well beyond the boundaries of his own field and into realms in which he is only modestly qualified. And "the odd outsider" ("der sonderbare Fremdling") encountered, he reports, a surprisingly inhospitable reception (vii).[15] The learned men shook their heads over his romantic raptures and were disdainful of his undertaking. And so, a loner *malgré lui* ("ein Eigenbrödler wider Willen," viii) he had to make his way alone in full awareness of the weaknesses he was unable to avoid. He acknowledges that this first volume does not offer what most readers might have expected: namely, investigations concerning Homer, *The Odyssey,* and other Greek legends—that investigation had to wait until Arthur Ungnad's brochure almost twenty years later—*Gilgamesch-Epos und Odyssee* (1923)—and Jensen's second volume (1928).[16] After an exhaustive exposition of the epic of Gilgamesh, Jensen sets out to demonstrate that Moses is the Gilgamesh of Exodus who saves the children of Israel from precisely the same situation faced by the inhabitants of Erech at the beginning of the Babylonian epic (125–58). He goes on for a thousand pages to depict parallels between Gilgamesh and Abraham, Isaac, Samson, David, and various other biblical figures and arrives inevitably at Jesus, who turns out to be "nothing but an Israelite Gilgamesh. Nothing but an adjunct to Abraham, Moses, and countless other figures of the saga" (1029). Just as the Babylonians once revered their Gilgamesh as a great, splendid sun vanishing in the mists, so Christianity worships its Jesus. "We children of a much-lauded time of wonderful cultural accomplishments who like to gaze with

a compassionate smile at the beliefs and customs of people of prehistory—
we in our cathedrals and houses of prayer, our churches and schools, in palace and cottage, we serve a Babylonian god, Babylonian gods!" (1029). His
fellow citizens, "a mighty cultural people of German brothers, tear ourselves apart in battle over the pretentiously ornamental state that has been
hung around this alien god; we block the sources of our native strength just
because in Rome a man sits on the throne who because of human delusion
and human arbitrariness is the representative of this Babylonian sun god!"
(1029–30).

Jensen correctly anticipated that his theory, which came to be known
as Pan-Babylonianism, could not expect much support in the immediate
future. People will continue, he says, "to try to beat to death the uncom-
fortable truth with clubs, to poison it with uncanny poisons or to repress it
with stony silence [. . .] in the service of religion, the service of science or
that of one's even more hotly loved own ego" (xiv).

Despite a few supporting voices from other Assyriologists, the attacks
came almost immediately from biblical scholars associated with the field
of *Religionsgeschichte* (history of religion) as it emerged around the turn of
the century—attacks focused on his methodology. In a leading theological journal, the Old Testament scholar Hans Schmidt considered Jensen's
presentation of his case and provided objections to his method.[17] He con-
cluded that Jensen wrote with a pronounced bias and that his work was
not the result of a calm historical investigation but "a passionate polemic,
assured in advance of its results, against the historical bases of the Christian
religion" (236). He hoped for "a general energetic rejection of the book"
that would discredit the widespread comparison of biblical narratives with
non-Israelite parallels—the "comparative mythology" that sought to overcome the odium clinging to its name.

There is no need to rehearse the lively controversy that Jensen's work
triggered in Germany and that was summarized by Hermann Gunkel in
a late and highly ironic review of that first volume.[18] By the time he published his review in 1909, the eminent historian of religion believed that
"the sensation and even excitement that this book first evoked have long
since subsided" (75). He observes that the reception of Jensen's work in
the learned world has been "almost universally and, in most cases, almost
without any major reservation rejected" and agrees with a fellow scholar
who calls Jensen's theories "wild phantasies" (75). In a careful analysis,

Gunkel denies the many similarities that Jensen purports to establish between the Babylonian epic and the biblical narratives and claims that even
the basic terms are not clearly and logically defined. He argues that Jensen
ignores the fundamental principles of comparative mythology by comparing series of stories rather than scrutinizing individual tales on their own
merits. Gunkel concludes with a general attack on Assyriologists, who for
all their accomplishments in their own field, had in the previous decade
entered the intellectual marketplace with a number of "conspicuous mistakes and remarkable aberrations" (84). Why have these misconceptions
always been advanced by Assyriologists? Because they have not famil-
iarized themselves adequately with the field of biblical studies that they
presume to enter. He ends with a bit of jovial schadenfreude toward his
Hellenistic colleagues because Jensen was now threatening to move on in a
second volume to "attack the Greek legends" (84).

The Babel-Bible controversy had largely exhausted itself by the beginning of the First World War, but the debate over the relationship between
the Babylonian epic and the Hebrew Bible has of course continued—
usually with less heat, but not necessarily with more light.[19]

The German Connection

It is no accident that the first serious cultural impact of the Gilgamesh epic
in the early twentieth century took place in German-speaking countries.
A general public awareness was kindled by the sensational controversy
over Babel and Bible—a controversy that goes unmentioned, by contrast,
in the 1910 (11th) edition of the *Encyclopaedia Britannica,* whose author
simply repeats the astral-mythological theory, advanced ever since Rawlinson, according to which the twelve tablets represent the zodiac and Gilgamesh exemplifies a solar myth. It was in Germany, moreover, that the
general public had access to the earliest complete and reasonably accessible translations. We have already noted Albert Jeremias's translation of
1891 and Peter Jensen's monumental edition and translation of 1900. But
the public attention was kindled by *Das Gilgamesch-Epos,* the more readable version of Arthur Ungnad (1878–1945), professor of Oriental philology at the University of Jena, which appeared in 1911 accompanied by an
"explanation" ("Erklärung") by Hugo Gressmann, which forty years later

one scholar called "the best commentary" on the epic.[20] In his extensive exegesis (81–232), the Berlin historian of religion proceeds systematically through the twelve tablets, taking up the various questions raised by earlier scholars, and then addresses such larger issues as the quest for life, the view of the epic as astral mythology (which he rejects), its poetic art as epic, the influence on world literature (where he dismisses Jensen's exaggerated views concerning analogies with the Hebrew Bible), a restrained comparison with other flood narratives, and the conjuration of death in Tablet XII. Gressmann provides a highly readable overview of existing scholarship, which can still be consulted with profit today. In the words of the preface: "In order to enable understanding even for those outside the narrow circle of specialists who are interested in the questions treated here, virtually nothing is presupposed as known."

It is no coincidence, then, that a lively interest was kindled that same year in two of the leading intellects of the day: Sigmund Freud (1856–1939) and Carl Gustav Jung (1875–1961). The information is scanty, but Jung's letter of October 4, 1911, from his temporary duty as a military physician in barracks at St. Gallen, suggests that the conversation between the two psychoanalysts had been going on for some time. Jung writes: "For our interpretation of the Utnapishtim episode in Gilgamesh I have found some rather weird parallels which shed light on Utnapishtim's gnomic utterances. I won't reveal anything yet, but must mull them over first."[21] Almost immediately, on October 13, Freud replied to Jung in his "military solitude" with his own contribution to their "conversations on the Gilgamesh material."[22] While he does not contest the interpretation of Gilgamesh and Enkidu (whom he still calls Eabani, according to the older translations) "as man and crude sensibility," it occurs to him that such pairs contrasting nobility and baseness constitute a motif that can be followed through world legend and literature: Don Quixote and Sancho Panza, the Dioscuri of Greek myth, or twins like the Roman Romulus and Remus: "One is always weaker than the other and dies sooner. In Gilgamesh this ages-old motif of the unequal pair of brothers served to represent the relationship between a man and his libido." Freud adopts the theory from Paul Ehrenreich's *General Mythology and Its Ethnological Foundations* (*Die allgemeine Mythologie und ihre ethnologischen Grundlagen,* 1910), as well as ideas from James Frazer's *The Golden Bough* (1890), to explain Enkidu as Gilgamesh's "afterbirth": "The weaker twin, who dies first, is the placenta, or afterbirth, simply because it is regularly born along with the child by the same mother."

Unfortunately neither the correspondence nor the biographies offer further hints regarding their conversations about Gilgamesh, nor does Gilgamesh occupy a prominent position in Freud's subsequent thought and works, which contain only a passing reference in the opening pages of his late monograph, *Moses and Monotheism* (1939). (In light of the prominence of dreams and their interpretation in the epic, this neglect is surprising.) ·

In contrast, their ruminations produced an immediate expression in Jung's early work, *Symbols of Transformation* (*Symbole der Wandlung,* 1911–12), where examples from Gilgamesh are frequently mentioned.[23] The epic is cited as an example for the unconscious incestuous tendencies of the mother (Ishtar's desire for Gilgamesh). Enkidu exemplifies the longing for regression back to childhood and into the mother's body. The monster Humbaba, who guards the garden of Ishtar, represents archetypally the father, "whose function it is to oppose pure instinctuality" and who is often "an object of neurotic fears for the son." In another context Gilgamesh is introduced as an example of the triumphant man who forgets his dependence on the unconscious: "He was so successful that the gods, the representatives of the unconscious, saw themselves compelled to deliberate how they could best bring about his downfall." Enkidu's death is cited as an omen of mortality like the death of Hiawatha's friend Chibiabos. Elsewhere, in another of his frequent comparisons of Gilgamesh to the Hiawatha legend, Jung claims that Hiawatha's appointment as ruler of the home-wind that protects him from death finds its "exact parallel" when Gilgamesh obtains from Utnapishtim "the magic herb which brings him safely over the sea to his native land, but which is stolen from him by a serpent on his arrival home." (Jung seems to forget that the magic herb has nothing to do with the return home but amounts to the gift of renewed youth.) Elsewhere he echoes Freud in his adducement of Gilgamesh and Enkidu as symbols of "the higher and lower man, ego-consciousness and shadow."[24] Although Jung frequently alluded to Gilgamesh in his later works, he never produced the study that he evidently had in mind in 1911.[25] But as late as 1948 he encouraged Rivkah Schärf Kluger, a newly minted doctor of philosophy whom he met at the Psychologische Club Zürich, to undertake the research that eventually resulted in her Jungian study *The Archetypal Significance of Gilgamesh: A Modern Ancient Hero* (1991).

Five years after the communications between the psychoanalysts, the poet Rainer Maria Rilke became acquainted with the epic of Gilgamesh in the adaptation by Georg Burckhardt that had just been issued by his publisher, Insel Verlag.[26] Burckhardt had undertaken his version in the realization that, despite the scholarly translation of Arthur Ungnad, the poem, "which in its grandiose simplicity can be numbered among the most significant works of world literature," was still too little known among nonspecialists.[27] He felt that the epic could be properly appreciated only if the historical material was recast "with the greatest freedom of phantasy into a unified form," whereby he hoped to enable "the primal saga ["Ur-sage"], which can only be sensed, to arise again in its elemental human-original simplicity." Burckhardt's success in popularizing the epic—in his afterword he even inadvertently sparked the baseless rumor that Nietzsche had known and valued Gilgamesh[28]—can be measured by the fact that his eminently readable prose paraphrase was reprinted in many successive editions, often accompanied by new illustrations, for the next half-century. It not only introduced Gilgamesh to thousands of readers but provided the source for many of the German writers and artists who subsequently took up the theme.

Rilke's poetic sense was evidently offended by Burckhardt's prose and inventive license—for instance, his Enkidu hastens directly to the city after his six days and seven nights with "the holy woman" but then almost immediately returns to his steppes, cursing the hunter and woman who took him away from them, and must be urged by the sun-god Shamash to go back to civilization. In any case, he soon sought out Ungnad's more literal translation. Rilke's enthusiasm is evident from his letter on December 11, 1916, to the publisher's wife, Katharina Kippenberg.

> Gilgamesh is tremendous! I know it from the edition of the original text and count it among the greatest that one can experience. From time to time I tell the story to one person or another, the whole sequence, and have every time the most astonished listeners. Burckhardt's summary is not wholly successful; it doesn't convey the greatness and significance—I feel that I tell it better.[29]

Indeed, he insisted with a good deal of cultural intuition, anticipating many later adaptations, that the story needed to be told orally. "I would

never relate the Gilgamesh other than orally. Every time I find more expression."[30] A few weeks later, on New Year's Eve, he asked his friend He-
lene von Nostitz if she had seen the Insel edition of what he mistakenly
calls the Old Syrian poem of Gilgamesh. "I have been concerning myself
with the precise scholarly translation (by Ungnad) and, in these truly monumental fragments, have experienced dimensions and figures that belong
to the greatest that the enchanting word of any age has produced."[31] The
poet tells his correspondent that he would prefer to relate it to her orally
and that Burckhardt's Insel edition, though tastefully designed, suppresses
the power of the ancient poem evident in Ungnad's text:

> In the (as I assume brilliantly translated) fragments there is a truly huge ac-
> tion and existence and fear, and even the extensive textual gaps have some-
> how a constructive effect by keeping apart the splendidly massive surfaces
> of the fragments. Here is the epic of the fear of death ["Todesfurcht"] that
> arose in primordial times among people for whom for the first time the sep-
> aration of death and life had become definitive and fateful.

Rilke concludes by saying that he has been living for weeks under the influence of the poem—a work that he read with poetic eyes wholly different from the psychoanalytic gaze of Freud and Jung.

Rilke encountered Gilgamesh during the years when he was associated in Munich with a group of thinkers obsessed with mysticism, Or-
phism, and the matriarchal theories of Johann Jakob Bachofen, whose
epoch-making study of matriarchy (*Das Mutterrecht,* 1861) he bought and
studied. In 1915 and again in 1917/1918 Rilke attended lectures by the Bachofen disciple Alfred Schuler, whose theory concerning the progressive
purification of humankind through the concept of death-in-life enthralled
him. "Just imagine," he wrote on March 18, 1915, to Princess Marie von
Thurn und Taxis-Hohelohe,

> that a man, from his intuitive insight into ancient imperial Rome, under-
> took to give an interpretation of the world, which portrayed the dead as the
> truly Being, the realm of death as a single incredible existence, and our brief
> period of life as a kind of exception thereto. And he supports this all through
> an immeasurable learnedness and through such a gradience of inner convic-
> tion and experience that the meaning of primordial myths, resolved, seemed
> to plunge into this bed of rhetoric.

Schuler claimed that human existence could be divided into two periods: a prehistoric time ("Urzeit"), which was characterized by the splendor of Paradise and the Heroic Age, and a historical age, in which that radiance becomes progressively weaker. He argued that periods of light alternate with periods of darkness and that humankind, driven by memories of the past, was evolving gradually toward enlightenment. Schuler's concept of the realm of death found expression in such texts of Rilke as his *Sonnets to Orpheus* (*Sonette an Orpheus*, 1923). We cannot know whether or not Schuler mentioned Gilgamesh to Rilke—the name does not figure in Schuler's own works—but Rilke's reading of the poem as the "epic of the fear of death" is absolutely consistent with the ideas that he heard in the circle of mystics and Orphists surrounding Schuler.

His contemporary Hermann Hesse responded to the work as exuberantly as did Rilke, and he appears not to have been troubled by Burckhardt's adaptation. In his 1916 review he called Gilgamesh "the most powerful poem that I have read in a long time."[32] The philological details can be studied elsewhere, he continues. But the work itself is "one of the very great primal poems along with the Indic myths and the best passages of the Old Testament." He recommended the book as "a treasure of gold, lately drawn to light again from mankind's most ancient crypts." Hesse cited the epic again in his essay "Library of World Literature" ("Eine Bibliothek der Weltliteratur," 1929), where he argues that "the oldest works age the least" and named Gilgamesh among the earliest books to be included in his ideal library: "the powerful song of the great hero who undertakes to do battle with death."[33]

Rilke and Hesse were merely the first in a succession of German-language writers who fell under the sway of the ancient epic. The earliest German literarization, Rudolf Pannwitz's *The Nameless Work* (*Das namenlose Werk*) appeared in a series entitled *Myths* (*Mythen*, 1919–1921), in which Pannwitz retold in various poetic forms such world myths as "Faust and Helena" (based on Goethe's *Faust*), the Egyptian "Fairy Tale of the Two Brothers," the myth of Psyche, and the Indic legend of Krishna's life. The enormously prolific Pannwitz (1881–1969), a poet and cultural philosopher, had shortly before enjoyed his single major success with his pre-Spenglerian essay *The Crisis of European Culture* (*Die Krisis der europäischen Kultur,* 1917). After his analysis of the decline of European civilization, Pannwitz concludes

that "there is no longer any way out of the crisis of European culture on
any hitherto tested path." The only possibility for Europeans, who have
reached the edge of the abyss, is "a merging of our European half-cultures,
which are already fused among themselves, with the great classic Oriental cultures."[34] But he cautions that one should not confuse that authentic
Orient with the spoiled Orient of globetrotters, mystagogues, adventurers,
research travelers, ministers, and dealers in colonial wares. The presuppo-
sition for both Buddha and Confucius, he continues, is "that most ancient
and greatest Oriental Weltanschauung, on which Nietzsche had already
drawn and which such Orientalists as Hugo Winckler and Alfred Jeremias have depicted in its tremendous unified extent" (182). At this point
Pannwitz offers a brief sketch of Babylonian culture and its astral mythology, concluding that of all our modern theories—conservation of energy, thermodynamics, social psychology—that exemplify the "complete
barbaric condition of the spirit," nothing will remain. "The Babylonian of
3000 B.C. in contrast has a classic spirit" (188).

So it is hardly surprising that, among his world myths, Pannwitz also
included the epic of Gilgamesh, "the unknown book." Pannwitz was exposed to Assyriology at an unusually early age. As a young teenager in a
small eastern German town, he was tutored at school in Greek and pri-
vately by Carl Bergemann, "an old recluse and private scholar" whose
wide-ranging interests had led him to the new field of Assyriology.[35]
"Through him I learned much in many areas and to direct my gaze in
many directions"—including the names and works of the Assyriologists
Hugo Winckler and Alfred Jeremias. Later, as a Gymnasium student in
Berlin, he lived in the home of his maternal uncle, an archaeologist who
had conducted excavations in Mexico and Guatemala. These exposures
during his impressionable years led Pannwitz at the University of Mar-
burg to pursue archaeology along with his studies in philosophy. It was no
doubt this unusual background that inspired him, during the turmoil of
the First World War, to "deepen my soul and spirit through the passionate
absorption of the cultures and religions of the ancient Orient, and above
all of the founders: Buddha, Laotse, Confucius, and Christ" (150)—and,
no doubt, Gilgamesh, whose epic he retold, tablet by tablet, in unrhymed
trochaic pentameter, basing his work primarily on the texts and research
of Jeremias but also on Burckhardt's recently published reconstruction.[36]
His poem, which uses the idiosyncratic capitalization and punctuation of

his mentor Stefan George, is a readable rendition of the epic that smoothes over the various gaps in the original text, adding and omitting nothing.

> Dieses ist ein namenloses werk
> Von dem helden und dem menschen schicksal.
> Alles sahe er der herr des lands
> Der erhabne der ausfragende
> Der gewichtge eines jeglichen
> Können und vollbringen wohl erfuhr er
> Jegliches verstand er er durchschaute
> Seiner leute treiben wie der gott
> Richtete und brachte es zurecht. (1)
> (This is a nameless work
> About the hero and human destiny.
> He saw all, the master of the land,
> The sublime one, the questioning one,
> The weighty one. Of everything's
> Possibility and completion he learned.
> He understood everything. He fathomed
> His people's actions. Like the god [he]
> Judged and set it right.)

Despite the efforts of Alfred Jeremias, who read and approved of Pannwitz's version and with whom the poet subsequently became acquainted and corresponded, the work appears to have had little public impact.[37] Even today it is largely unknown even among specialists, although Pannwitz possessed a much deeper knowledge of Assyriology and the epic in particular than almost any of the other modern adapters. Forty-five years later Pannwitz returned to Gilgamesh in a major philosophical work that we shall consider in its proper context (see chapter 4).

One of the most extraordinary adaptations of Gilgamesh by any standard was published in 1927 by Wilhelm Wendlandt (1859–1935), a minor poet who also served as a provincial parliamentarian and as founding secretary of the National Industrial League. Wendlandt, who heralded the epic as the nucleus of the noblest ancient wisdom and the archetype of all mythological figures, was convinced that several tablets were missing from the end of the work: "After all, according to historical tradition Gilgamesh is the 'redeemer-king' of the Assyrians, the prototype of a *Christ* and his heavenly ascension!"[38] But the extant tablets end disappointingly with the hero's disconsolate death: "The ascension and the eternal life are missing." In his *Gilgamesh: The Battle with Death: A Song of Life* (*Gilgamesch. Der Kampf mit dem Tode. Ein Lebenslied,* 1927), Wendlandt argued that it was necessary to fill out the missing tablets in order to restore the true purpose and meaning of the epic.

To this end he assigns a new function to Ishtar, who begins as the goddess of sensual love but evolves into the image of heavenly rapture. For much of the poem Ishtar fulfills her traditional role: as the spurned lover, she uses all the means in her power to humiliate Gilgamesh. But when Gilgamesh succeeds in defeating Death himself, who implores Gilgamesh to be his friend and to liberate him from his hateful task, Gilgamesh ascends to heaven, where a transformed Ishtar, acknowledging that he has prevailed and redeemed the world, now takes him by the hand in eternal marriage. Wendlandt's adaptation, based wholly on Burckhardt's translation, is arranged in twenty-four cantos divided into twelve "tablets." But the story as we know it (that is, through Uta-napishti's story of the flood and the "wonder plant") is recapitulated in the first ten tablets: the last two comprise the author's wholly invented account of Gilgamesh's defeat of Death and his ascent to eternal life.

A secondary theme of Wendlandt's adaptation, and hardly surprising in view of his own involvement in government and industry, hints at the political activity in contemporary Germany. When the citizens of Uruk become dissatisfied with Gilgamesh's rule, "they sat down in the conspirators' corner and founded first of all a party" (27) that agreed on a single point: "We're going to take the government in hand!" But the idea of a unified fatherland soon gives way to partisan goals, whereupon the chief agitator becomes its president and demands an oath of loyalty from all his followers.

The radical Christianization and politicization of the epic is not Wendlandt's only change. Inspired by Shakespeare, he was determined to present his epic in stanzaic form but felt that most forms—notably *ottava rima* or the strophes of the *Nibelungenlied*—were not lofty enough for the grand theme of Gilgamesh. To accommodate "the greatest and richest content" he settled on "the greater measure of the so-called 'antique sonnet'" (5–6): three quartets with flexible rhymes followed by a rhyming couplet. In the end, he accomplished the astonishing feat of retelling the story of the Mesopotamian epic in some four hundred sonnets, as illustrated by the lines in which Ishtar acknowledges her defeat:

> Du hast gesiegt!—Vom Tod' hast Du erlöst!
> Und Niemand mehr den Untergang beweint,
> Da Du die Welt zum Göttlichen erhöhst,
> Mit mir und allen Seligen vereint.
> Du hast Dein heißes Menschenherz bezähmt,
> Hast meine irdsche Lust zurückgewiesen
> Und eine Göttin kalten Bluts beschämt,
> Bezwungen alle meine stärksten Riesen,
> Die ich zur Rache Dir entgegenstellte,
> Chumbaba, Enkidu, den Himmelsstier!
> Der Schöpfung ganzes Heer an Dir zerschellte,
> Allmächtger Herrscher über Mensch und Tier.—
> Mir blieb nur eine Macht, Dich zu bezwingen:
> Doch selbst den Tod sah ich Dich niederringen. (204)

> (You have won!—You have redeemed from Death!
> And no one still weeps over decline
> Since you raise the world to divine heights,
> United with me and all the Blessed.
> You have tamed your hot human heart,
> Have spurned my earthly lust
> And coldbloodedly shamed a goddess,
> Defeated all my mightiest giants,
> Whom I sent against you for revenge,
> Humbaba, Enkidu, the Bull of Heaven!
> Creation's whole army was smashed by you,
> Almighty ruler over man and beast.—
> Only one power to tame you was left for me:
> But I saw you defeat even Death.)

While Wendlandt's verses are facile and readable, they are not memorable as poetry, and his prolific work has never established itself in German literary history. But his adaptation is notable for the sheer accomplishment of retelling the epic in hundreds of sonnets; it anticipates more recent versions in its exploitation of the ancient epic for contemporary political criticism; and his Christianization of Gilgamesh represents, as we shall see, a constant tendency extending from the earliest scholars down to various recent poets.

The succession continued with two further Nobel Prize recipients in addition to Hermann Hesse. In his autobiography, Elias Canetti, known above all for his novel *Auto-da-Fé* (*Die Blendung,* 1935) and his study of mass psychology *Crowds and Power* (*Masse und Macht,* 1960), calls the encounter with Gilgamesh "the most significant experience" of his Gymnasium years in Frankfurt am Main (1921–24).[39] Moreover, he first experienced the work precisely in the manner that Rilke claimed to be the most effective: orally. At a Sunday matinee at a Frankfurt theater, he heard the actor Carl Ebert read a work previously unknown to him. "It was older than the Bible, a Babylonian epic." The young Canetti knew only that the Babylonians had also had a legend of the flood and that it had made its way from there into the Bible. That alone would not have attracted him, he confesses, but his teenage excitement about the matinee idol prompted him to attend. "Gilgamesh's lament on the death of his friend Enkidu struck me in the heart," he wrote. In his search for eternal life, to be sure, Gilgamesh fails, "but that simply strengthens one in the feeling of the necessity of his undertaking."

In this manner Canetti felt for the first time the effect of a myth: "as something that in the half-century that has passed since then I have contemplated in many ways and turned this way and that in my mind but never *once* seriously doubted. I absorbed as a unity that which has remained a unity within me." It is not a question of belief in the story, he emphasizes. The question is simply whether one willingly accepts death or rebels against it: "Through the revolt against death I have earned my right to the glory, wealth, misery and despair of all experience. I have lived in this endless rebellion." The grief that he felt for the loss of those closest to him was no less, he believed, than Gilgamesh's grief for Enkidu: "But I have one advantage over the lion-man: that I am concerned with the life of *every* human being und not only that of my nearest and dearest." As in Rilke's case, it was the theme of death that attracted Canetti to the tale of Gilgamesh: not Rilke's acceptance of death-in-life but revolt against that death.

Again and again, during these early decades of the twentieth century we encounter an awareness of Gilgamesh in the minds and works of leading German writers. In *Young Joseph* (*Der junge Joseph,* 1934), the second volume of Thomas Mann's tetralogy *Joseph and His Brothers,* the myth of Gilgamesh is one of the many things that the young Joseph learns from his aged tutor Eliezer (in Mann's fictional version of the Babel/Bible controversy). Eliezer owns many examples of Babylonian writing, we are told, which Joseph learns to decipher, among them the story of "that Gilgamesh, whose body was divine flesh and who nevertheless could in no way succeed in gaining eternal life."[40] He read, too, about the Akkadian hero Etana, legendary king of Kish, who was borne up to heaven by an eagle but—with an implicit allusion to the novel *Steppenwolf* of Mann's friend Hesse—preferred Enkidu's taming by Shamhut:

> Better than that story [about Etana] he liked the one about the forest-man Enkidu and how the prostitute from Uruk, the city, converted him to cultivated behavior: how she taught the animal man to eat and drink with manners, to salve himself with oil and to wear clothes. It appealed to him, he found it excellent how the prostitute tamed the wolf from the steppes after she had made him susceptible for refinement through a love life of six days and seven nights. The Babylonian language flowed in dark splendor from his lips when he recited these lines.

That same year, in his novel *Babylonian Tour, or Arrogance Comes before the Fall* (*Babylonische Wandrung oder Hochmut kommt vor dem Fall,* 1934), Alfred Döblin mentioned Gilgamesh in passing in a manner implying his assumption that readers were already familiar with the epic. The satirical novel is based on the fiction that "a Babylonian-Chaldean-Assyrian god" awakens from a Rip Van Winkle sleep of several millennia to find himself suddenly in the twentieth-century—a fictional technique already exploited by André Gide in *Le Prométhée mal enchaîné* (1899) and Stephan Wolpe in his opera *Zeus und Elida* (1928). From Iraq in 1933 he travels with two companions to Constantinople, Zürich, Paris, and other cities to experience in his newfound penury and powerlessness and in retribution for his own earlier sins the depravity of modern European society. On his way the god, now named Konrad, meets a German archaeologist who is excavating the ruins of what once was ancient Baghdad and who cites such predecessors as Austin Henry Layard and Hormuzd Rassam. A little later Konrad tells his companion Georg, a minor deity who becomes a corrupt business tycoon, the story of Astarte, also known as Aphrodite and later as Beatrice, who sent Tammuz to the underworld, transformed other lovers into birds, wolves, and vegetables, and amused herself sexually with horses and lions: "Then Gilgamesh, Young Siegfried, came down from his father's fortress. And the story took a turn and found an end that Konrad did not conceal but that we, out of respect for Astarte, decline to relate."[41] In short, the reader already knows that Gilgamesh rebuffs Ishtar and that she descends to underworld.

But the first major literary exploitation of Gilgamesh, in German or any other language, was yet to come.

The Spread of the Epic

Between the two world wars, despite little literary activity in the form of adaptations, public acquaintance with the epic of Gilgamesh spread gradually through new translations and illustrated editions.[42] In Germany it was especially Burckhardt's 1916 version and the dramatic potential of the story that attracted artists of the Expressionist generation. In 1919 a limited deluxe edition of the popular prose version was published (in only 175 numbered and signed copies), with ten striking etchings by the painter Richard Janthur (1883–1950).[43] The artist presented his figures nude and drawn with the strong lines favored by the German Expressionists. Opening with two rather sexy drawings depicting Enkidu with the temple prostitute and Gilgamesh with Ishtar (see figure 1), he went on to depict such scenes as Enkidu's dream, Gilgamesh rowing the boat with the mighty oars, and Gilgamesh with the youth-restoring plant. A year later the Dresden artist Josef Hegenbarth (1884–1962), who in the course of an almost fifty-year career illustrated well over one hundred literary works, created eleven drawings for a new edition of the same translation (reprinted in 1991 in a luxury edition). In 1922 Rolf Nesch (1893–1975), whose early work was influenced by Ernst Ludwig Kirchner, produced an extremely rare portfolio with twenty etchings based on the same translation— etchings displaying the rough linear contours characteristic of much Expressionism. (The illustrations by all three artists have been displayed in several recent German museum exhibitions of art based on the Gilgamesh theme.) That same year, Hans Steiner illustrated yet another edition of Burckhardt's version with lithographs.

Figure 1. Richard Janthur, *Enkidu and the Temple Prostitute.* From *Das Gilgamesch-Epos,* trans. Georg Burckhardt (Berlin: Fritz Gurlitt, 1919).

The year 1924 saw two new versions adapted especially for general reading. The film theoretician Hermann Häfker, convinced that the epic belonged to world literature alongside Homer, the Old Testament, Dante, and Goethe's *Faust,* published in 1924 a "German setting" in free verse based on the existing scholarly translations by Jensen, Jeremias, and Ungnad: "The meaning everywhere is literally retained and whenever possible with the same words."[44] He sought to produce a recitable text by bridging certain gaps and providing for each tablet an introductory prose overview to aid comprehension. Häfker calls attention to the circumstance that here, at the beginning of world literature, the question of the meaning of life and death plays a central role; this proves its eternal appeal. He emphasizes, further, the significance of eros as exemplified by Ishtar and points to its influence on the Homeric poems. The Assyriologist Hermann Ranke offered a smoothly readable translation that was hand-printed in three hundred copies for the League of Book Friends (Bund der Buchfreunde) in Hamburg.[45] In 1926 a further scholarly translation by Erich Ebeling was published in an anthology of ancient texts relevant to the Old Testament.[46] And in 1934 Albert Schott's translation (*Das Gilgamesch-Epos*) appeared in a widely accessible (and frequently reprinted) Reclam edition.[47]

Perhaps the earliest adaptation in English after Hamilton's was created by the Armenian-English writer and painter Zabelle C. Boyajian (1872–1957), who became acquainted with the epic as a child in the Kurdistan highlands. In 1924 she published, in a handsome limited edition, her *Gilgamesh: A Dream of the Eternal Quest* with her own striking illustrations (see figure 2), which are inspired by the Babylonian seal-cylinders and Assyrian bas-reliefs, and an introduction by the Assyriologist Wallis Budge.[48] Her blank-verse poetic drama is essentially a free paraphrase of the original, interweaving various Sumerian myths into the basic epic tale. Based primarily on translations by Morris Jastrow (who until his death in 1921 was supposed to provide the introduction) and other "distinguished Assyriologists" (7), it uses the names and interpretation provided by Jastrow (8). The author shows a marked deference to the original, considering it "almost sacrilegious to use it as the base for another work" (7) and appreciating its multiple roles as nature myth, epic, and religious poem. The work, divided into three acts preceded in each case by an explanatory prologue, for the most part omits the epic action. In the first scene of act 1 Ukhat

(Shamhat) persuades Ea-bani (Enkidu), largely through her rhetoric, to go to the city to meet Gilgamesh. By the second scene the Khumbaba episode, narrated as a lay by the hunter who first encountered Ea-bani, is already past and Ishtar makes her advances, which Gilgamesh rejects. In the short third scene Ea-bani is already dead and Gilgamesh in mourning.

Act two begins in Sabitum, the palace of the maiden goddess (Sabitu), who tries to persuade Gilgamesh to stay with her rather than cross the perilous sea, but in the second scene Gilgamesh is already on his way to Hasis-Adra (Uta-napishti), who relates the story of the flood and warns Gilgamesh: "Seek not to probe the mysteries of death: / Thy work is life; life wants thy utmost thoughts" (84–85). In act 3 Gilgamesh finds and loses the plant of life; in the final scene the now-aged Gilgamesh summons up the spirit of Ea-bani, who tells him, when he desires to know the mystery of the underworld: "Seek not to know it. . . . Nothing can save thee, Gilgamesh, from death." But he consoles Gilgamesh with the closing thought

Figure 2. Zabelle C. Boyajian, *Gilgamesh on the Waters of Death*. From Zabelle C. Boyajian, *Gilgamesh: A Dream of the Eternal Quest* (London: George W. Jones, 1924).

that "there is no death for him who fears not death." With her vivid illustrations and graceful verses, Boyajian provided a competent poetic adaptation of the epic as it was known in English around the turn of the century,
albeit without the often grim realism of the original. But in Germany, as
we have seen, and imminently in England, the epic as we know it today
was gradually becoming available.

The first complete translation into English after the partial versions
of Morris Jastrow and Stephen Langdon (1917) was presented in 1928 by
R. Campbell Thompson (1876–1941) in *The Epic of Gilgamish* (*sic!*), which
was based on a new collation of the tablets in the British Museum and
introduced in a handsome edition as "one of the most interesting poems
in the world."[49] The Oxford Assyriologist, who two years later issued a
new scholarly edition of the cuneiform text with transliteration and notes,
praises "the poetic beauty of the Epic," which in its simplicity succeeds in
describing "the whole range of human emotions in the aptest language,
from the love of a mother for her son to the fear of death in the primitive mind of one who has just seen his friend die; or from the anger of
a woman scorned to the humour of an editor laughing in his sleeve at
the ignorance of a savage" (unnumbered page 6 of the brief preface).[50]
Thompson chose to render the epic into rather ponderous and sometimes
coy hexameters.

> The girl, displaying her bosom,
> Shew'd him her comeliness, (yea) so that he of her beauty possess'd him
> Bashful she was not, (but) ravish'd the soul of him, loosing her mantle,
> So that he clasp'd her, (and then) with the wiles of a woman she plied him,
> Holding her unto his breast. (13)

Six years after Thompson's translation, the American poet and translator William Ellery Leonard (1876–1944) offered in his *Gilgamesh:
Epic of Old Babylonia* (1934) a wholly different version for the general
reader: a rendition into free verse of Hermann Ranke's earlier German
translation. The poet and the German scholar, "now Egyptologist at
Heidelberg but formerly himself a research-man in things Assyrian,"
had become acquainted before the First World War during the research
year that Ranke spent at the University of Pennsylvania in 1905–6 while
Leonard was working in Philadelphia as an associate editor for the

Lippincott's Dictionary.[51] Their friendship was resumed when Ranke came as a visiting professor to the University of Wisconsin and collaborated on what Leonard calls "the Englishing" of his translation.[52] The difference between Thompson's hexameters and Leonard's free verse is instantly apparent if we consider Leonard's energetic version of the seduction scene:

> Then the priestess loosened her buckle,
> Unveiled her delight,
> For him to take his fill of her.
> She hung not back, she took up his lust,
> She opened her robe that he rest upon her.
> She aroused in him rapture, the work of woman.
> His bosom pressed against her. (8)

Like Thompson, Leonard cites the timeless themes of the epic: "sex-love, combat, friendship, adventure, valour, loyalty [. . .] the mystery of birth and death." He does not forget to mention the early occurrence of such motifs as "the flood and the tree of life and the evil serpent which are to this day believed by many millions in three religious faiths" (x). Leonard's work was greeted enthusiastically by reviewers in all the leading newspapers and journals—*The Boston Transcript, The New Republic,* the *Saturday Review, Poetry,* and others—who praised the felicity of the verse. For instance, Peter Monro Jack in *The New York Times* (July 22, 1934, Book Review, p. 10) hailed it as a "lovely English poem" in which "the eternal themes of literature are here, with what freshness!" In most cases, surprisingly and despite some fifty years of controversy, the epic was treated as a previously unknown work.

These were the two translations, complete with Tablet XII, through which British and American readers became acquainted with the Babylonian epic for the next few decades. Other readers no doubt were exposed to the epic by the full recapitulation, according to Leonard's translation, in Will Durant's *Our Oriental Heritage* (1935), the first volume of his phenomenally successful *Story of Civilization.*[53]

In these same years, translations and fictional or poetic retellings (often based on other modern versions and not on the original) were gradually being produced in other languages: for instance, Russian (1919 by N. S.

Gumilew), Polish (1922 by Józef Wittlin), Hebrew (1924 by S. Tchernich-owsky), Dutch (1925 by J. H. Eekhout and 1941 by Franz M. T. Böhl), French (1939 by Georges Contenau), Danish (by F. L. Østrup), Turkish (1942 by Muzaffer Ramazanoglu), Finnish (1943 by Armas Salonen), Italian (1944 by G. B. Roggia), and Swedish (1945 by Kn. Tallqvist), thus opening the way for a truly international reception of the ancient myth. World War II precluded any immediate literary response to these initiatives, but the adaptations began to take shape rapidly in the postwar years.

2

Representative Beginnings (1941–1958)

Modes of Modernization

Since the mid-twentieth century, the Gilgamesh story has been treated in a variety of aesthetic forms: fiction, poetry, drama, opera, film, painting, and beyond. These treatments, however varied they may be, use one of four basic modes of modernization. First, and most straightforward, is translation, ranging from highly literal to free (as we have noted in the early examples already considered). In the following pages we shall not be concerned primarily with translations, except as sources; any detailed consideration would require an authoritative command of the original languages. However, the very frequency of translation is in itself an indication of the popularity of the topic.

Second, we will encounter a number of fictionalizing and dramatic revisions of the theme: that is, works that retell the story in its original period and setting while imposing upon it a viewpoint and values characteristic of the writer's own age. Familiar examples based on other myths are Thomas

Mann's tetralogy *Joseph and His Brothers* (1933–44), Robert Graves's *King Jesus* (1946), or Thornton Wilder's *The Ides of March* (1948).

The third mode may be called postfigurative: that is, works set in the writer's own time but whose action clearly follows a pattern identified with a mythic model. The most famous example, and the one that established the genre in the twentieth century, is doubtless James Joyce's *Ulysses* (1922). As T. S. Eliot observed in a frequently cited essay on *"Ulysses,* Order, and Myth" (1923), Joyce's "parallel use of the Odyssey" has the importance of a scientific discovery. "In using the myth, in manipulating a continuous parallel between contemporaneity and antiquity, Mr. Joyce is pursuing a method which others must pursue after him. . . . It is simply a way of controlling, of ordering, of giving a shape and a significance to the immense panorama of futility and anarchy which is contemporary history."[1] Other familiar cases are the postfigurations of the Faust legend in Thomas Mann's *Doktor Faustus* (1947) and John Hersey's *Too Far to Walk* (1966) or of the Gospels in Ignazio Silone's *Bread and Wine* (1936) and Graham Greene's *The Power and the Glory.*

Finally, there is a catch-all category that might be called broadly thematic or motivic analogues: that is, works sometimes known as "pseudonyms" or *imitatio* that seek by certain means—notably titles, names, mottos, textual allusions—to establish a loose thematic connection with the source work. A well-known example is James Joyce's *A Portrait of the Artist as a Young Man* (1914), in which the hero's name Stephen Dedalus, the motto from Ovid's *Metamorphoses,* and Stephen's vision of a "hawklike man whose name he bore" as a symbol of the artist associate the novel with the myth of Daedalus and Icarus, although the plot is not a postfiguration of the myth as we know it from Ovid.

In the following pages we shall encounter works from all four categories or modes.

Four Poets in English

The first significant postwar English adaptation of the epic was *Gilgamesh: King of Erech* (1948) by the prolific British poet and critic Frank Laurence Lucas (1894–1967). Apparently Lucas did not trust his audience as being hardy enough to deal with the unadulterated Babylonian poem, which is "brief, bitter, yet intensely dear" and offers "no consolation beyond the grave" in its "eternal gloom" (6).² His work, neither translation nor paraphrase, is "a free retelling" of the epic in free verse, which "alters, or expands, or abridges, the often fragmentary or unintelligible original in many small details" (62). The author not only omits many figures and episodes—the "rather tedious premonitory dreams (with a noticeable homosexual tinge)," which he considers "uninteresting" (57); the deities, whom he regards as "more tedious than most" (58); the Siduri scene; the "Stone Things." He even changes several names out of consideration for delicate English sensibilities: he uses "Ziusudra," as he confides in his notes, because Ut-napishtim is "more grotesque than poetic to English ears" (56), and "Engidu," because Enkidu is "slightly grotesque in English" (56); he avoids the name "Humbaba" altogether because it is "as impossible in English verse as Wordsworth's Jones" (57). His adaptation, which is based on several earlier translations—the notes cite Ungnad, Ranke, Campbell Thompson, and Alexander Heidel (see below)—rearranges the entire story, recasting it as a narrative that Gilgamesh recounts retrospectively to Ziusudra. By the time he reaches the ancient wise man,

> I had tasted of battle: it sickened me.
> I had built mighty walls: I was weary.
> I had loved women: they loved not me—
> Only my gold, or my power,
> Or my flesh. (22)

Then he meets Engidu. After the fight over the courtesan who brought the wild man in from the steppes, they become fast friends and immediately set out to obtain cedar for the roof of the great House of Ishtar. After they kill the unnamed demon (Humbaba) and chop his body into a thousand pieces without keeping a trophy head, Ishtar appears to Gilgamesh at night in the forest and offers him her hand and body.

> I gazed in her eyes, her eyes that shone even in the shadow of the cedars,
> And lo! I saw again,
> In the green light of growing dawn,
> The green eyes of the courtesan that had betrayed Engidu.
> And I thought "Like servant, like mistress." (28)

Listing her earlier lovers, he rejects her—an act that leads to the fight with the wild bull and Engidu's death. When the grieving Gilgamesh wonders why he should continue to live in that "night without dawn" (33), the priests send him to seek answers from Ziusudra. After passing the scorpion man, who offers the thoughts otherwise attributed to Siduri; a dark valley; and a garden whose trees have branches that glitter "like jewels" (37), he reaches the ocean. Although in his initial anger he tears "the sails" of Sur-Sunabu, he reaches Ziusudra and asks him to "tell me the secret of immortality" (42). Ziusudra relates the story of the flood and then offers the test of sleep and bread. Not immediately but after five days and nights Gilgamesh falls asleep and dreams of the god Ea, who tells him of a red stone, the "fruit of Immortality" (45), which he recovers and loses to the serpent.

"Long afterwards," Gilgamesh, now white-haired, returns to Erech, and his hand, heavy before in tyranny, "now weighed justice" (48, 49). Still longing for news of his friend, in the temple of Ereshkigal he summons the spirits of the dead, among whom he sees the shadow of Engidu, but they all disappear "like a thin smoke" (52). Later he dreams that Engidu comes but refuses to tell of his fate in the land of shadows. "Forget Death, / Fear not that Death will forget *Thee,*" he reports. "I knew it, I knew it," Gilgamesh laments, "there is no justice / In the world of Death, as in the world of Life." He returns to Erech, determined to fulfill his human responsibilities as a just judge for his people.

Lucas's version manages almost completely to de-Sumerianize the epic, rationalizing away most of the supernatural and uncanny elements, which are largely relegated to dreams, and smoothing over what he regarded as the harsher tones of the original to make it suitable for a postwar British public that he apparently regarded as unready to handle the bleak message of the Mesopotamian myth—even the small public that had access to the elegant limited edition of five hundred copies that were printed.

A much broader and evidently hardier audience was reached by the dramatic poem *The Quest of Gilgamesh* by Douglas Geoffrey Bridson (1910–80), for many years the chief cultural editor for BBC. First broadcast in 1954 on BBC's Third Programme (and repeated in 1956 and 1969), the work covers the entire story of the epic, bridging the gaps, rationalizing and psychologizing the action, and employing a vigorous colloquial language with none of Lucas's concern for the delicate ears of his audience.[3]

(In addition to an expository narrator, the text was distributed among fifteen speaking roles against a background of incidental music composed by Walter Goehr.) Bridson tells us in his foreword that his work is meant neither as a translation nor as a paraphrase but rather as "a complete re-thinking" of the Gilgamesh story (7)—a story embracing two main themes: "man's conquest of his environment and his search for the secret of immortality" (89). In particular Bridson rejects, without naming him, Lucas's reading of the poem as "a plea for submission to our human lot or a homily upon resignation" (92): instead, he presents it essentially as "a poem of revolt" (92) and "the first great onslaught of rationalism upon the forces of superstition" (95).

The narrator is clearly a voice from the twentieth century capable of drawing cultural analogies. Gilgamesh and Enkidu resemble other familiar pairs from the Bible and classical mythology—David and Jonathan, Achilles and Patroclus: "find the parallels for yourselves" (23). He uses modern science to rationalize the seemingly miraculous events: the battle with Humbaba is explained as man's conquest of the environment.

> And there were no more battles like that one
> till Franklin began to fly his kite, and Faraday
> ran rings round an iron core, and Rutherford
> first knocked spots out of an atom, and Cockcroft
> drew his bead upon lithium. (35)

The Bull of Heaven is simply a huge bull that Enkidu as matador dispatches in a bull fight, as Gilgamesh plants the banderillas and a huge festive crowd looks on (43). And Utnapishtim's flood is the tidal wave resulting from an atomic explosion:

> there was a blinding flash of light that up-ended
> half the heavens like an immense cauldron! The very air
> caught fire and burned! And a dark pall spread over the earth
> which coiled up into a giant mushroom . . . while the skies emptied
> in one torrential downpouring of death. (65)

Other incidents are interpreted psychologically: the snake that steals the magical plant is "Man's distrust of his own sufficiency" (74). "It was the doubt there at the heart of you / that fostered the snake" (74), Gilgamesh realizes.

> Only by faith
> in what he is can Man ever hope to have
> that answer within his reach. . . . Only by will
> can his future be mastered for him. . . . Only by pride
> can he compel the Gods. . . . Only by knowledge
> can he become a God himself. (75)

Cursing the years wasted on his futile quest, years he might instead have used to seek knowledge to replace his illusions, Gilgamesh returns to Uruk. In the concluding epilogue the author looks back from the ruined walls of present-day Uruk, where even the course of the river has changed.

> More answers are needed, it would appear,
> than Gilgamesh demanded—as there are many problems, now,
> that Uruk never contended with . . .
> Yet most of them
> are by-products of that first failure. (78)

Ishtar continues about her business today. The tamed heart of our contemporary Humbaba is the cyclotron (79). Even immortality is within our grasp, but biophysics and not mythology, the mutation of our genes rather than of our beliefs, will synthesize for us the prickly plant (79).

Bridson's re-vision of the epic is enlivened by its vivid language. Gilgamesh's Uruk was much more in those days "than a rewarding dig for a squitter of archaeologists" (17). The temple girl is "bosomed up, ripe as a Soho stripper" (14). When their fight ends in a draw, Gilgamesh asks Enkidu, "Is the world large enough for the two of us?" (21). The scorpion people speak a broad Scottish dialect:

> He's a braw fella aa richt, Angus—an' twa thirrds
> o'him'll be God, aiblins . . . But for the thirrd thirrd,
> he's nae nair than the maist o'men, as I weel ken. (53)

When she first catches sight of the bedraggled Gilgamesh, Siduri the Ale-Wife wonders "whether he wasn't a class of customer / that might be bad for the house" (55). And Utnapishtim's message for Gilgamesh is simply this:

> And if you have an ambition to do as well
> for yourself as I did—first you will have to prove
> your usefulness to the Gods in a similar way! (67)

It is this message that makes the hero realize that the years of his quest were squandered in futile dreams rather than useful action.

Bridson's striking poetic re-vision transforms the epic into a positive statement consistent with the postwar optimism of a generation confident in its ability, through determination and science, to tame the gods and nature to its own useful purposes. Bridson states in his postscript his own belief in the human ability "through research into the origin and nature of life . . . to synthesize it for ourselves"—a result that he confidently expects to have been achieved by the end of the twentieth century (95). As we shall see in the next chapter, the generation that followed him no longer shared that confidence and began, instead, to lament man's violence against nature.

The three leading scholarly advocates of Gilgamesh in the postwar United States were foreign-born but received their advanced educations at U.S. universities.[4] Argentinean-born Alexander Heidel (1907–55), a research scholar at the University of Chicago's Oriental Institute, studied first in Brazil and at Concordia Theological Seminary in St. Louis before obtaining his Ph.D. at the University of Chicago. He included a translation of the epic—celebrated for its tactful rendition into Latin of the sexy scenes—in his *Gilgamesh Epic and Old Testament Parallels* (1946), which carried on the discussion that reached back past Jensen to George Smith. Polish-born Ephraim Avigdon Speiser (1902–62) studied at the University of Pennsylvania before obtaining his Ph.D. at Philadelphia's Dropsie College of Judaic Studies. His influential translation of the epic was included in James B. Pritchard's standard sourcebook *Ancient Near Eastern Texts* (1st ed. 1950). His colleague, Russian-born Samuel Noah Kramer (1897–1990), who studied at Dropsie College before completing his Ph.D. at the University of Pennsylvania, translated the earlier Sumerian myths about Gilgamesh for the second edition of the same volume (1955). Both Speiser and

Kramer became distinguished Assyriologists at the University of Pennsylvania, where Kramer worked primarily on Sumerian and Speiser on Akkadian. Their translations in *Ancient Near Eastern Texts* provided the basis, as we shall see, for several of the American adaptations of the following years.

Likewise of interest in this context is Theodor H. Gaster (1906–92), the British-born and American-trained historian of religions, known for his abbreviated edition of Sir James Frazer's *The Golden Bough* (1959). He included Gilgamesh in his book *The Oldest Stories in the World* (1952), which was also intended for a general audience. But though "based on original translations by the author," his version is actually an abbreviated prose retelling of Tablets I–XI, omitting such passages as the introductory material or Enkidu's stay with the shepherds and abbreviating others, such as Gilgamesh's return to Uruk.[5] Gaster is primarily interested in the folkloristic motifs of the epic, which he catalogues without argument in his commentary: Enkidu as an "imposter"-figure, the Bull of Heaven as a storm god, the garden of delights as earthly paradise, Siduri as Calypso and Circe, and so forth.

The two unlikely heralds of Gilgamesh in American popular culture were the omnivorously erudite poets Charles Olson and Gregory Corso, both of whom, for wholly different reasons, had become disenchanted with a culture based on Socratic rationalism and sought to go back to more ancient sources. Educated at Wesleyan and Harvard universities, Olson (1910–70) received a Guggenheim Fellowship for his graduate studies on Herman Melville, which later resulted in his book *Call Me Ishmael* (1947). But, dissatisfied with academia, he gave up the fellowship and served during the Second World War in the Office of War Information.

In 1951 Olson published a key essay entitled "The Gate and the Center," which begins with the assertion that "KNOWLEDGE either goes for the CENTER or it's inevitably a State Whore—which American and Western education generally is, has been, since its beginning."[6] Without mentioning Nietzsche, Olson attributes the loss of center to the rationality that produced "the rash of multiples" caused by the impulse to analyze and categorize. He believes that thoughtful people were just beginning to break through the notion that culture began with the Greeks and to look farther back: "to the Phoenicians, to the Babylonians, behind them the Akkadians, and, most powerful of all, the Sumerian poets, those first makers, better than 2000 years prior to Homer, Hesiod & Herodotus" (171). Olson, an admirer of C. G. Jung, detected the "archetype" of "the EXCEPTIONAL man," with his "WILL TO COHERE" among his beloved Sumerians (172). He concludes his short exhortatory essay, which maintains that that original "FIRST WILL" is again rising within the American people, with a reference to "the subtle tale" of Gilgamesh, which (unaccountably) he assumes his readers know: how "the rude fellow Enkidu" was sent to correct Gilgamesh because he had lost his center and become a burden, in his lust, to his city's people: "As I read it, it is an incredibly accurate myth of what happens to the best of men when they lose touch with the primordial & phallic energies & methodologies which, said this predecessor people of ours, make it possible for man, that participant thing, to take up, straight, nature's, live nature's force." That year he applied, apparently unsuccessfully, for a Fulbright Fellowship to go to Iraq in order to deepen his studies of Sumerian history and culture.[7] Then, presumably hoping to put his educational theories into practice, he accepted an appointment at the experimental Black Mountain College in North Carolina and soon became its rector.

It was not the new scholarly translations that first made Olson aware of the huge Gilgamesh, to whom the poet at 6'7" may have felt a special kinship. As early as 1941 one of his first poems, "Tomorrow," began with the lines:

> I am Gilgamesh,
> an Ur world is in me
> to inhabit.[8]

The poem, which presumably is based on Leonard's recent felicitous translation from the German, speaks of "the fathers" who told him of the flood and said "the heart / knows no evolution: / it is as it was when it is." Already here, then, Olson was familiar with the story of Gilgamesh, and his idea of a primal "archetypal" human nature, which it is the individual's responsibility to discover within him- or herself, was at least tentatively present.

We next hear of Gilgamesh in mid-May 1949, when his correspondent and epistolary lover Frances Boldereff—a typographic designer and writer whose first book, *A Primer of Morals for Medea* (1949), had just appeared—sent Olson an offprint of an article by Samuel Kramer, whom she had met at the University of Pennsylvania's Museum, entitled: "The Epic of Gilgameš and Its Sumerian Sources: A Study in Literary Evolution."[9] (Her accompanying letter mentions Leonard's "very nice translation.")[10] Olson reported a few days later (May 23, 1949) that he had begun reading Kramer's article and enclosed in his letter a copy of his still-unpublished poem "Tomorrow." Two days later he sent Bolderoff a new poem with the notation: "recognize it? my thanks."[11]

This poem, "La Chute," clearly based on Kramer's account of the Sumerian poem "Gilgameš, Enkidu, and the Nether World," is Gilgamesh's lament for his drum and lute—the *pukku* and *mikku* of the Sumerian work—and his wish for someone to bring them up from the world below.[12] (Today the terms *pukku* and *mikku* are more commonly translated as *ball* and *mallet,* but, as we shall see, many writers have preferred the musical implications of Kramer's rendition as *drum* and *drumstick.*) Olson regarded this poem, as well as others like it, as "transpositions" of the original material.[13] Of interest here are in particular the specific borrowings from Kramer's text. Olson assumes, no doubt thinking of the Humbaba episode in the epic, that Inanna's *huluppu* tree is a cedar tree, which Gilgamesh felled for the goddess. But like Kramer, who tells that he fashioned "of its crown a *mikku,*" Olson writes: "o my lute / wrought from the tree's crown."[14] Kramer renders the following lines: "My *pukku* whose *lustiness* was irresistible, / My *mikku* whose *pulsations could not be drowned out*" (emphasis in original). Olson retains the italicized nouns:

> my drum whose lustiness
> was not to be resisted
>
> my lute from whose pulsations
> not one could turn away.

And where Kramer's version ends with the formulation: "My *mikku,* who will bring it up from the 'face' of the nether world?", Olson offers: "my lute / who will bring it up / where it fell in the face of them."[15] According to his essay two years later, the drum and lute symbolize the primal power and sexuality that Gilgamesh has lost and that will be recovered when, through Enkidu, he is reunited with his lost center.

In another "transposition" written that summer, "La Chute II," Olson took up the same theme, going on to the next phase of the story: namely, Gilgamesh's instructions as Enkidu prepares to "go down to the dead" to recover the lost drum and lute.[16] Again, the wording suggests Kramer's translation as the source: Kramer's "lest the outcry of Kur will seize thee" becomes "lest the outcry shall seize you"; "Kiss not thy beloved wife, / Strike not thy hated wife" becomes "And when you met the wife you loved / do not kiss her / nor strike the wife you hated"; and Kramer's note that the mother "was lying stark naked in the nether world" yields "there, lies naked / the mother."[17] As John Maier acutely sensed, "The very fidelity with which Olson keeps close to the Sumerian is evidence of his listening closely, his avoidance of 'the lyrical interference of the individual as ego'"—in sum, Olson's effort through his "transpositions" to overcome modern subjectivity in the service of a primal directness.[18] A third poem of that summer, "La Chute III," sounds like a Sumerian poem of descent-to-the-underworld—Ishtar, Enkidu, Gilgamesh—filtered through Jung and Sartre's *Huis clos* ("L'enfer, c'est les autres"). The descent, we learn there, to the womb or to the underworld, is not the end in itself.

> the hell
> is the present descent, the hell
> is the guilt present, the descent
> is not to the past, the descent is
> the pursuit, the desire and the door.[19]

The two "Bigmans" poems written the following year (1950) clearly refer to Gilgamesh, but here the source is no longer Kramer's article but Speiser's translation of the epic as Olson presumably found it in Pritchard's *Ancient Near Eastern Texts*. Indeed, "Bigmans II" amounts to a sometimes literal transposition of the opening lines of the epic. "He who saw everything, of him learn, of my land," the poem begins (Speiser: "He who saw everything, [to the end]s of the land").[20] And it continues for some five pages with allusions to Gilgamesh's "long journey to cut down / the dirty tree" and to him "who did build a wall, who saw his job as civilizer." The speaker goes on to invite people to inspect the wall with its bricks, timber, and vaulting (Speiser: "Inspect the base terrace, examine the brickwork"). It goes on to complain that he "made bull trouble among his folk, / he was so rampant, wild and unacknowledged to himself" (Speiser: "He is made fearful like a wild ox") and concludes with the people's appeal for "his equal": "make a man of impetuous heart, the two of them / will struggle with each other, / and give the rest of us some rest" (Speiser: "Create now his double; / His stormy heart let him match. / Let them contend, that Uruk may have peace!").

Allusions to Sumerian culture generally occur with frequency in Olson's writings of the 1950s and 1960s. It is reported that he owned over one hundred books and articles on the subject in his personal library.[21] And references to Gilgamesh occur in several of his later poems, for example "Tale of the Two Spiders, Cross-Legged in Eternity" (c. 1960), with its apparent allusion to the episode of the scorpion-men in the epic. But the main point remains constant: Olson turned to the epic as a specific exemplification of the archaic Sumerian "will to cohere" that he regarded as the answer to modern futility and disintegration.

During those same years the Beat poet Gregory Corso (1930–2001) became similarly addicted to Gilgamesh. But unlike Olson, who read the epic while he was a graduate student at Harvard or shortly thereafter, Corso probably became acquainted with the work as part of his autodidactic education as a teenager serving three years in prison for theft, where his voracious reading extended from the Greek and Roman classics to the English Romantics and beyond. While Gilgamesh does not enter directly into his poetry, Corso seems to have mentioned the work to his friends and interviewers in every possible context. He was fond of calling Gilgamesh and Enkidu "proto–Jack Kerouac" and "proto–Neal Cassady," referring to his fellow beatniks from San Francisco days: "two friends in search of the mystery of everlasting life."[22] And he liked to test interviewers by asking them to identify the world's oldest book or to name Gilgamesh's best friend.

Most importantly, however, and very much like Olson, from whom as a poet Corso could scarcely have differed more: he felt that Gilgamesh was significant "because I like to go back to the sources"—that is, beyond the rationalism of the Greeks and Romans to an earlier primal unity. Not surprisingly, when he taught a series of seminars at the Naropa Institute in Boulder, Colorado, in the summer of 1977 for its "Jack Kerouac School of Disembodied Poetics," he devoted one full session to Gilgamesh, in which he discussed such issues as Gilgamesh as a tragic seeker, the relationship of Enkidu to Gilgamesh and the animal world, and immortality and impermanence.[23] What matters is not Corso's originality or lack thereof—in fact his views of the epic are quite conventional—but rather his early obsession with the epic as a sign of its importance within a particular group of American poets and his identification of Gilgamesh's search with their own "howls" and quests "on the road."

Apart from Bridson's radio play, which reached a wide audience, the other three poetic works in English had little general impact. Lucas's version had a very small print run while Olson and Corso, regardless of their standing within their separate coteries on both coasts, were hardly known to the public at large, which in any case during the Eisenhower era was hardly in a mood to listen to their message of social futility and moral disintegration. While these works indicate a growing awareness of the epic of Gilgamesh within the literary communities in England and the United States, the broader acquaintance had to await developments of the 1960s.

Four German Initiatives

The situation was different in Germany, where writers in the immediate postwar period, confronted with the harsh reality of death in war, with the disintegration of the world as they had known it, and with the problems of exile and the homecoming wanderer, drew often in their novels and poems on such myths as that of Odysseus and on the life of Ovid, in which precisely those problems are reflected.[24] So it is hardly surprising that they turned as well to the epic of Gilgamesh, which had already established itself among prewar German writers and thinkers, because it reflects precisely those issues—plus others that the writers, depending on their personal concerns, recognized in the Babylonian story.

    The first postwar "translation"—actually more of a "transposition" almost in Olson's sense—was Bruno P. Schliephacke's "narrative from the primal time of all culture," *Gilgamesh Seeks Immortality* (*Gilgamesch sucht die Unsterblichkeit,* 1948).[25] The author was by profession a folklorist who applied Jungian methods (in a sublimation of his earlier nationalistic inclinations) to folktales and myths in an effort through their "soul and symbol" to find "new ways to ancient knowledge."[26] Using Ungnad's translation of the epic plus Gressmann's version of other Akkadian myths, Schliephacke manufactured a prose account of Sumerian myth beginning with the creation and Adapa's fall (as tales told to Gilgamesh by a priest named Sumu). The principal episodes of the epic are related summarily: after civilizing Enkidu, "Mashiana" (a name taken from an ancient Persian legend of the first couple) becomes friends with Gilgamesh without the traditional fight, and they quickly kill Chumbaba and the heavenly bull. After Enkidu's death, Sumu sends Gilgamesh to Ut-napishtim. He encounters Sabitu in her lovely garden and hears the flood story from Ut-napishtim. After the snake steals the miracle-working plant, Gilgamesh vainly seeks advice from the spirit of Enkidu. Then Sumu tells him the story of Ishtar's descent to the underworld and her return with Tammuz. Gilgamesh is consoled, having learned that "the dead like Tammuz rise to escape the dark womb of the earth. . . . Living things die, but not life itself" (34). Gilgamesh returns happily to his city and continues to build his great wall.

Schliephacke states clearly that he has no desire to practice philology, only philosophy: "For that reason in the entire presentation particular value was placed on the clarity of the symbolism, which in Sumer—at the end of a mythic age—still appears in a splendid und unfalsified form" (38). Following his brief and optimistic recapitulation of the epic, he appends a lengthy essay "On the Culture of the Sumerians," which consists essentially of a Jungian and ethno-anthropological reading of the story he has just told, with Bachofen's theory of matriarchy thrown in for good measure. We learn that the Sumerian creation legend anticipates the theory of relativity (40); that the androgynous god of creation is still present in German folktales (40); that Mashiana's taming of the wild man reflects early matriarchy (48) and that modern socialism reveals a "motherly tendency" stemming from its synthesis of matriarchy and patriarchy (50); that Chumbaba, with his threat against culture, embodies the existential experience of endangerment and angst, while Ishtar exemplifies the redemption from that threat (51); that Sabitu in her garden anticipates the Virgin Mary in her *hortus conclusus* (54); that in Gilgamesh "the separation of the egocentric world of the subject from the world of objects is for the first time completed following difficult struggles" (60); and so forth. In sum: the epic of Gilgamesh, with some of its troublesome passages excised— most notably, those that are not useful to his interpretation—is set within

a broader context that allows the author to present it as a reassuring solu-
tion to the problems of Germans shortly after World War II: while many
may have died, life goes on; socialism affords a kinder, gentler order that
protects human values against the ruder impulses of patriarchy and capitalism; love can transform the individual in such a manner as to offset the
threats of existence; and people should get back to the business of rebuild-
ing the nation.

A year earlier, the German poet and essayist Hermann Kasack (1896–
1947) had published one of the most striking postwar novels, *The City beyond the River* (*Die Stadt hinter dem Strom,* 1947), which received a major
literary prize and, with Kasack's own libretto, was scored for an opera by
Hans Vogt (1955). This novel, which combines in Kafka's manner a surreal vision with detailed realism, depicts a place that strikingly resembles a
German city destroyed by the bombs of World War II. Kasack tells us that
in 1941 he had a dream that took him into "the realm of the dead . . . who
still seemed to have traces of life that, more or less rapidly, dissipated until
the individual consciousness submerged into the anonymous, in the wholly
dead."[27] Soon thereafter, early in 1942, he experienced a vision of "a ghostly
city of ruins, which edged off into the infinite and in which people moved
like groups of captive puppets."[28] He immediately began to write an account combining his dream and his vision, and soon enough—through the
bombing of Berlin, where Kasack had worked for years as an editor and
then as a pioneer in radio broadcast—reality caught up with the vision.
The second part of the novel, written directly after war's end, depicts the
harsh existence in the postwar ruins.

In the cellars and catacombs of the "city beyond the river"—reminiscent
of the various rivers or waters separating the realms of life and death in
world mythologies—the narrator encounters people he has known and
presumed dead: his father, his lover, his best friend, and others. It gradually dawns on him that they are indeed dead: "phantoms, empty images
that mimic life" (257), their shadows are brighter than his, their skin cooler
to the touch, their actions meaningless repetitions of various occupations.
It turns out that they are temporarily inhabiting an "intermediate realm"
(329) or "forecourt of death" (403) from which eventually they move on
into absolute nothingness as their shades disintegrate.[29]

Gilgamesh enters the story indirectly: we learn early on that the pro-
tagonist, Dr. Robert Lindhoff, was for five years a research scholar at the

Institute for Research in Cuneiform Languages and that his special field embraced Akkadian studies on the epic of Gilgamesh. He has been hired as the archivist for this "city beyond the river" because his own studies have taught him that "the written word most faithfully serves the spirit" (23). If the Gilgamesh epic, the songs of the Upanishads and of Homer, the Tao Te Ching, or *The Divine Comedy* had not been written down, "the world of mankind today would no longer be distinguishable from the world of ants." The archives contain "the spiritual legacy of the Eurasian world" (68). Consistently enough, books that have no obvious spiritual value simply disintegrate into dust (73). Lindhoff is housed in a hotel with no other guests, and when he glances at the register he sees that it holds very few entries for past centuries—an unspoken hint that it was the special resort for earlier visitors to that realm from Dante by way of Aeneas and Odysseus back to Enkidu. Even though the Gilgamesh theme is not again stated explicitly, the reader inevitably identifies Lindhoff's venture into the realm of death with Enkidu's nightmare of descent into the nether world (Tablet VII). When Anna, his onetime lover, eventually recedes beyond the intermediate stage into a stony realm where she utters sphinxlike truths, she represents, Lindhoff is informed, "the homecoming of the logocracy into the age of the matriarchy, of gynecocracy, or—to leave aside the clever professional terms—the return of the spirit to the heritage of the mothers" (400). Following her ultimate loss and his stay in this "forecourt of death," where as a living human being he was viewed with suspicion by most of the shades, Lindhoff returns for a time to the real postwar world. Unable to adjust again to its reality, he remains in a boxcar of the train that takes him back, relating his experiences—essentially the novel we are reading—to skeptical listeners. Finally, upon his own death, he returns to the "city beyond the river"—not unlike Enkidu, who, too, after his visionary descent to the underworld and his report to Gilgamesh must return to the dead.

Kasack's novel was not only a realistic depiction of the deathlike existence in Nazi Germany of the years 1942–44 and of life amid the postwar ruins but also a powerful pacifistic appeal. In one scene, Lindhoff watches a procession of soldiers from armies of centuries past, each bearing a placard stating the number of dead they represent—a "great deathbook of world history" (294). "The end of all great battles is never peace. The end and the heritage that wars leave to the survivors is always a defiled piece of the

world, a defiled piece of humanity" (291). But its thematic allusions to Gilgamesh support the powerful and moving vision of the realm of death that
motivated Kasack and, along with many other cultural references, exposes
the direct relevance of the world's most ancient epic to the experiences of
men and women in postwar Germany.

In 1950, Franzis Jordan, inspired with romantic enthusiasm deriving
from his visit twenty years earlier to the German excavations at the site of
Uruk/Erech, published a popular anthology of ancient Babylonian myths,
In den Tagen des Tammuz ("In the Days of Tammuz"), which contained—
along with the Akkadian versions of Ishtar's Descent to the Nether World,
Etana's flight to heaven, and the creation myth—the author's own poetici-
zation of the Gilgamesh epic based on the earlier translations by Ebeling,
Ungnad, Schott, and Thompson (and omitting most of Tablet XII). Jordan's version is what he calls "an organic reconstruction of the epic"[30] based
on a comparison of the available material and employing basic four-beat
lines of full sentences without lacunae:

> Da lag im Blute der Himmelsstier Ishtars,
> Ihm rissen die Helden das Herz aus der Brust.
> Dem Sonnengott boten sie's dar zum Opfer,
> Vor Schamasch' Antlitz verneigten sich beide
> Und setzten sich hin, wie Brüder es tun. (57–58)

> (There lay in blood Ishtar's heavenly bull,
> The heroes tore its heart from its breast.
> They offered it to the sun god in sacrifice,
> Both of them bowed before Shamash's countenance
> And seated themselves as brothers do.)

Following an account (in the lengthy appendix) of earlier interpretations,
which focused principally on the question of death and immortality, Jordan's exegesis stresses the themes of sexuality and the conflict between matriarchy and patriarchy: "This mighty epic of humanity embraces the two
great ur-problems, the problems of death and love, of will to life and the
battle of the sexes. No other myth created more powerful images" (193).
In light of the circumstance that none of the other Sumerian myths have
a tragic outcome, Jordan also believed that there had been hitherto too little emphasis on the epic as a song of praise to the legendary builder of the

city wall of Uruk. However, he did not go so far as to add or embroider the relevant passages for emphasis, relying simply on the text to illustrate his argument.[31]

A fourth work, Joachim Maass's *The Gouffé Case* (*Der Fall Gouffé,* 1952), does not share the postwar characteristics of the first three. Maass (1901–72), a popular novelist and radio dramatist, emigrated in 1939 to the United States, where he wrote *The Gouffé Case,* his most successful work, and spent most of his remaining years.[32] The first part of the 600-page novel amounts to a detective story à la Dostoyevsky followed by a court-room drama after the fashion of Perry Mason (to whom Maass was no doubt exposed during his American years), all set in the France of 1889–90; the second part is a tale of passion and quest involving two of the principals from the first part and moving across the United States from east coast to west. There is nothing either German or contemporary about the action. In part I a young man named Jaquemar goes to the Paris security police, specifically to its famous chief-of-investigations Goron, to report that his brother-in-law, a well-known businessman named Gouffé, is missing. In a leisurely narrative filled with almost pedantic procedural detail, we learn that the body turns up in a suitcase near Marseilles and that Gouffé was murdered by a team consisting of a gorgeous young woman and her brutal companion in a plot to get his money. The interest revolves principally around the personalities of three figures: Goron, with his incorruptible will to punish crime; Jaquemar, with his insatiable desire to understand the reasons for his brother-in-law's death; and Gabriele Bompard, the irresist-ibly beautiful and utterly amoral seductress.

Bompard comes freely to the police to confess and obtain the reward offered by Jaquemar, saying that she was an unwitting accomplice who invited Gouffé to her apartment in the hope of tempting him into mar-riage. She accuses her companion Eyraudt of the murder out of jealousy and greed, counting on her demeanor of total innocence to confirm the truth of her statement. Even though Goron is convinced of her guilt, pub-lic sentiment and even many in the police, including her female warden in jail, are won over by Bompard, who serenely and cleverly woos general affection. Pamphlets crying "J'accuse!"(several years before Dreyfus) and accusations of police incompetence in the case undo Goron, who is forced to resign and soon thereafter dies of a heart attack. During the trial, a bril-liant lawyer, abetted by an inept prosecutor, easily manages to persuade the judges of his client's innocence. Eyraudt is convicted; Bompard is acquitted, marries a wealthy benefactor, and goes off to America.

In the second part, Jaquemar, dissatisfied with the verdict and filled with contempt for Bompard, pursues her to America in the hope of winning a confession from her. The search leads from Saratoga Springs, New York, by way of Four Corners, Vermont, to Moonstone Valley, California. Along the way even Jaquemar allows himself to be seduced by Bompard's sexual allure. Although she never confesses, her final action—she shoots him in Monterey and leaves him for dead—speaks her guilt more loudly than words. The ending of the story leaves it open whether Jaquemar lives or dies from his wound.

What does Gilgamesh have to do with all this? The novel opens with a motto attributed to the epic: "Death resides in my quarters, and wherever I flee, there is death." We soon learn that the epic is one of Jaquemar's favorite books—so much so that he is known as "Gilgamesh-Edmond" to his friends (105) and as "Gilgamesh-Jaquemar" by the author (616), who seems not to realize that in 1889 the epic still existed only in the partial translation of George Smith, where the hero was still known as Izdubar. Early on, when Goron goes to question Jaquemar, at the door he hears a voice inside reading the unidentified lines: "If I told you the order of the earth that I saw, you would sit down and weep" (from Tablet XII). It is Jaquemar's friend, Germaine Chottin, who later in a letter wonders "who is now reading to you from the song of Gilgamesh?" (554). Shortly before Gouffé's murder, Jaquemar asks his brother-in-law and friend if he knows the story of Gilgamesh, the mighty king of Uruk who had a friend named Enkidu, whom he loved beyond everything and who suddenly died. What did Gilgamesh do?

> He ran through the world and wailed: Death resides in my quarters, and wherever I flee, there is death. . . . He left everything and went into the world that lies behind power: there live the spirits of the ancestors, the dragons and the demons. He fled there to find some means against the death that threatened to overwhelm him. (69)

He found it, Jaquemar continues, "but the important thing is, that he yielded totally to his need, that he put everything aside and wandered to the end of the world in order to master his need"—a passage that anticipates

Jaquemar's behavior in the second part of the novel. In his last letter to Jaquemar, written on the eve of his death, Gouffé even wishes Gilgamesh-Edmond "happiness on your way to the demons" (105). We hear no more about Gilgamesh until part II, which is entitled "Mystical Final Battle." There, after he has succumbed to Bompard's blatant sexual charms and to rationalize his weakness of the flesh, he recalls the Gilgamesh of Tablet XI, "whose mortal weakness on his heroic demon-journey the old song sings: 'Like a snowy drift, sleep stormed in on him.' But Gilgamesh raised himself from the failed test; otherwise his song would end at this point" (526). In her letter, Germaine tells Jaquemar that she consulted their friend, the doctor Lebigot, about his possible whereabouts: "Deep thinking, deep thinking is my entire misery! That's what happened to Jaquemar's Gilgamesh. When his drum-brother Enkidu kicked the bucket, he wanted to know, come what may, what was behind it, and his deep thinking dragged him from one awkward situation into another" (550). In the last paragraph, the author apostrophizes his hero: "Hey, Jaquemar! Gilgamesh in our time, where are you?" (639).

These allusions make it clear that we are to think of Jaquemar's quest, which leads him from Europe across the United States to the Pacific coast, in terms of Gilgamesh's search for understanding. Other hints indicate that the villainess of the piece, the wicked seductress Bompard with her pure sexuality, is to be construed as a modern Ishtar. At one point her defense attorney even talks about the combination of "virginity and the craving for the orgiastic" that Bompard shares with such goddesses as the Babylonian Ishtar, the Egyptian Isis, and the Greek Aphrodite (369–70). In fact, as we look back at the action, we can see certain hints of the role of Ishtar in the epic. It is Ishtar who causes the death of Enkidu (Gouffé). Despite his sexual craving, Jaquemar, like Gilgamesh, rejects marriage with Bompard/Ishtar and confronts her insultingly with the list of her rejected past lovers, most of whom have been ruined or killed (604). And, like Ishtar, Bompard tries to kill Jaquemar/Gilgamesh. Other motifs occur as well: in the California monastery at Yoshua Springs, Jaquemar encounters Old Gabriel, reputedly the oldest man in the world, but unlike Utnapishtim he has no words of wisdom for the hero.

In sum, a compulsive psychological mystery story—not a page-turner but a leisurely read for the pre-television public—has been decked out with motivic hints that add to a popular bestseller a mythic dimension meant to appeal to the new postwar interest in the epic of Gilgamesh. (It is no accident that the ship that transports Jaquemar to America is named "Orphée.")

A Major German Thematization

During these same years, on the island of Bornholm off the coast of Denmark, the German playwright, novelist, and organ-builder Hans Henny Jahnn (1894–1959) was writing one of the most remarkable novels of the twentieth century—and one in which the Gilgamesh theme plays a central role: his more than 2,000-page trilogy *River without Shores* (*Fluß ohne Ufer*, 1949–50, 1961). Jahnn's works have been surrounded by controversy ever since the appearance of his first drama, *Pastor Ephraim Magnus* (1919), which won a major literary prize along with public outrage. For the sadomasochism, the perverse sexual practices, the violence of his works, he was reviled as a "prophet of indecency," and "Jahnnism" became a code word for degeneracy.[33] At the same time, while his novels remain largely unknown to the general public at home and abroad, Jahnn has been compared favorably to the greatest twentieth-century novelists, beginning with his first novel *Perrudja* (1929; still untranslated into English), which shows in its interior monologue and other stylistic devices the clear influence of Joyce.

The trilogy consists of three parts: a short novel, *The Wooden Ship* (*Das Holzschiff*, 1949), a massive two-book central section, *The Deposition of Gustav Anias Horn after He Had Become Forty-Nine Years Old*, 1949/50), and an unfinished *Epilog* (1961). We shall be concerned principally with the second part, which, however, refers constantly to the cryptic events of *The Wooden Ship* (the only part of the trilogy hitherto translated into English).[34] There the "Lais," a handsome vessel with hidden passageways and a mysterious cargo overseen by a shipper's representative, sets sail for an unannounced destination, accompanied by the captain's daughter Ellena and her young fiancé Gustav, who has stowed away on the ship to be near her. From the outset the crew is infected by a strange sense of malaise and menace, which is heightened when Ellena disappears. Led by Gustav, the crew mutinies and, in search of the missing girl, breaks into the cargo rooms, causing a leak that sinks the ship. As the crew escapes by lifeboat, they see the figurehead of a voluptuous woman—which no one had previously noticed—rise from the sea and then disappear along with the ship and, presumably, Ellena.

Although the novel, written from 1934 to 1936, has invoked comparisons as a sea story to Conrad, as an allegorical detective story to Poe, and, as a tale of the uncanny to Kafka, it left open so many questions—about the cargo, the destination, Ellena's disappearance—that it was repeatedly rejected by leading publishers before finally appeared in 1949. As a result, Jahnn began writing an explanatory concluding chapter, which soon turned into the immense second part, on which he worked from 1936 until 1945.[35] Here, some thirty years later, Ellena's fiancé Gustav is provoked by the cynical comments of a stranger, whom he meets in a local inn and who claims that the past is useless, to pursue with Proustian perseverance his own memories of the past, including specifically the fateful journey of the wooden ship. His account falls into thirteen monthly chapters as he sets it down over the course of a calendar year during which past and present are interwoven inextricably until, in the last few sections, the past catches up with the narrative present.

Gustav is now forty-nine years old and a famous composer, living in isolation on an island, Fastaholm, off the coast of Denmark in a house with a large chest containing the embalmed body of his friend and lover, Alfred Tutein, who died some years earlier and had been "the force that changed my life" (I.33).[36] (That Gustav is a composer and that music, as we shall see, plays such a central role in the work has led critics to compare Jahnn's novel to Thomas Mann's almost contemporaneous *Doktor Faustus* [1947].) It turns out that Tutein, at the time an ordinary seaman on the "Lais," murdered Ellena—perhaps accidentally and for obscure reasons. When the crew in their lifeboats were rescued by a slow freighter and the two young men were thrown together as bunkmates, Tutein confessed his crime to Gustav, who for complicated reasons decided not to surrender the murderer to the law.

> I became his friend; not because he was innocent or only seemingly guilty: he became a part of me because he was guilty. He wanted me to kill him after he had made his confession. He feared the court and the scaffold. Because I did not want to be his judge and executioner, but his friend, he demanded of me that I never leave him. (I.674)

Hearings take place, first on board and later when the freighter docks in South America, with no clear explanation about the cargo, the murder, or the sinking. However, from the shipper's representative, who commits suicide, Gustav inherits a sum from whose interest he and Tutein are able to live with a degree of independence for the rest of their lives.

In the first five chapters (November through March) Horn recalls the journey and adventures of the two friends as they make their way with various sadomasochistic sexual adventures with girls and boys from South America to Capetown and then up the coast of Africa to the Canary Islands and, finally, to a village in Norway. There, Horn, a trained pianist in his early years, begins to compose on his Bechstein piano—an oeuvre that later encompasses fifty published compositions including two symphonies, a quintet, preludes, fugues, piano sonatas, and short orchestral pieces— while the untutored Tutein begins to show considerable skill in architectural drawing. Four years later they move to a town in Sweden, where Tutein becomes a shrewd horse trader while Horn gives his first concerts and enjoys critical and popular success. In the course of these years, despite occasional flings with partners of both sexes, the two men develop an intimate homosexual love. The most serious threat to their affair develops when Tutein gets close to his assistant, Egil, and Horn becomes involved with the seductive Gemma. In all cases the erotic episodes function as a sedative in the face of life's threat. "The fear is great," Tutein says. "But there is no salvation from the fear, only anaestheticization" (I.729). When the friends reject Egil and Gemma, who in turn get married, Horn and Tutein seal their own love with a mystical blood bond: a friend, a physician helps them to exchange half their blood—a scene depicted in considerable medical detail.

Tutein, apparently weakened by the exchange of blood that strengthens Horn, dies of flu at the age forty-two after the two men have been living together for some twenty years—twenty years during which "we explored, fought, tormented, hated and, even more, loved each other" (II.171). In a physiologically detailed description, we learn how Horn, concealing his lover's death, embalmed his body, enclosed it in a copper container, and kept the container within a handsome teak chest. Later he hires workmen to blast into a nearby rock a large hole—whether eventually to bury the chest there or for some other purpose remains unclear. When Horn reaches August in his account, he gets an unexpected visit. In his effort to recover the past, he had earlier written to invite a former crewman from the "Lais" to come for a visit. The sailor is already dead, but the letter falls into the possession of an exploitative and vicious young man named Ajax von Uchri, who persuades Horn to take him on as an assistant for a three-month trial and soon tries tyrannically to seize control of his house and life. Having gained Horn's confidence, he learns the secret of the chest and the embalmed body of Tutein. He persuades Horn to bury it at sea and then blackmails him for the suspected murder of Tutein and even that of Ellena. In November, exactly a year after Horn began his account and when he is experiencing visions of dead acquaintances from his past, Ajax murders him and flees from the island. *Epilog* offers the response of some of the survivors to Horn's death and their experiences with him.

The immense length of the novel is a product of the inclusion of frequent digressions: extended memories about Horn's childhood as well as novella-length narratives about other characters, lengthy descriptions of animals and nature, and long technical discussions of music (especially Baroque music) and Horn's own artistic development as a composer, which begins when he tentatively adds additional voices to the rolls that control mechanical player pianos and proceeds through his experiments in composition, with occasional examples of scores from his works. As fascinating as some of these digressions are, we limit our discussion here to those aspects relevant to our larger topic.

Horn observes toward the end of his account that his personal life provided the instigation for his music. "My angst, my grief, my desolation, my health, the disturbances within me and the periods of equanimity, the manner of my senses and my love, my possession by it—all have also shaped my musical thoughts and feelings" (II.674). Accordingly, the novel displays a number of autobiographical features.[37] From his schooldays on, Jahnn was attached in a homoerotic relationship to his friend Gottlieb Harms, with whom during the First World War for reasons of pacifism he moved to Norway and settled in circumstances much like those portrayed in the novel. (It is no coincidence that Gustav Horn has the same initials as Gottlieb Harms.) Like Horn, Jahnn was an accomplished musician, well known in Germany for his restoration of Baroque organs and for his many writings on organs and organ music. In 1926 Jahnn married Ellinor Philips, who supplied the name for Horn's murdered fiancée in *The Wooden Ship,* and the couple lived together with Harms and his wife, Ellinor's half-sister

Sybille, in an artists' community they founded in North Germany. When Harms died in 1931, Jahnn was devastated. With his wife, his sister-in-law, and his mistress/assistant Judith Kárász, he moved to the Danish island of Bornholm, where he acquired a farm much like the one portrayed in the novel and where he lived until his return to Hamburg in 1950.

While his personal life provided many of the details in Jahnn's work, its meaning resided elsewhere. "Year in, year out I have sought a subject—a mirror image of my destiny," Horn confides (II.684). He found it, he continues, when the epic of Gilgamesh fell into his hands. Jahnn had long been familiar with the Babylonian masterpiece in Ungnad's translation. As early as June 21, 1925, in a joint letter to his wife and Harms, he enclosed what he called "a canon from the Gilgamesh epic"—a reference to the musical canon that Jahnn composed in 1924 and reproduced with its score both in *Perrudja* (with no reference to the source) and later in *The Deposition of Gustav Anias Horn*.[38] It constitutes a duet based on Tablet XII of the epic (in a lightly modified version of Ungnad's translation), where Gilgamesh asks Enkidu to tell him about the order of the nether world, while Enkidu steadfastly refuses:

> "Sag an mein Freund, sag an mein Freund,
> Die Ordnung der Unterwelt, die du schautest!"
> "Ich will es dir nicht sagen, mein Freund,
> ich will es dir nicht sagen.
> Wenn ich die Ordnung der Unterwelt, die ich schaute,
> dir sagte,
> Würdest du dich den ganzen Tag hinsetzen
> und weinen."[39]

> ("Tell me, my friend, tell me, my friend,
> The order of the underworld that you saw!"
> "I won't tell you, my friend,
> I won't tell you."
> If I told you the order of the underworld
> that I saw,
> You would sit down the whole day
> and weep.")

Fifteen years later, midway through the composition of the second part of his great novel, Jahnn wrote to his wife that it had just occurred to him that his novel is "the Gilgamesh epic, modern."[40] This suggests that the explicit inclusion of the Gilgamesh material, which occurs only in the second half of the work, was in fact a later addition as the theme became clear to the author. (In the first half the sole allusion to ancient Assyria is a lengthy discussion of the Babylonian calendar [I.335–38].)

Howsoever that may be, Gilgamesh clearly emerges as a dominant theme in the second volume of the novel.[41] As he embalms Tutein's body, Horn recalls the exchange from the twelfth tablet (II.180). In the days following Tutein's death, it occurs to him that he had long ago wanted to write music for all twelve tablets of the epic and had failed, composing only a trumpet fanfare that appears in his first symphony (II.232; the score of the fanfare is reproduced at I.819). He considers the words in which Enkidu refuses to tell Gilgamesh about the underworld but realizes that he needs a different text "for myself as guide through the labyrinth of the gloomy and dark harmonic and rhythmic streams" (II.233–34) and chooses for that purpose the passages from Tablet X in which Gilgamesh explains his grief three times in precisely the same words: first to Siduri, then to Ur-shanabi, and finally to Uta-napishti: "Why should my cheeks not be hollow, my face not sunken, / My mood not wretched, my visage not wasted?"—and so on for some thirty more lines. "The song of death was still in my heart," Horn realizes (II.236). Directly he begins work on a second symphony, his Gilgamesh symphony, on which he labors steadily until its completion two years later. The symphony becomes an enormous international success, but Horn asks himself, "What does all that have to do with those lonely days and nights in which I wrote it down? Millennia-old words, are they suddenly worn-out and without effect? Can they not stand up to a premiere performance? The spirit of Enkidu, has it dissipated into the never-existent?" (II.276). Later Horn confesses that he had hoped to score the entire epic as a memorial for Alfred Tutein, "but my pain prevented me from doing so" (II.530). We last hear of Gilgamesh in Horn's final pages, when he recalls his search for the words and stories in which his own destiny might be recorded, as was Mozart's in *Don Giovanni*. He found it in the Gilgamesh epic,

> that Babylonian poem about the friendship between Enkidu and Gilgamesh, about their shared deeds, about the dying of the one, about the unrestrained desire of the other to penetrate the underworld in order to find

again the one robbed by death.—That poem in whose fragmentary ending the curse of the flesh becomes evident—flesh which is exposed to decomposition, which cannot remain the seat of the soul, whose inmost value goes into exile and falls prey to the yammering of the underworld. (II.684)

Thinking again of the exchange between the two friends upon Enkidu's return from the underworld, he had tried to find new and more melodic, more singable sounds for the text: "After many years I returned to the first version, tore up the sheets on which the tragic strophes sparkled a bit. Only the lamed, unbelieving stammering is related to my soul when I think of Tutein's death—of mine—of everyone's" (II.685). After writing music for the first tablet and composing a boys' chorus for the last one, he had stopped, inscribing the words "in vain" on his score. His second symphony had arisen from the fragments of his Gilgamesh-Enkidu canon; the trumpet fanfare introduces both works. At this point (II.686–89) Horn includes the full score of the canon, the same one that figured years earlier in *Perrudja*. He concludes with the sad realization that "I won't see him again, even if I descended to the bottom of the ocean. I could wander to Ut-napishti, but I wouldn't see him again" (II.689–90).

Clearly Gilgamesh provides the central thematic line for Jahnn's novel: the theme of homoerotic friendship and an almost Sumerian horror of death, which is announced in the first pages: "My spirit is not prepared to accept death with open indifference" (I.24). But the novel reveals, as well, a number of structural parallels. One scholar suggests that the girl Gemma, whom Horn intends to marry until he discovers that she is pregnant, whereupon she curses him frightfully, represents a fictional parallel to the Ishtar of the epic.[42] Indeed, one might even wonder, given the earlier discussion of the Babylonian calendar, if the chapters themselves are meant as an analogy to the twelve tablets. The novel, to be sure, has thirteen chapters; but the thirteenth is incomplete, ending as it does with Horn's murder early in the month (on November 8).

Other parallels are clearer. Horn, from a genteel background and like Gilgamesh with his drum and lute a musician, represents the forces of civilization, while the earthy Tutein, the seaman and horse trader, exemplifies the powers of nature. As in the epic, the two meet in what Tutein intends to be a fight over a woman when he confesses the murder of Ellena to Horn; but Horn refuses to turn him in and—with no more motivation than in the epic—the two become close friends. The early years of their friendship are spent in adventurous travels and bisexual seductions. Horn, like Gilgamesh, spends the years following Tutein's death in mourning and in the search for meaning in the face of "the terrifying indifference of nature toward its creatures" (II.621)—a search that leads him finally to visionary interviews with spirits of the dead. He even has a great opening blasted in a rock: "I wanted to possess this hole in the stone, this entrance to the underworld" (II.429).

In sum, both for thematic and motivic reasons it is fitting to regard Jahnn's novel as, in his own words, "a modern Gilgamesh."

The First Musical Settings

Gilgamesh, that virtuoso of drum and (perhaps) lute, was not slow to make his presence felt in the postwar musical world, where he enjoyed a lively career. The sounds that Jahnn's composer-hero heard only in his imagination resounded almost simultaneously in the imagination of several musicians. In 1943–44 the Swedish composer Ture Rangström (1884–1947) wrote his opera *Gilgamesj*, which was orchestrated by his friend John Fernström and had its premiere in 1952 after the composer's death. In 1956 Alfred Uhl (1909–92), the Austrian composer and professor at the Vienna Music Academy, based his oratorio *Gilgamesch* (revised 1968) on the text by Franzis Jordan as arranged by himself and A. Liess. And around 1960 the German composer Raimund Schwedeler (b. 1925) composed a three-act opera, *Gilgamesch*.

The earliest performance of which I am aware is *Gilgamesh* (1947) by the Russian-born violinist and composer Nicolai Berezowsky (1900–53): a cantata for chorus, orchestra, solo voices, and narrator.[43] The cantata, commissioned for the occasion with a libretto based on Leonard's translation, had its premiere in May 1947 in Columbia University's McMillin Academic Theater as part of a festival featuring American compositions. According to some reports the work was favorably received, but that statement is hardly borne out by Olin Downes's review in *The New York Times* (May 17, 1947, p. 8). Downes cites the themes of Gilgamesh as stated in the program notes: "sex-love, combat, friendship, adventure, valor, loyalty, Nature and the mystery of birth and death." But he found in the work itself nothing but "bad, flimsy, tedious music, only entertaining when it was funny; as for example the place where the orchestra imitated the snortings, tramplings and bellowings of the heavenly bull." Despite this excoriation of the work itself, he found that the chorus and soloists, trained by Robert Shaw, sang the difficult music quite creditably and that the conducting of a difficult score was competent. In sum, nevertheless, "'Gilgamesh' absorbed valuable time."

In 1958 audiences in Basel experienced the premiere of a musical *Gilgamesh* that has subsequently made its way into the international repertoire—a work that comes fairly close to the musicalization of the entire epic that Jahnn's Horn envisaged. In 1954–55, only a few years before his death, the enormously prolific Bohuslav Martinů (1890–1959), along with Leoš Janáček one of the two leading Czech composers of the twentieth century, wrote his oratorio *The Epic of Gilgamesh,* his most ambitious and extensive vocal work and the one commonly regarded as his greatest achievement. Martinů had already turned to Babylonian mythology for one of his earliest successes, *Istar* (1922), a ballet in the form of a symphonic poem. For that work, which deals in three acts with the love of Ishtar and Tammuz, his loss through death, and their reunion and immortality, Martinů did not use any original sources but rather a poem by the Czech writer Julius Zeyer.[44]

For his later work, written in Nice during his long exile from his homeland and shortly before his return to the United States and the Curtis Institute in Philadelphia, the composer wrote a libretto based on the English translation of the twelve tablets by Campbell Thompson. (The first Czech translation, by Lubor Matouš, did not appear until 1958.) He acquired the translation in 1949 and was initially impressed, as had been many earlier scholars and writers, by the flood story in Tablet XI.[45] He studied the text carefully for several years before undertaking the composition and libretto, which was translated into Czech by Ferdinand Pujman and which, paradoxically, omits the flood story that first caught the composer's attention. His adaptation, which emphasizes the tragic sadness of the original, falls into three major sections: "Gilgamesh" (based on Tablets I and II), "The Death of Enkidu" (Tablets VII, VIII, IX), and "Invocation" (Tablet XII).[46]

The powerful and hauntingly lovely work, perhaps more accurately called a cantata, features a chorus, four soloists singing different roles, and a speaker—supported by a large orchestra providing a rich background in a variety of moods and musical modes that draw on the early

Baroque forms favored by the composer (as well as Jahnn/Horn). Part 1 ("Gilgamesh") begins with the choral lament about the tyranny of their ruler and an appeal to Aruru for help. This is followed immediately by the encounter of Enkidu and the woman, in which the successful climax is suggested by a lovely orchestral interlude culminating in the sustained sensual "Ah!" of the chorus. The section ends with a choral account of the fight between the two men, punctuated by violent orchestral effects. When the next section ("The Death of Enkidu") begins, Enkidu is already sick and near death. Enkidu (tenor) tells Gilgamesh his nightmare of the underworld in its darkness and dust and then dies. In a long solo, Gilgamesh (baritone), wandering across the steppe, laments and expresses his own fear of death: "I, too, shall I not die like Enkidu also? Sorrow hath enter'd my heart, I fear death as I range o'er the desert!" In the concluding "Invocation," Gilgamesh, "having failed to learn the secret of eternal life" and supported by a chorus of wailing women, summons his friend Enkidu from the dead and appeals to the gods for their assistance. "Open a hole in the earth, that the spirit of Enkidu may from the earth issue forth!" The spirit (now a bass) emerges, and the cantata continues with an exchange based on the same passage that inspired the canon of Jahnn/Horn: "Tell me, my friend, I pray thee, o tell me what thou hast seen of the laws of the Underworld!" But here, in contrast to Jahnn's work, Enkidu reports what he has seen: the one who fell from a pole, the hero slain in battle, the one whose ghost has none to tend it, and others. As the work dies away with gentle harp arpeggios and sustained strings in the highest register, echoing its opening strains, Enkidu and the chorus simply sigh the words repeatedly: "I saw, I saw!" In his program notes the composer relates that

> I have come to realize that in spite of the immense progress we have made in technical science and industry, the feelings and problems which move people most deeply have not changed and that they exist in the literatures of the oldest peoples of whom we have knowledge just as they exist in ours. They are the problems of friendship, love and death. In *The Epic of Gilgamesh,* the desire is expressed with almost painful urgency for an answer to these questions to which to this day we have failed to find a reply.[47]

As we have seen, Martinů deals with these various problems successively: sexual love (part I), love and friendship (part II), and death (part III). Jahnn, almost precisely Martinů's coeval, would have been impressed; but since the successful premiere took place only a year before the deaths of the composer and the novelist, it is unlikely that he knew of it.

During and after the Second World War German artists were as strongly attracted to the theme as they had been following the First. Willi Baumeister (1889–1955), fascinated by the visual possibilities of Near Eastern themes and images, created several series based on biblical legends (for example, Saul, Esther, Salome).[48] But no other theme occupied him as obsessively as Gilgamesh. In 1943, in response to the war and his own inner exile, he created a series of sixty-four illustrations to the Gilgamesh tale, based again on Burckhardt's version—a theme to which he occasionally returned over the next ten years.[49] Baumeister's style was wholly different from the more starkly realistic renditions of the Expressionists of the 1920s. Using frottage and collage techniques, he created abstract reliefs and hieroglyph-like figures to depict scenes that usually involved dialogue situations: the fight between Gilgamesh and Enkidu, Gilgamesh's quarrel with Ishtar, the battle with Humbaba, or the talks with Ur-shanabi (see figure 3). In each case the often otherwise unidentifiable illustration and its motifs were explained by a quotation from Burckhardt's version, as for instance: "Chumbaba saw them coming, he had claws like a lion."

During that same period, and apparently unbeknownst to one another, several other artists turned their attention to Gilgamesh. In 1943 the Swiss

Figure 3. Willi Baumeister, Sheet 22 of *Gilgamesh Series*: "Und sie erschlugen den Riesen, den Förster Chumbaba," 1943 ("And they slew the giant, the guardian of the forest, Humbaba"). Staatsgalerie Stuttgart. © 2010 Artists Rights Society (ARS), New York/VG Bild-Kunst, Bonn.

Expressionist painter and art critic Walter Jonas (1910–79), known for his illustrations of other literary classics, produced a series of twenty aquatints depicting episodes from the epic. Emil Schumacher (1919–99), regarded as one of the founders of abstract art in Germany, had been interested in the epic since before the Second World War; in his fascination with the Near East he produced a sketchbook entitled simply *Irak* as late as 1990. But it was in the years 1949–50, in the same postwar mood as the other writers and artists, that he created a series of linocuts illustrating Gilgamesh. In 1958, yet another edition of Burckhardt's version was published as an Insel-Buch with woodcuts by the popular illustrator Hans-Joachim Walch.

The first ten years after World War II produced wholly different responses to Gilgamesh in Germany and Anglo-America. The German novelists and artists, drawing on a literary reception that can be traced back some thirty years and that involved many of the most prominent writers of the interwar period, were able to assume in their audiences at least a passing acquaintance with the story and for that reason felt free to introduce its themes and motifs into their own works as an ancient prototype for the postwar experience of grief and the search for renewed meaning. In England and the United States, in contrast, there was no similar ground of understanding. As a result, the poetic treatments had either to introduce the themes, in particular the quest theme, in a popularly accessible manner (as did Lucas and Bridson) or to allude to it as an in-group shibboleth (as did Olson and Corso). As for the musicalizations, both Berezowsky and Martinů became familiar with the epic in English translation. It is impossible to know to what extent the mixed reception of Berezowsky's cantata can be attributed in part to the unfamiliarity of the epic in the United States. But the enthusiastic response to the premiere of Martinů's oratorio is probably indebted at least in some measure to the more knowledgeable receptivity of the German-speaking audience in Basel. Both works, as well as Rangström's, demonstrate the strong appeal of the epic for treatment in operatic or cantata form—modern forms that reflect at least in part what many scholars assume to have been ancient performances of the story, both as bardic recitation and dramatic representation. However, these poems, novels, radio plays, operas, and cantatas from the immediate postwar era represent only the first stage in what was gradually to develop into a much broader public reception of the ancient epic.

The Popularization of Gilgamesh (1959–1978)

Whereas the immediate postwar reception of Gilgamesh from 1945 to the late 1950s was largely a consciously cultural affair involving cult poets, controversial novelists, experimental artists, and the opera-going public, the next fifteen years witnessed a significant popularization of the epic and a broadening of its thematic uses. A host of translations made the work available for the first time to audiences in Czechoslovakia (1958 by Lubor Matouš), Japan (1965 by F. Yajima), and Romania (1966 by V. Servanescu), while French, Italian, Russian, and Arabic readers were presented with new translations (1958 by Paul Garelli; 1958 by Giuseppe Furlani; 1961 by Igor Diakonoff; 1967 by A. Fariha).

The Epic of Gilgamesh, Nancy Sandars's English version (1960), published by Penguin and frequently reprinted, remained for several decades the version of choice for many college courses.[1] Her smoothly readable prose text, based on the translations by Alexander Heidel, E. A. Speiser, and Campbell Thompson, is divided into seven chapters rather than twelve tablets and, omitting the formulaic repetitions, lacks much of the grim dignity of the original. At the same time, the edition provided an informative introduction surveying the history, background, theology, and diction of the epic. (Sandars's version remained the standard Penguin text until it was replaced in 1999 by Andrew George's original and now authoritative translation.)

Meanwhile, translations in Germany continued apace. In 1958 Albert Schott's 1934 translation was revised and updated by the eminent Assyriologist Wolfram von Soden for the popular Reclam series.[2] That same year, Georg Burckhardt's enduringly popular adaptation was reprinted with woodcuts by Hans-Joachim Walch. In 1966 Hartmut Schmökel, a German scholar of the ancient Near East, brought out a faithful yet eminently readable translation of the epic (*Das Gilgamesch-Epos*) into blank verse, arguing that the rhythms of that basic German metrical form correspond to the rhythms of the common four- or five-beat Assyrian line.[3] The translator allowed himself a degree of flexibility: for instance, to avoid tedious repetition he used different terms to vary certain stock phrases in the original ("underworld," "realm of the dead," or "Hades"; a variety of expressions for "he said"). Although the translation indicates its progression from line to line and from tablet to tablet, the translator divides his version into seven major sections with numerous subheadings to assist the reader's comprehension.

Against this background of availability, the popularizations of the epic began to emerge. On May 19, 1958, "The Epic of Gilgamesh" was performed by a student organization at Wageningen in the presence of Queen Juliana of the Netherlands (in a dramatization based on the 1941 translation by Franz Böhl). The highly praised performance, its dramatic dialogues introduced by a narrator, was produced essentially without textual changes and without distracting modernizations.[4] In the summer of 1960, the Los Angeles radio station KPFK—an affiliate of the progressive Pacifica Radio, which featured such cultural programs as readings of *The Odyssey* and performances of Stravinsky—offered an eight-part reading of Sandars's translation by Mitchell Harding, a local radio celebrity. In 1964 the Museum für Gewerbe und Kunst in Hamburg sponsored an exhibition entitled "Gilgamesch" featuring graphic works by artists we have already encountered: Richard Janthur, Josef Hegenbarth, Rolf Nesch, Willi Baumeister, and Emil Schumacher.

In 1966 Young Scott Books brought out Anita Feagles's *He Who Saw Everything,* a retelling of the epic for youthful readers with illustrations by Xavier Gonzales. A year later *Gilgamesh: Man's First Story* (1967) was published by Bernarda Bryson, wife of Ben Shahn and a prize-winning author and illustrator of children's books. Her "highly personal account," which is based on readings from the time when she first became acquainted with the epic in the late 1920s, contains no mention of the hero's womanizing: we hear simply that "our girls languish without lovers" (14) and that Enkidu feels "great contentment in merely sitting beside" the young woman sent to tame him.⁵ Utnapishtim comes across as an angry old man, who ridicules Gilgamesh and scornfully tells his wife "how deceitful are the ways of mortals! I must prove to this one that he is not fit to dwell among us" (84). In a final section, "Gilgamesh At Last Finds Enkidu," he goes to the gate of the underworld and pleads with Nergal to release his friend; when that proves to be impossible, he chooses to stay with Enkidu and dies "a mortal's death" but leaves behind an "everlasting name" (92ff.).⁶

A decade later in Germany several versions for children and teenagers appeared, including Edgar B. Pusch's "Little Gilgamesh" (*Der kleine Gilgamesch,* 1978); "When the Gods Still Spoke with Men" (*Als die Götter noch mit den Menschen sprachen. Gilgamesch und Enkidu,* 1981), by Victoria Brockhoff and Hermann Lauboeck, with illustrations by Katharina Lehmann;⁷ and *Gilgamesch und Enkidu* (1981), a theatrical adaptation for children by the film and TV actor Tilo Prückner and Roland Teubner.⁸

In 1968 the Polish composer Augustyn Bloch (1929–2006) conducted the premiere of his *Gilgamesz,* a ballet-pantomime in one act accompanied by orchestral music characterized by intense chromaticism with twelve-tone chords creating archaic sound effects and punctuated by a chorus singing quasi-Gregorian chants depicting the hero's initial exultation and subsequent grief. In 1970 Hope Glenn Athearn submitted "Gilgamesh: A Novel"—a retelling of the epic "as it actually might have happened"—to San Francisco State College as her thesis in partial fulfillment for her Master of Arts degree.⁹ Elizabeth Jamison Hodges's *Song for Gilgamesh* (1971) imagined the voice of a boy poet who accompanies Gilgamesh to recount episodes of the epic for teenagers. In 1975 the British jazz fusion band Gilgamesh, which had its debut performance in January 1973 and lasted until 1978, released its first album, also called *Gilgamesh.* And in 1977, in the

introduction to his anthology *The Road to Science Fiction,* James Gunn pro-
phetically devoted three pages to a retelling of the epic, in which he found
foreshadowed all the elements of later science fiction: a culture hero who is
partly divine, controls the elements, and saves the people—and which even
contains "a bit of technology" in the weapons used by the two friends and
the bricks with which the walls of Uruk are built.[10]

Poetic Adaptations

While the foregoing examples suggest the extent to which Gilgamesh was
penetrating the popular cultural consciousness of all generations in Europe
and the United States, the literary adaptations continued apace. In his first
book, *Sarmatische Zeit* (1961), the East German poet Johannes Bobrowski
(1917–65) looked in several poems beyond Eastern Europe to ancient Babylon. His hymn to the Sarmatian steppes ("Die Sarmatische Ebene") ends
with an allusion to "the heavy beauty / of the unfaced clay head /—Ishtar
or some other name—/ found in the mud" ("die schwere Schönheit / des
ungesichtigen Tonhaupts /—Ischtar oder anderen Namens—/ gefun-
den im Schlamm").[11] Another poem, "On the Road to Tauris" ("Auf der
Taurischen Straße"), describes an incident one evening at the edge of the
steppe near the Caspian Sea, where the camels were resting: "In the distance Enkidu: / as he approached / from the gazelles' watering hole, / with
a dark face. I was born on the steppe, / he says, I shall fight / in the cedar
forest" ("Dahinter Enkidu: / wie er nahte / von der Gasellen Tränke, / fin-
stren Gesichts. Ich bin auf der Steppe geboren, / sagt er, kämpfen werd ich /
im Zedernwald"). It is worth noting that Bobrowski's volume, with its
allusions to the Gilgamesh epic, also includes a poem in memory of Hans
Henny Jahnn ("Trauer um Jahnn").

    Herbert Mason, a Harvard Ph.D. in Near Eastern languages and litera-
tures, characterized his *Gilgamesh: A Verse Narrative* (1970) as "a personal
attempt to revivify the *Gilgamesh* in a free form as a living poem" (105).[12]
His almost embarrassingly confessional "autobiographical postscript" relates the author's obsession with the poem from the time he first encountered it in 1954 as an undergraduate and his sense that the poem exposed
wounds stemming from his father's early death and the discovery that a
close friend was dying of Hodgkin's disease. The second experience clearly

affected his rendition of Gilgamesh's conversation with Enkidu on the eve
of his friend's death:

> Everything had life for me, he heard Enkidu murmur,
> The sky, the storm, the earth, water, wandering,
> The moon and its three children, salt, even my hand
> had life. It's gone. It's gone. I have seen death
> As a total stranger sees another person's world, . . . (48)

Throughout Mason gives a personal slant to the narrative, which often
takes on a contemporary tone. Thus the prostitute sleeps with Enkidu
"until he was used to her body. / She knew how gradually one stops / De-
siring to run with old companions" (20), much as a jealous woman weans
her new husband away from the drinking buddies of his bachelor days.
Mason's Siduri appears to have sexual designs on Gilgamesh: "She moved
her lips across his chest / And caressed the length of his tired body / And lay
over him at night until he slept" (64). Gilgamesh's conversation with Utnapishtim sounds very much like a college seminar discussion, and the older
man regards the sleeping hero "with hostile irony" (81). Mason's version,
based, like that of Sandars, on Heidel, Speiser, and Campbell Thompson
but omitting the twelfth tablet, ends with Gilgamesh's return to an Uruk
that has forgotten the name of Enkidu "As if to say it is impossible / To
keep the names of friends / Whom we have lost" (91–92). We are left wondering what Gilgamesh has learned from his own experience, since, in the
concluding lines, "for a moment—just a moment—/ All that lay behind
him / Passed from view." Between Sandars and Mason, readers of English
had a wide variety of choice, between prose and free verse, between a busi-
nesslike breeziness and an emotion-soaked intensity.

Mason's adaptation was one of the sources used by the Québécois poet
and dramatist Michel Garneau in *Gilgamesh,* his poetic dramatization of
the epic, along with the versions of Sandars and Jean Marcel and the studies of the Assyriologist René Labat.[13] "I fell in love with the history, the
themes, the symbolic course, and the personages of Gilgamesh," he writes,
"because I am fascinated by the fact of being a human being within all
humanity and not just in my own circumstances and because I love all
the spaces of possible song." His *Gilgamesh* was first performed in 1974
by students at l'École Nationale de Théâtre in Montreal and subsequently

executed as a one-hour puppet play some 150 times in Canada and French-speaking Europe.[14] Like Mason's version, it is also intensely personal, as indicated by the dedication to the memory of his deceased brother ("p'tit frère") and by the author's "Prologue," in which the singer, in words repeated by the chorus, tells us that this oldest story, one that still deserves to be told, is "the story of a friend who loved his friend and lost him through death, the story of Gilgamesh and his friend Enkidu, the story of Enkidu and his friend Gilgamesh":

> C'est l'histoire d'un ami
> Qui aimait son ami
> Et qui l'a perdu dans la mort
> C'est l'histoire de Gilgamesh
> Et de son ami Enkidou
> C'est l'histoire d'Enkidou
> Et de son ami Gilgamesh
> C'est l'histoire de Gilgamesh.(15–16)

Accordingly, Garneau shifts the emphasis from the second part of the epic to the first, although he scrupulously follows the sequence of the tablets and, to a great extent, the words of the various translations. The story is related by two narrators and two singers (male and female) with a chorus, all using the iterations characteristic of the original. (The author tells us in a prefatory remark that his text should be imagined as "sustained, penetrated, enveloped, caressed, understood, illuminated, unveiled, read, loved by the music" of his friend André Angélini [7].) The narrative is interspersed with scenes, often with dramatic ingenuity, acted out by the major figures of the epic. The seduction scene, for instance, takes place with Enkidu and the "fille de joie" on one side of the stage while on the other Gilgamesh relates his dreams of the falling star and the axe to his mother, Ninsoun. The fight between the two heroes comes to a draw, after which "they look at each other now in the silence and begin to smile" (37). During the death monologue of Enkidu, the hunter and the "fille de joie" reappear in person as he first curses and then blesses them. But while the first part of the epic is related or enacted almost in full, the second part is radically cut to roughly a quarter of the text. We again sense Mason's influence in the scene with Siduri, who implores Gilgamesh to stay with her and "take in me the love you are missing—I am going to rock you with my whole womb":

> Et tu peux prendre dans moi
> L'amour qui te manqué
>
> Je vois te bercer avec tout mon ventre (100)

Otherwise, the later scenes are drastically abbreviated. The ferryman Our-shanabi is given the speech that traditionally belongs to Siduri—that Gilgamesh should return to Uruk and take joy in his wife and child—but we hear nothing about the mysterious stones; the crossing of the Waters of Death is not depicted; Outnapshtim does not relate the story of the flood; and the search for the "rose de juvence" (110) and its theft by the serpent is mentioned by the chorus almost in passing. At the end Gilgamesh returns to Uruk and regards its walls, recognizing that it is "wisdom itself that leads men to such a lovely work" (114; "la sagesse elle-même / Qui mène les hommes à la si belle ouvrage"). As the chorus assures us in the last canto, even after the spirit of Enkidu has reported to him what he has seen in the underworld, Gilgamesh "lives each day of life in the reality of things" (120: "vit chaque jour / Chaque jour dans le réel des choses"). The work has been wholly refocused to highlight the hero's friendship with Enkidu, to play down his search for immortality, and to emphasize the satisfaction he ultimately finds in life itself.[15]

One of the strangest adaptations of Gilgamesh appeared in 1975 in canto 23 of the vast poetic cycle that Louis Zukofsky created over the course of fifty years under the title "*A.*"[16] Zukofsky (1904–78), a protégé of Ezra Pound, is often identified as a founding member and principal theorist of poetic Objectivism, which he introduced and defined in 1931 in a special issue of the journal *Poetry* and showcased a year later in *An "Objectivists" Anthology* (1932). The characteristics of that movement—notably a prioritization of form over content, of word over meaning—are fully evident in the poetry of the man who has been called "the most formally radical poet to emerge among the second-wave modernists."[17] (The analogy of objectivism to such contemporary developments in music as twelve-tone serialism is not accidental, since Zukofsky was himself the husband and father of professional musicians and knowledgeable in its history and theory.)

The cycle as a whole consists of twenty-four separate poems or cantos of radically varying length, form, and subject matter. While the poems reflect many of the political and economic issues of the half-century they cover, ranging from the depression of the 1930s and the wartime fall of Paris to the death of John F. Kennedy and the Vietnam War, they grow progressively more personal and include many autobiographical details. In addition, the twenty-four poems are linked by certain recurring cultural themes, most notably the music of Johann Sebastian Bach. A performance of his *Passion of St. Matthew* in Carnegie Hall is described in "A-1"; his fugal form is imitated in several of the poems; and his "innocence" is cited in the closing lines of "A-23."[18] Many of the poems include translations of, fragmentary quotations from, and allusions to a variety of works of world literature, including the epic of Gilgamesh. In form they vary from sonnets to haikus and in length from the four words of "A-16" to the thousand lines of "A-23."

Each of the thousand lines of this poem, which has been called "perhaps the most obscure poetry written in English in this century," consists of exactly five words—sometimes Zukofsky cheats by counting long hyphenated words as one—and the subject matter roams widely.[19] The poem begins with one hundred lines citing the "unforeseen delights" of common household objects—lamps, cushions, cats, gardens, flowers—and moves on to several lines of sheer wordplay, with the phrase "Ye nó we see hay / io we hay we see" and so forth, followed by a scene involving "sun hot bright" and "golden tile" (36). Suddenly, at line 133, we find the words: "Praise! gil . . gam . . mesh . ." (In Zukofsky's wordplay, which resembles that of Stanisław Lem, who, as we shall see, was also interested in Gilgamesh, it is not unlikely that the poet is referring here also to the stockinged [mesh] legs [gams] of his wife Celia, who figures in the poem.) The memory of Gilgamesh is presumably suggested by the hot sun and golden tiles of the preceding section, because the poem continues with the lines:

> excellent body sunned whose world
> journey wore out His wisdom
> building: wall God and Goddess
> copper-crowned cornice under Firmament . . . foundation
> terrace . . . masonry . . . proved fired brick (37)

There follows a 136-line recapitulation (37–40) of the Gilgamesh epic in which the familiar scenes and figures appear, but with new names:

Gilgamesh is called "Strongest" and Enkidu becomes "One Kid, a hillga-zelle" or, after his defeat to Gilgamesh, simply "Stronger."[20] The story is of course radically compressed. The entire episode of hunter and temple prostitute is reduced to two lines: "Strongest sent, his harlot went, / One Kid exulted until unmanned" (37). Ishtar's fury—she is designated simply as "a Goddess"—leading to Enkidu's death becomes:

> She raged,
> grappled, Stronger harrowed, hers—Strongest
> sobbing, "Why you not me
> dying." (38)

In this extreme compression, however, Zukofsky recapitulates the entire epic in a manner readily comprehensible to any reader familiar with the original. We hear of Gilgamesh's dreams, the fight and friendship with Enkidu, the battle with Humbaba ("The Spirit," "It"), Ishtar's proposal and rejection, Enkidu's death, and Gilgamesh's mourning:

> "Like him I shall be
> dust vanish unless my father
> everlasting—stirps my wander seeks—
> make me so and my
> friend brothers everlasting together."(39)

(Zukofsky uses the Latin word *stirps*, "stock" or "stem," to suggest the pri-mal ancestor, Utnapishtim, whom he seeks in his wandering.) We hear how Strongest tunnels "12 leagues of treemountain," passes through the jeweled garden ("flower carnelian, bud sapphires"), and is told by Siduri ("a veiled girl") to give up his search.

> Better
> a bath's clean linen, the
> glad wife embraced, a child
> fondling you. . . . (39)

But Strongest, having destroyed the "holy stones" of the pilot, makes his way to Utnapishtim, who is called simply "Everlasting" and who sends him home again with the gift of the plant "*Alive-Old-Stay-Young.*" At this point the recapitulation ends, and the poem continues with praise of "order, / loveliness, universe not improved upon" (41).

It is not necessary for our purposes to discuss the remaining three-quarters of the long poem.[21] The poet's concluding argument for "An art of honor, laud—" (57), which parallels the opening paean to the beauty of homely objects, makes it clear why Zukofsky, like Olson before him, introduced the Mesopotamian epic into his poem: it exemplifies a poetry praising the values of friendship, love, and simple order and beauty. Zukofsky's poem posits a universal cultural order capable of embracing values ranging from Gilgamesh to Bach and of synthesizing the various qualities represented by the many fragmentary quotations hidden in the text. As we shall see, his adaptation of the epic of Gilgamesh in "A-23" is consistent with the use by other American writers of the decade, most notably that by John Gardner in the person of his Sunlight Man: Sumerian culture is idealized as an archetypal paradigm for the life of eternal values in the midst of an often corrupt or degraded modern civilization.[22]

The First Fictionalization

The first in what would become a wave of historical novels based on the epic was published in 1959: *Gilgamesh: Romanzo* by Gian Franco Gianfilippi. In his novel the author takes a number of drastic liberties with the original, not only adding many figures but also extensively expanding it. The first half, with its emphasis on romantic love, is more of a romance than a swashbuckling adventure. Indeed, the action scenes are downplayed throughout. The story begins when the temple girl Belit is sent out to tame Enkidu, but she immediately falls in love with the man leitmotivically called "the panther from the steppe" (la pantera della pianura).[23] Enkidu and Gilgamesh, who is married to Ninguesirka, an earthy and ultimately unworthy queen, become friends after their fight; Gilgamesh's mother Rishat adopts Enkidu; and Enkidu immediately offers to show Gilgamesh the road to Kumbaba, "the lord of the cedar forest sacred to the gods" (26). When Gilgamesh balks, Enkidu returns to the steppe while Belit pines for him. She persuades her friend Sarug, who turns out to be a Hebrew, to bring Enkidu back to her. Meanwhile Iskara, the high priestess of Ishtar, with whom Gilgamesh has coupled in sacred marriage rites, tries unsuccessfully to woo him and makes threats against his pride and power. When Sarug brings Enkidu back to the city, the two heroes immediately go off to kill Kumbaba, an incident recounted as briefly as the following fight with the heavenly bull. Gilgamesh is somewhat saddened when Enkidu marries Belit but is then distracted by a great boat that Sarug is building for him (in a culture that hitherto knew only river rafts). Sarug tells him the story of Noah's ark, which arouses his dreams of immortality. Then Enkidu dies from injuries suffered when he dashes into a burning house to save a neighbor's infant boy. After Enkidu receives a hero's burial, Gilgamesh goes out onto the steppes, plagued by his grief.

While Gilgamesh is abroad, Uruk reverts to its wild ways—including Sarita, the girl whom the devout Sarug marries against his father's wishes and who now revels drunkenly and sleeps with other men. Leaving her, Sarug goes back to his own people in the north, where he marries Noemi. Meanwhile Gilgamesh, who has learned of Utnapishtim from his wise friend and adviser Sinka, makes his way past the giants guarding the Mountain of Maru and past Siduri to the ferryman Sanabi, who takes him across the sea to Utnapishtim. But Gilgamesh is disappointed by what he learns from the aged sage because he has already heard the story of the flood from Sarug (the author's hint that the Hebrews did not borrow the flood story from the Babylonians). He discards the fine clothes given to him by Utnapishtim, puts on his lionskin, and makes his way back to Uruk by the same route by which he had come (with no detours to seek a plant of rejuvenation). At this point, not even halfway through the novel's 320 pages, the tale known from the epic ends.

In the second half the emphasis shifts significantly as the spice of religion is added to the stew of romance. In his "Author's Premise" Gianfilippi informs us that he has been concerned "not so much to give an explanation of the myth as, rather, to extract its moral conclusions, comforted not only by the knowledge of the new findings by scholars of the history of religions but above all by a loftier conception of religion" (7). He does so in lengthy conversations and monologues that often resemble academic discourses.

Back in Uruk, summoning the nobles and elders, Gilgamesh confesses to them that his journey to the east gave him no satisfaction: Utnapishtim himself in all his wisdom has found only an illusory tranquility. Yet he still believes in the possibility of a better life, even if the law of death is harsh. So Gilgamesh institutes a new and gentler order in Uruk, and the city prospers again. With the inauguration of a great dike the security of the city is established. Gilgamesh, following a violent disagreement with the haughty and ambitious Ninguesirka, marries the lovely Ninlil, his mother's handmaiden. As the years pass Gilgamesh learns from his conversations with Sarug and Sem, his wise father, the beliefs of the Hebrews: "Only the soul is eternal. And God leaves us free to choose between good and evil" (192). When the high priests, who oppose all doubt and uncertainty and increasingly seek to conflate religion with politics, incite the people of Uruk against the Hebrews, whose encampment they burn, Gilgamesh reclaims the authority they sought to usurp. "In this manner Gilgamesh, the fifth king of Uruk, albeit not in any strictly official form, restored anew his power on the religious forces of his land, casting a new foundation for the relationship of his state and the religious one" (226)—in effect, establishing religious tolerance and a spirit of free inquiry. He points out—much in the spirit of dissidents in modern totalitarian societies—that the walls of Uruk, while they protect the city against attack, cannot keep out ideas (244).

Much of the plot in this second half revolves around his son Urnungal, nicknamed Gilghi. Gilgamesh, having grown old, is known as "Old Gilga"; his mother, Sinka, Sem, Istara and others from his past are dead. Meanwhile, his son, who has come under the influence of Sarug and his father and accepted their belief in a single God, falls in love with Miriam. His father points out that laws and tradition prohibit the future king from having a foreign wife and introduces him to Enlil, the daughter of his friend Muzudi and a beautiful, thoughtful young woman. Gilghi is torn between love and ambition. In his confusion he tries to follow in his father's footsteps to Utnapishtim but gets no farther than the Mountain of Masu, where he is overwhelmed by a vision of the god Samash. Returning to Uruk, he forsakes Miriam and his Hebrew beliefs and marries Enlil for essentially religio-political reasons: "Once supported by Enlil, he would have obtained the religious power that his father had handed over to the high priest and would have become a king similar to those who had preceded his father" (275). But on their wedding night, Enlil, disgusted by his arrogant calculations, refuses to sleep with him and returns to her father's house.

To avoid public scandal, Gilgamesh spreads the word that the newlyweds have gone off for a honeymoon and gathers them all—Enlil and her father, himself and Gilghi—on the great ship that Sarug once built (its first mention since Sarug's departure from Uruk many pages earlier). The water journey works its magic, and the two young people are reconciled in genuine love and understanding, whereupon Gilgamesh can die in the tranquil knowledge that the future of Uruk is assured. He has come to realize that any reign depends on order and discipline but must be tempered by love and understanding (314). As far as religion is concerned, mankind was not created solely for a mindless devotion to the cult of the gods. Rather, the individual's sole religious obligation is the search for God (316). And for this insight he is able, at the end of his life and for the first time in his life, to thank God for giving him life. In the last sentences of the novel the author reminds us that "Gilgamesh was sculpted in stone as the man who slays the wild animals, who liberates men from the fear of death. Whoever sculpted him knew the law of God" (325).

In this first fictionalization, which lacks most of the background trappings characteristic of the later historical novels, the author—in what might be regarded as a poetic resolution of the old Babel/Bible debate—has turned the monarchistic epic of the polytheistic Mesopotamians into a Judeo-Christian paean to the monotheistic God and a hymn to modern liberalism. Gianfilippi's novel is not so much a re-vision of the epic as a totally invented extension of its plot.

The Gay Gilgamesh

The year 1966 witnessed in Germany the publication of a novel that has established itself as an early classic of a genre the Germans call queer literature ("schwule Literatur") and that bears a warning facing the title page that "the owner of this book has obligated himself to keep the volume closed away and not to make it available to youths."[24] Swiss-born Guido Bachmann (1940–2003) studied piano at the Bern conservatory before going on to the university to take up music history and theater studies. His postfigurative *Gilgamesch*, the first of his many prize-winning novels and stories, recounts the bildungsroman of a musically talented Swiss teenager, Roland Steinmann, who undergoes terrible emotional crises between his seventeenth and nineteenth years, although most of the crucial action takes place between the actual narrated events and is related in flashbacks.

Having discovered his homosexuality, he steals money from his school and runs away with his friend Christian. They are promptly caught, and

Roland is sent to an observation station, where he is treated by psychiatrists and forced to labor in the fields. Shortly after his release, Christian dies, and Roland succumbs to despondency. Following a suicide attempt, he runs away from home and lives for a time with a prostitute. He is rescued by his piano teacher, Kissling, who enters him in a competition for the solo part in his piano concerto. Roland moves in with his teacher, practices hard, performs triumphantly, and wins the competition. But before the performance he spits blood into his handkerchief and is warned by his physician that he needs either mountain or sea air. He runs away again and works as a cigarette salesman at a fairground until he is taken by Ruben, a sinister friend from his boyhood, to the villa of a wealthy acquaintance. But Roland is too edgy to stay there: he goes to Marseilles and, in the nearby mountains, meets the shepherd Eustache, with whom he stays for several days in a homosexual liaison. Then he travels by ship to Hamburg and finally by car to Prague. Having experienced mountains, sea, and the city, he finally goes home again, where his mother soon dies. When he has a nervous breakdown in the cemetery and tries to dig up the grave of his friend Christian, he is taken away for psychiatric treatment. After his cure, Kissling takes him back to the estate where Christian's body has been removed and reburied in a marble sarcophagus. Now healed and composing his own music, Roland is adopted by Kissling, moves in with his family—and presumably lives happily ever after. As he recapitulates his life: "Premature birth, childhood, boyhood, love, prison, grief, hatred, pianist, waiter, mountaineer, ship's boy, adventurer—grave defiler?" (221).

This straightforward if sometimes sordid tale is narrated in a phantasmagoric language shot through with literary references and feverish visions. On one level it is a Faustian narrative in which Roland signs a pact with his Mephistophelean friend Ruben to forsake God and the order of human society—presumably to achieve his genius. At the end he recovers the burned parchment on which the pact was signed in blood. On another level, he consistently regards himself as a Gilgamesh mourning the loss of his friend Enkidu. A priest, who later turns out to be gay and a Nietzschean believer in the collapse of civilization, warns him to stay away from Ruben and urges him to return to Kissling and give up his wild dreams. "'Don't attempt the impossible—to reach Christian. No mortal has succeeded in doing so. You may have no contact with Christian—or you'll go crazy! I'm telling you, Roland: You are not Gilgamesh!' 'Gilgamesh?

Gilgamesh? Yes, I am Gilgamesh. And Christian is Enkidu'" (88). The priest warns Roland not to plunge into nothingness:

> "Go on building! Be yourself, become and grow! Climb from step to step. Stay on the step you have reached, without falling in between, until you can climb further. From step to step: from success to success: from truth to truth all the way to eternal truth. Let ascent be your experience—ascent to illumination. Into the embrace by light: primal darkness—the vision of the mountain of light—and its mystical ascent." (123)

In the mountains outside Marseilles, "Utnapishtim spoke to him, to Gilgamesh" (in words based closely on the tenth tablet):

> "Why are your cheeks wasted away, your figure bent, your spirit sad, your features worn out, grief in your thoughts, like a wanderer your face, burnt by dampness and the heat of the sun?" Gilgamesh said to him, to Utnapishtim: "Why should my cheeks not be wasted away, my figure not bent, my spirits not sad, my features not worn out, grief not in my thoughts?" (179–80)

Roland and Eustache sacrifice a lamb, whose blood they drink and whose pelt Roland keeps. Then they couple: "So they climbed upon each other, rider and horse. Roland's thighs pressed Eustache's body. He groaned beneath him. They exchanged roles. Eustache also pressed his thighs together and exclaimed: 'Alas, Gilgamesh!'" (189).

At this point the musical theme enters. In Prague Roland suddenly realizes that he doesn't want to die: "Not die now! Set the Gilgamesh epic to music. Ripened for three years like good wine" (202). He wants only a small room with a piano. We learn that he has completed two works and sent them to Kissling: "The duet of Gilgamesh with Enkidu is profoundly moving, and the string quartet is absolute music. . . . The string quartet is a single scream, like one of Trakl's night-dark poems" (232–33). Kissling invites Roland to live with him and work: "You still must learn a lot if you now set to music the tablets of the Gilgamesh epic. Work! Mythos and logos flow through time together like two streams. Somewhere the two streams come together. This is the only water you should enjoy" (238). The narrative contains many other allusions to the epic, as when Roland circles Christian's sarcophagus and hears in his imagination the music he composed for the now-familiar lines from the twelfth tablet: "Tell me, friend, the order of the world that you saw" (245).

In general one senses throughout the novel various influences that are hardly unexpected in the 1960s from a first novel by a university-trained literary scholar. Particularly noteworthy is the musical theme, which is reminiscent of Jahnn's novel; Roland and Horn even set the same passage of the epic to music. Most significant, however, is Bachmann's early and frank adaptation of Gilgamesh and Enkidu as an exemplification of gay love, which in the earlier treatments by Jahnn and Franzis Jordan was still understated. Previously, as we have seen, it was especially the theme of death and the search for immortality and meaning that primarily attracted writers and musicians. In 1946 the Italian Assyriologist Giuseppe Furlani had suggested that the emphasis of interpretation should be shifted to give more weight to the theme of friendship.[25] But not until the 1960s—at the end of which the Stonewall riots in Greenwich Village galvanized the gay rights movement in the United States—could the theme be treated frankly. From this point on, as we shall see, Gilgamesh repeatedly provides the subject for gay treatment in German and English, a status confirmed by the epic's inclusion (in selected passages from Sandars's translation) as the opening text in *The Columbia Anthology of Gay Literature* (1998) and its discussion in such critical studies of gay literature as *One Hundred Years of Homosexuality*.[26]

Another early adaptation of Gilgamesh with a gay agenda, thematically and not postfiguratively, occurs in the monumental fiction *Saturn* (1974), the magnum opus of the Danish novelist Henrik Bjelke (1937–93). This vast Joycean work, by any measure one of the oddest adaptations of the legend, leaps around temporally between the First World War and the author's present day and moves spatially from Venice to St. Petersburg, from Menton to Königsberg. In a first-person account we follow the narrator's search for himself as he experiences affairs with a series of male and female lovers, including an enchanting Italian woman, a young American hippie, and finally the woman he marries. Gilgamesh enters the phantasmagoria in a chapter entitled "I Am Not Going Back to Limbo Anymore," which features a psychiatrist, Dr. Rod Steiger, who is at the same time identical with the film director Rod Schamasch.[27] Having long planned to film the epic of Gilgamesh, he is as profoundly fascinated by the mythical subject as he is with the various psychological types he is studying in an effort to understand how the process of maturation takes place, or stagnates, in them. One of his patients, jaundiced and "Syrian" in appearance, strikes him as perfect for the role of Enkidu when he returns, ill and weakened, from the underworld. He is the counterpart to the American hippie who takes on the part of the virile Enkidu. Meanwhile, a Parisian lady friend introduces him to Otto Georg Rosenquist (one of the various hypostases of the narrator himself), who strikes him as the ideal Gilgamesh and who, appropriately, becomes engaged in a homosexual relationship with the hippie. Gilgamesh's preoccupation with death in the epic reflects precisely the problematics of Rosenquist's own existence since his childhood in an utterly dysfunctional and perverse home situation.

Another figure who contributes to the undertaking is Jean Auger, known as Jean la Gazelle because he succeeded in taming the wild boy of Rio de Oro, who grew up among the gazelles (in analogy to Jean-Marc-Gaspard Itard's famous account of "the wild boy of Aveyron" [1801]). The widespread travels of this poet-painter-philosopher had led him, among other places around the world, to Iraq, where he saw the walls of Uruk and became acquainted with the Gilgamesh epic, experiences that equipped him to become a ideal adviser for Steiger's film. While this chapter constitutes only one episode in the huge novel, the homosexual theme introduced there, as with many motifs from the epic (the gazelle motif, the name Schamasch), plays a conspicuous role throughout the novel. (Bjelke later returned to the theme in his novel *To Maend eller Hvad ingen skrev om Gilgamesh og Enkidu* [1982; "Two Men or What No One Wrote about Gilgamesh and Enkidu"].)

Gilgamesh and the Philosophers

It was not only the homosexual potentialities of the epic that received an impetus in the 1960s. We have already encountered Rudolf Pannwitz's version of "the unknown work" in 1920. Almost fifty years later, Pannwitz, who in his *Crisis of European Culture* (1917) was among the earliest users of the term *postmodern,* returned to the epic in a major study entitled "Gilgamesh—Socrates: Titanism und Humanism" (*Gilgamesch—Sokrates,* 1966).[28] According to Pannwitz's broad cultural-historical scheme, titanism and humanism are the two opposing poles of human nature and its history. In the first part of his study, the author introduces Gilgamesh as the personification of titanism: the figure in whom the spirit of megalithic culture was embodied (76). To this end he recapitulates, in prose and with a running commentary, the story of the epic, which for Pannwitz exemplifies symbolically the history of human cultural development. Enkidu represents an early stage: prehistoric mankind that preceded both the nomadic hunter-gatherers and stabilized agricultural communities. Accordingly, his death is a necessary stage in human history. Their defeat of Humbaba and the bull and Gilgamesh's subsequent rejection of Ishtar's advances represent "the break with the old religion [of matriarchy] and the violent elevation of a new one: the solar and titanic religion of the Übermensch" (79). The megalithic culture that Gilgamesh exemplifies sought to compel immortality titanically, not through rituals and mysteries; yet the effort ultimately fails. "Throughout the vast poem resounds a cry of lament of a sort that could never have sounded in Egypt: It is all in vain! Man is hopelessly mortal!" (95).

Modern cultural man, with his self-awareness and awareness of the world, has roots reaching immeasurably far back in history and has conquered vast realms of time and space. But what modern man lacks, according to Pannwitz, is greatness and even the belief in its possibility or desirability: "For it is its [titanism's] very excesses that created an Übermensch like Gilgamesh as the final witness of many epochs and, in him, integrated man and mankind" (96). What replaced titanism was its opposite: a historical-suprahistorical humanism exemplified by Socrates. "Humanism and titanism stand in an agonal relationship to each other" (342): they either submit one to the other or join together in cultures in which the one or the other more or less predominates. It is mankind's challenge to attain the integration of pre- and posthistory (96). Only then will mankind be able to rise from chaos to cosmos and, as an epoch, once again achieve "Europe," a concept that for Pannwitz symbolizes the unity of Gilgamesh's titanism and Socrates' humanism (344). Pannwitz's scheme is indebted both to Jung's theory of archetypes and to Nietzsche's dualism. His synthesis of titanism and humanism results, as does that of Nietzsche's Apollonian and Dionysian, in a truly "European" man or Übermensch. It was in particular Pannwitz's revitalization of Jung's theory of archetypes, as we shall see, that manifested itself in various subsequent German literary treatments of Gilgamesh.

Whereas Pannwitz was writing on a lofty philosophical level for students of cultural history and philosophy, another work of the 1960s addressed itself to a broader audience of readers newly interested in the epic Gilgamesh.[29] With the help and advice of numerous experts in Europe and the United States, Vera Schneider in *Gilgamesch* presented a general introduction to the epic, moving from topic to topic ("The Creation of Gilgamesh and Enkidu," "Enkidu's Death," "Ishtar and Her Lovers") and illustrating each one with passages from various English and German translations (notably Speiser and Schott, but also Kramer, Landsberger, and others) to demonstrate the difficulties of the text and its translation. In chapters dedicated to such specific topics as "Pukku and Mikku," "The Six Loaves of Bread," and "The Plant of Life," the author discusses the theories offered by various scholars to explain those perplexing issues. While offering no broad philosophical interpretation of the Gilgamesh story, as does Pannwitz, Schneider provides a thorough and incisive reading as an introduction to the epic and the Sumerian world: "Its interpretation has been attempted repeatedly. If one now strikes out on new paths, one must be prepared for deep skepticism on every side" (10). Instead, as a necessary precondition for understanding she invites the reader to attempt "a spiritual-intellectual reorientation, which may not be easy for contemporary Westerners. The scholar has acquired it; the lay person must learn to adopt it: the turn away from our purely rational, analytical mode of thought—the return to that intuitive grasp in which the senses, soul and intellect, are still one" (10).

A Comic Interlude

One of the most amusing treatments of this often grim literary monument was provided by the Polish philosopher and popular science-fiction author Stanisław Lem (1921–2006). His *A Perfect Vacuum* (*Doskonała próżnia*, 1961) is a collection of "pseudo-reviews" by fictitious writers of books that don't exist, such as Marcel Coscat's *Les Robinsonades,* Kuno Mlatje's *Odysseus from Ithaka,* or Wilhelm Klopper's *Culture as a Mistake.* In Lem's own introductory "review" of *A Perfect Vacuum,* the "reviewer" points out that writing reviews of nonexistent books is not Lem's invention—that Borges and Rabelais had already done the same. He states that the review of Patrick Hannahan's *Gigamesh* pleases him least of all: "Is it really worth-while to dismiss masterpieces with jokes of that sort?" (8).[30] He suggests that the work constitutes "a book of unfulfilled dreams" and "a history of what one would like to have, but doesn't have" (12). That review (34–47) begins with the claim that Hannahan is "a writer who envies Joyce for his fame" and points out that he admires *Finnegans Wake* but doesn't respect *Ulysses* because "the *Odyssey* represents plagiarism in decline because it de-stroys the entire greatness of the Gilgamesh-struggle. . . . The destiny of man as struggle that inevitably leads to defeat, that's the ultimate meaning of Gilgamesh."

Accordingly, Hannahan takes the Babylonian epic as the basis for his own book *Gigamesh,* the story of "the notorious gangster, the paid mur-derer and American soldier G.I.J. Maesch (that is, G. I. Joe, Government Issue Joe)," who is betrayed by his pal N. Kiddy and sentenced by a mili-tary court to be hanged for rape and murder. The 395-page novel, which depicts only the thirty-six minutes during which the hero is taken from his cell to the place of execution, is followed by the author's own 847-page exegesis. It provides explanations of such matters as, for instance, the name Gigamesh, which means among other things the "GIGAntic MESS" in which the hero finds himself when sentenced to death. It also hints at his murder technique because he covered his "giggling" victims with cement and then sank them in a small "gig." And so on for ten ingenious pages. The reviewer cites earlier critics who attacked Hannahan for having pro-duced the greatest logogryph of literature, a monstrous semantic rebus, a truly hellish charade. But this reviewer begs to differ: "Where should one actually draw the line between ambiguity, as an expression of genial inte-gration, and an enrichment of the work by intellectual contents that rep-resent the pure schizophrenia of culture?" He accuses the anti-Hannahan literary scholars of a simple fear of unemployment since Hannahan pro-vided his own exhaustive interpretation of his complex work. "Either 'Gigamesh' is the summa of modern literature or neither it nor the story of Finnegan along with Joyce's Odyssey has the right to ascend the belletristic Olympus."

Lem returned to Gilgamesh in his novella "Golem XIV" (1981), the account of a long conversation between a supercomputer and scientists at MIT and from Princeton's Institute for Advanced Study. We learn that the Golem series was preceded by prototypes known as HANN (for

Hannibal), ULVIC (for Ultimative Victor), AJAX, ULTOR, and GIL-GAMESH.[31] Lem's hilariously comic treatment of the ancient epic, which differs so drastically from the usually more serious adaptations, suggests how well-known the theme had become to European readers by 1961, for parody depends upon familiarity.

Three American Fictional Exuberances

Although American literature at this point still offers nothing to match the postfigurations and extensive thematizations we have encountered in German and Swiss works, the prominent allusions to Gilgamesh in three novels of the early 1970s suggest the growing popularity and influence of the theme. John Gardner's *The Sunlight Dialogues* (1972), with its vast and richly complex cast of characters over the course of some seven hundred pages, recounts a series of events that take place in September 1966 in Batavia, New York—events that expose the character and values not only of one small town but also of the contemporary United States. The plot comprises three murders involving Taggert Hodges, the scion of a prominent family who, having disappeared from Batavia for many years, returns as a seemingly mad philosopher (or philosophizing madman) and, unrecognized at first, simply calls himself the Sunlight Man. He is pursued by Fred Clumly, Batavia's fat and aging chief of police, who is profoundly disturbed by the direction in which he sees society, and particularly its youth, headed. "What's the matter," he asks his desk sergeant,

> "don't you read the papers? All over the world there's kids gone wild. . . . And why? I'll tell you what the article says—a piece in *Look*. Urbanization, the rapid growth of towns. Unemployment. Parents have been raised in the country or in towns like Batavia use to be, and they got small-town or country values, but the kids want to live the way city kids live, or the way they think they do." (248–49)[32]

On another occasion he tells his patrol-car driver that contemporary prosperity has produced "misery and crime and despair. More violence than ever before in history. More sorrow and hopelessness and rage. America leads the world in it" (640). His response to the moral and social disintegration is Law and Order, his constant refrain.

The "dialogues" of the title are four conversations that take place between Clumly and the Sunlight Man. In each case they are dramatically staged by the Sunlight Man, who in addition to his weird sense of humor is also skilled in magical effects and manages each time to disappear more or less in a puff of smoke. It is in the third of these dialogues that the Gilgamesh theme enters the novel. As we learn from all four dialogues, the Sunlight Man—and his chosen sobriquet hints at this—is in fundamental disagreement with Clumly's gloomy Old Testament moralism. In its place he enthusiastically advocates what he sees as the joyousness of the Babylonians and the Mesopotamian gods. "I'm Babylonian," he announces, "and you, you're one of the Jews" (360). For the Mesopotamian lore, using what he himself calls a "collage technique," Gardner drew liberally on A. Leo Oppenheim's standard work *Ancient Mesopotamia: Portrait of a Dead Civilization* (1964).[33] "Cities of hanging gardens and magnificent towers, devoid of slums," he exclaims—"compare miserable Jerusalem or Rome or Athens, or London and Paris in the fourteenth century!" (349). In matters as diverse as sex, politics, and human progress, the Sunlight Man finds the Babylonians superior: "One of the most remarkable differences between the Babylonian and the Hebrew mind is that the Babylonian places no value whatever on individual human life. Got that? Individual. Human. *Life.* Every Babylonian lives his life as fully as he can, but to the culture he is, himself, nothing, a unit, merely part of a physical and spiritual system" (353). Above all, he challenges Clumly's Judeo-Christian view of Law and Order:

> "I mean your laws are irrelevant, stupid, inhuman. I mean you support civilization by a kind of averaging. All crimes are equal, because you define the crime, not the criminal. It's effective, I admit it. But it has nothing to do with reality. There is good and evil in the world, but they have nothing to do with your courts." (360)

His lesson on Babylonian civilization continues in the second dialogue. It is only in the third, "The Dialogue of the Dead," that he mentions Gilgamesh: "A splendid epic, but very obscure, difficult for people like us—undramatic, one thinks at first glance" (586). Basing his own reading on Sandars's translation, Gardner provides a brief but incisive analysis of the epic's poetic effects. Then speaking of the framework embracing the

poem—the parallel scenes concerning the walls of Uruk at the beginning
and at the end of Tablet XI—Gardner offers (in the Sunlight Man's words)
his own interpretation.

> "The same walls that are the hero's only glory seal his doom. To get the
> walls built, Gilgamesh is forced to make all the inhabitants of his city work
> for him like slaves. The people cry out to the gods, the gods are enraged and
> resolve to destroy him. There you have the paradox. The rest of the epic
> elaborates it, describing the kinds of immortality Gilgamesh tries for and
> misses—eternal youth, lasting fame, and so on. . . . In Babylon—I leap to
> essentials—personal immortality is a mad goal. Death is a reality. Any strug-
> gle whatever for personal fulfillment is wrong-headed. Mankind is walled
> in from the outset: the very walls man builds around his city to lock out his
> enemies are the walls around his tomb." (587–88)

The conclusion that the Sunlight Man draws is that "one acts to maintain
the freedom to act, but the ultimate act, the act which comes when the gods
command it, is utterly impersonal, a movement of the universe, a stroke
by, for, and of sole interest to—the gods." He asks if one should act within
the cultural order in which one does not believe or within the cosmic order
in which one does believe—or simply stand indecisive between the two
orders: "Which shall I renounce, my body—of which ethical intellect is a
function—or my soul?" (589).

Although the novel contains yet a fourth dialogue, in which the Sunlight Man calls the towers of Babylon "the crowning achievement of ancient civilization" (696), the Gilgamesh theme does not reappear.[34] Despite
his growing obsession with the epic—to which he returned ten years later
in his collaborative translation with John Maier—Gardner did not set out
to construct even a loosely analogous postfiguration of the story. But the
theme plays a central role inasmuch as Gilgamesh represents the heroic
personification of the values of Mesopotamian civilization that the Sunlight
Man embraces and opposes to the Judeo-Christian Law and Order of Chief
of Police Clumly. The novel ends with a gesture toward a Hegelian synthesis of the two theses.[35] When the Sunlight Man is killed—accidentally shot
by a panicked desk sergeant when he comes in to surrender—Clumly's
hitherto rigid values are jolted. Instead of a speech on Law and Order
that he was supposed to give to a civic group that evening, he speaks

extemporaneously, wondering where the justice was in the Sunlight Man's death:

> "Justice *did* triumph, and we can be proud that we live in this great free country where that can happen. Yes! But also justice didn't triumph, in a way of course. I can't explain that if you don't see it in your heart, it's just the way it is, maybe always was and always will be. You have to have laws, the best you can, and this is democracy, as we all know, and we're dedicated to the idea of liberty." (742–43)

But his hard-and-fast conceptions have been tempered by his dialogues with the Sunlight Man: "'We may be wrong,' he said. 'We have to stay awake, as best we can, and be ready to obey the laws as best we're able to see them.'" Yet, he adds in his final words, "Blessed are the meek, by which I mean all of us, including the Sunlight Man" (745). The final insight of Gardner's novel is surprisingly close to that of Gianfilippi's liberalizing revision of the epic.

Another American novel of the following year featuring Gilgamesh peripherally is bitter in its irony. In the undisciplined fantasy of Philip Roth's *The Great American Novel* (1973), one of his least successful works, Gilgamesh is simply one among a parade of heroes from world myth who provide the names—Big John *Baal*, Roland *Agni*, Frenchy *Astarte*, Mike *Rama*, Hothead *Ptah*, Wayne *Heḳet*—and sometimes ironic parallels to figures from the realm of baseball as depicted in the novel.[36] The narrator, Word Smith ("Smitty"), author of a once renowned syndicated sports column and now patient in a nursing home, recounts the history of the fictional Patriot League in the 1930s and 1940s up to the its demise after the Second World War under accusations of communist infiltration. He focuses in particular on the Ruppert Mundys, the lowest-ranked team in the league, where during the 1933–34 season "Gil Gamesh" was the unparalleled pitching sensation.

Gil, we learn, is "the enraged son of a crazed father" and one of the only two Babylonians "in the whole damn U.S.A."[37] He develops his pitching arm by throwing rocks at the kids of various other ethnicities who call him "a lousy little Babylonian bastard" and "dirty bab" before he becomes, for one brief season with his almost perfect record of shutouts "the Talk of the

World" (55). He displays all the arrogance of his Babylonian antecedent: "Nothing shy, nothing sweet, nothing humble about this young fellow" (55), who "knew a hundred ways to humiliate the opposition" (56) and who, when chastised for his behavior, rashly insists that "I'm Gil Gamesh! I'm an immortal!" When his actions become too outrageous, the league director brings a tough but fair official, Mike "The Mouth" Masterson, out of retirement to umpire Gil's games and discipline the unruly pitcher. The season, along with Gil's spectacular career, ends when Gil, enraged by one of the umpire's calls, hurls a fastball into his throat, rendering mute forever "the Mouth."

At that point Gil Gamesh disappears from the novel for many years, although we learn later that, during that incredible season, he had an affair with the beautiful and seductive Angela Whittling Trust, manager of a competing team, whose charms had already ensnared and rejected a series of earlier lovers including Ty Cobb and Babe Ruth. In 1944, after several chapters recounting other incidents from the history of the team and the Patriot League—including one where members of the team are caught in a scandal involving a group of women surrounding one known as "the Eternal Mom" on Euphrates Drive (156–59)—Gil reappears in the story and relates the history of his wanderings: across the United States and then to Moscow, where he became a Communist and was trained to return to the United States as an agent of espionage and sabotage. Gil, however, has a change of heart. He becomes manager of the Mundys and inspires them to occasional victories yet eventually destroys the entire Patriot League by unmasking the alleged Communists within its management and players. Gil returns to Russia in 1946 but only two years later is sentenced to death as a double agent and executed.

Clearly this career has very little to do with the Gilgamesh theme. Gil has the youthful arrogance and greatness of the Babylonian hero. He defeats a postfigured Humbaba (Mike the Mouth), but he submits to, rather than refusing, the advances of an Ishtar-like siren. He then wanders for many years and returns home again—but to destroy, not to build. In fact, his story is simply one among many mythological reverberations underlying Roth's novel, which is in part a parody of other baseball novels with a mythological prefiguration (notably the Parsifal theme in Bernard Malamud's *The Natural*) and in part a satirical attack on such Cold War institutions as the hearings of the House Un-American Activities Committee

and the war in Vietnam.[38] It would, however, be an exaggeration to suggest
that the novel amounts to any systematic postfiguration of the Gilgamesh
epic of the sort evident in other novels.[39]

As unlike Mesopotamia as northern New York State may be, or perhaps
precisely because of the unlikely difference, it produced in the year after
the *Sunlight Dialogues* another wildly imaginative novel in which Gilgamesh has a walk-on role. Rhoda Lerman's *Call Me Ishtar* (1973) is a
raunchy monologue by the goddess Ishtar, who has returned to the world
in the person of a Syracuse, New York, housewife who is married to a
manufacturer of polyester and is herself manager of a rock-and-roll band.
In words often reminiscent of Gardner's Sunlight Man, this earthy heroine, who styles herself variously Queen of Heaven/Angel of Death/Whore
of Babylon/Great Goddess, has come back, she informs us in her opening
statement, because "your world is a mess. Your laws are inhuman. Your
religion is without love. Your love is without religion and both, undirected,
are useless. Your pastrami is stringy, and I am bored by your degeneracy"
(xi).[40] The work is not a systematic postfiguration but simply the author's
often outrageous visualization of the ancient Ishtar confronted with the
modern world. It is of interest here, however, because among the various
flashbacks to her earlier metamorphoses one recalls the occasion when the
goddess, dazzled by Gilgamesh, invites him to be her husband and is rejected and insulted, whereupon—unlike the account in the epic—Ishtar
simply mounts to heaven and "abandoned her people" (50–52). On a second occasion, to illustrate her diatribe against the electronic forces that "directly affect the basic biologic activity of our cells," she recalls the creation
and seduction of the wild creature Enkidu (168–69).[41]

Along with the Gardner and Roth books, Lerman's novel suggests the
growing interest in, if not any general acquaintance with, Babylonian mythology, in which the epic of Gilgamesh figures conspicuously. More generally, her work reflects the tendency toward what has come to be known
as Goddess Spirituality. While the study of matriarchy goes back at least to
Johann Jakob Bachofen's works of the mid-nineteenth century, the topic
was injected with its post–World War II energy by Robert Graves's *The
White Goddess: A Historical Grammar of Poetic Myth* (1948), in which the
poet argued on the basis of mainly literary evidence that goddess wor-
ship was the original form of all world religions. Although his work

was severely criticized by scholars, Graves's eloquence stimulated others into further elaborations of the notion. We have already noted allusions to matriarchy as early as 1950 in the works of such German writers as Schliephacke and Jordan, but the theme began to emerge prominently in the 1980s with such works as Edward C. Whitmont's *Return of the Goddess* (1982), a Jungian analysis of the recovery of feminine aspects of the human personality, and Gerda Lerner's *The Creation of Patriarchy* (1986), which argued for the primacy of matriarchal society. In a series of widely translated studies, the German philosopher and aesthetician Heide Göttner-Abendroth has dealt with questions of matriarchal aesthetics, as in the essays collected in *The Dancing Goddess* (1982).[42] In recent years the interest in goddess theology has generated wide interest and resulted in such works as David Adams Leeming and Jake Page's *Goddess: Myths of the Female Divine* (1994), Thomas Cleary's *Twilight Goddess: Spiritual Feminism and Feminine Spirituality* (2000), and Judith Laura's *Goddess Spirituality for the 21st Century: From Kabbalah to Quantum Physics* (1997) and *She Lives! The Return of Our Great Mother. Myths, Rituals, and Meditations* (1999). We shall see evidence for the broadening influence of these ideas in several of the works yet to be treated.

The Operatic Gilgamesh

It was not only writers and thinkers who approached Gilgamesh with new ideas. As in the last chapter, which ended with the high point of Martinů's great cantata, the following period reached a major culmination with the opera *Gilgamesh* (1972; premiere 1973) by the Danish composer Per Nørgård (b. 1932).[43] As daringly experimental with the subject matter of the epic as with its musical form, Nørgård achieves strikingly eerie effects throughout with his spectral harmonics. The work's subtitle, "Opera in Six Days and Seven Nights," indicates a wholly new dimension—one with distinct biblical overtones—that the composer has added to the epic. It is not divided into traditional acts but into a number of short scenes identified as day, evening, and night of seven days, beginning with the creation of the gods, demons, animals, and human beings and ending with the hero's awakening to a new consciousness following his various adventures. The ethereal aspect of creation and awakening is suggested by the eerie electrophonic effects that supplement the orchestration at beginning and end.

The opera, which (as specified in the stage directions) is performed in a rectangular space with the audience seated along two sides, includes several other striking effects. Uruk lies to the north, while the Kingdom of the Dead and Utnapishtim's realm are situated in the south; the two realms are separated by the Forest in the center. Each of these three realms has its own orchestra and distinctive instrumentation (for example, for the night music that Aruru plays on the "soundwaves of the Forest"). During the performance the conductor moves around the room in a circular motion once a "day" to suggest his role as Shamash, god of the sun; and each "evening" is signaled by a piece called the "Evening Howl" ("Aften-Brølet").

The opera follows generally the sequence of the epic, but some scenes are compressed and others are radically changed. Following his creation by Aruru, Gilgamesh asserts his egotistic self-awareness by repeated shouts of "Me, me!" ("Jeg, Jeg!") and by numerous repetitions of his name in various distorted forms. Ishara's seduction of Enkidu is accompanied by highly sensuous music. The fight between the two men passes surprisingly quickly, but the long fifth day—along with the seduction scene by far the two longest scenes of the opera—compresses the battle with Humbaba, the rejection of Ishtar, and the fight with the Heavenly Bull into a single flowing action. Particularly effective here is the scene with the Bull, whose role is played by a trombonist on the stage, who accomplishes astonishing braying sounds until he is killed when Gilgamesh finally manages to tear the slide out of his instrument. Then the Scorpion People appear and cover the heads of Humbaba and the Bull with black sacks. Later that evening, when Enkidu dies, they place a sack over his head and conduct him, along with the other two, to the Kingdom of the Dead. When Gilgamesh reaches Utnapishtim, the wise man counsels him that nothing lasts eternally but offers him a chance for immortality if he can stay awake for seven days on the mountain Nisir. As the Creation Symphony is played in the background, Gilgamesh sleeps and dreams: he sees Enkidu but, finding that he is bound to the corpses of Humbaba and the Bull, is unable to free him. Finally Gilgamesh awakens with his new insight ("indsigt," as Utnapishtim tells him) and without the whip with which he had tyrannized Uruk at the beginning. Aruru has created him anew, and on the seventh day a glorious light falls on Uruk, Gilgamesh returns, and everyone prepares to sing and play—whereupon the opera ends. It is an immensely effective aesthetic creation.

In 1976 the American composer George Belden (b. 1939) offered a brief (11-minute) atonal composition, *Gilgamesh: An Aria for Contralto, Piano, Percussion, and Tape*.[44] The piano and percussion provide a mostly lively rhythmic foundation, while electronic effects produce occasional melodic riffs against which the contralto sings and sometimes howls the fourteen lines (in Speiser's translation) in which Siduri consoles Gilgamesh ("Gilgamesh, whither rovest thou") and tells him that it is "the task of mankind" to enjoy life and family pleasures. While the oddly compelling music is boldly experimental, the text is removed entirely from its larger context—assuming the audience's acquaintance with the source, perhaps—and adds no new insights into the epic. Two years earlier, Claire C. J. Polin had published her score for *Musical Scenes from Gilgamesh*.[45]

L'Épopée de Gilgamesh (1977) by the Syrian-French composer-singer Abed Azrié, in contrast, amounts essentially to a 75-minute musicalized version of the standard epic in thirty-three episodes with an Arabic text written by the composer. The work is alternately narrated and sung by Azrié himself in his warm, flexible baritone to the simple and often repetitive accompaniment of a small group of mainly Near Eastern instruments (oud, ney, qanun, and various percussion instruments and cymbals along with a few strings and a harp) using characteristically Near Eastern rhythms.[46] As a bold mixture of Eastern and Western styles, it is a fascinating musical experiment; however, as a fairly literal reproduction of the original, it adds no new dimensions to our understanding of the epic. At the same time, it affords yet another example of the readiness with which the ancient epic lends itself to a mixture of narration and dramatization, as in the earlier performance by students in the Netherlands—and, presumably, by bards in third-millennium Sumer.

Two years later Azrié published a French version of the entire epic based not on the original but on earlier Arabic translations (by T. Baqir, 1950, and A. Fariha, 1967).[47] Azrié's adaptation, which is handsomely and liberally illustrated with photographs of ancient cylinders, bas-reliefs, and statues, includes a brief introduction and notes on Babylonian mythology. It is again divided into thirty-one short sections with monologues punctuated by narrative passages. The narratives, in a straightforward standard French, contain considerable material omitted from the libretto, but the monologues, employing a more formal and archaic language, are largely identical with the text of the musical version. Again, there is no appreciable modification of the basic storyline or any attempt to impose an original interpretation on the epic.

In sum, the novels, stories, plays, poems, operas, drawings, readings, performances, and new interpretations of the Gilgamesh theme in countries extending from Italy to Poland, in both Europe and North America, make it quite clear that by the late 1970s Gilgamesh had emerged from what had been primarily a German and English cultural context to become an increasingly familiar name and story in the world at large. It is also apparent that the reasons for this appeal had moved beyond the initially more somber attraction of immediate postwar audiences by its message of consolation after death and depression. During the 1960s such social themes as homosexuality begin to be stressed along with the philosophical-psychological recognition of the archetypal significance of the epic's figures, the representation of the shift from matriarchy to patriarchy, the struggle between titanic action and humanistic contemplation, science fiction, and questions of religion. As John Maier and Parvin Ghassemi suggest in an incisive essay, writers used ancient Near Eastern myth "to proclaim the end of male, white, bourgeois, uptight, unsharing, and guilt-ridden society" in favor of "a more primordial reality" and a "cosmic"—that is, freer and more fully human—relationship to the universe.[48] Finally, the story had become familiar enough to lend itself to the zany humor of Stanisław Lem and the exuberances of the American novelists.

4

The Contemporization of Gilgamesh (1979–1999)

New Contexts

The Near East thrust itself upon world attention in 1979 when the Iranian Revolution overthrew the Shah. Other violent events that kept the region in the international headlines included the Iran-Iraq War, the Soviet invasion of Afghanistan, the Israeli incursion against the PLO in Lebanon, the U.S. air strikes against Libya in retaliation for its support of terrorism, and the first Intifada in the Gaza Strip and West Bank.

One of the intellectual beneficiaries of that public turmoil was Edward Said and his book *Orientalism* (1978). The study, controversial at the time of its publication and now extensively qualified for its historical inaccuracies as well as its bias and political agenda, was extremely influential in certain circles, including such budding postmodernist movements as feminism and postcolonialism.[1] Said does not mention Gilgamesh and, indeed, shows little interest in the ancient Near East. His animus is directed principally against what he considered the prejudices and imperial interests of

Britain, France, and the United States during the nineteenth and twentieth centuries in their assessment of the history and culture of the Middle East and in their engagement with the lands there.[2] Moreover, his ignorance of Near Eastern studies by German scholars sorely handicapped and slanted his work. However, the political events of the times along with the sometimes opportunistic scholarship inspired by the occasion inspired and intensified among many an interest in the Near East and its culture. The epic of Gilgamesh profited directly from this enhanced attention.

In 1981, for instance, the prominent German artist Anselm Kiefer (b. 1945), long fascinated by mythology and mysticism both Germanic and Near Eastern, followed in the footsteps of earlier German illustrators by publishing a series of three striking photomontages entitled "Gilgamesh and Enkidu in the Cedar Forest" ("Gilgamesch und Enkidu im Zedernwald," 1981)—one of several similar series in which Kiefer portrays himself in the part of Gilgamesh and his wife as the spirit of the Sacred Cedar.[3] The first, a photograph of two young men in long gowns standing in a dark forest and covered with spiraling scrawls of black ink, is followed by a painting in blacks and grays of a fallen tree, its stump, and an axe; the series is completed dramatically by "The Lament of the Sacred Cedar," a photo-montage of the same two young men holding hands, standing beside the tree stump from the previous painting, and gazing up at the large face of a weeping woman. Kiefer's series strikingly anticipates the ecological theme that becomes pronounced in German fiction of this decade. During these same years the Polish artist Marek Żuławski (1908–85) produced a series of fourteen bold graphics to illustrate a second edition (1987) of Józef Wittlin's poetic retelling of 1922 (*Gilgamesz: powieść starobabilońska*).

On another level, the video game *The Tower of Druago* (by the Japanese company Namco), in which it is the goal of the hero Gilgamesh to rescue the maiden Ki from the demon Druago, initiated in 1984 what turned out to be a succession of pop-culture works capitalizing on the name of the epic and its hero: for instance, characters in the 1995 TV series *Xena: Warrior Princess* and the 1992 Canadian science-fiction series *Highlander* as well as such comic book series as Jim Starlin's "Gilgamesh II" (1989) and the popular 1990s science-fiction tetralogy *Tymewyrm*. Part of the epic, notably Gilgamesh's lament for the dead Enkidu, was recounted to a broad audience in the TV series *Star Trek: The Next Generation* (in the 1991 "Darmok" episode).[4] In 1989 the popular crime-story writer Jo Bannister published a murder mystery under the title *Gilgamesh.*

The popularization was enriched by new and often excellent versions of the epic for children. In 1992 the first in a trilogy for young readers by Ludmilla Zeman, the Czech-born Canadian author-illustrator of children's books, appeared: *Gilgamesh the King,* in which Shamhat is not a temple harlot but a beautiful singer who tames Enkidu through her music.[5] In *The Revenge of Ishtar* (1993), Humbaba attacks Uruk and kills Shamhat, whereupon Gilgamesh and Enkidu seek their revenge. After they slay Humbaba and the Bull of Heaven, Ishtar casts an illness on Enkidu, but the spirit of Shamhat comes in the shape of a bird and bears him away to the underworld, where they live happily ever after. *The Last Quest of Gilgamesh* (1995) is a startlingly faithful retelling of the final section of the epic with its monsters and complete with Siduri and Utnapishtim. At the end Ishtar sends a serpent to eat the plant of youth, but the spirit of Enkidu consoles Gilgamesh and takes him back by air to show him Uruk, his great achievement: his immortality.[6]

In 1998 Irving Finkel, Assyriologist in the Department of Western Asiatic Antiquities at the British Museum, brought out an informative introduction to the epic, *The Hero King Gilgamesh,* which retells the story in very precise detail but puts everything into a form accessible to young readers: "It is easy to imagine children in those days, wide-eyed as they listened to the dramatic events concerning gods and heroes which had been handed down from such remote times" (4).[7] The narrative is illustrated with images from photographs of ancient relics. As is usual in children's versions, the temple prostitute is introduced simply as "a certain young woman," and Enkidu is "transformed by her beauty and passion": "His mind had broadened, and his humanity had developed" (9). When Ishtar is rejected she becomes "absolutely furious" (24); after Enkidu's death, "Something had changed inside Gilgamesh. While still weeping for his friend, going over and over Enkidu's death in his mind, he had begun to reflect bitterly on his own mortality" (32). When Siduri slams the door in his face, he becomes "considerably annoyed": "You can hardly blame him for this reaction, under the circumstances" (33). And Utnapishtim's wisdom consists of the advice that "a certain period of grief for another was wholesome, but he argued that it was always man's responsibility to make the most of his life" (39). Accordingly, when Gilgamesh gets back to Uruk, he feels "an unexpected sense of peace." That same year, children in Germany could turn for their amusement and edification to *Gilgamesch von Uruk* (1998) by Arnica Esteerl and Marek Zawadzki.

The period saw, as well, another wave of translations and adaptations of the epic: French (1974 by Hubert Comte, based on Sandars's English version; 1979 by the French-Canadian writer Jean Marcel); Spanish (1980 by Hyalmar Blixen and another by Federico Lara Peinada); and German (1988 Schott's version revised by Wolfram von Soden). In 1984, finally, the translation of *Gilgamesh: From the Sîn-Lequi-Unninnî Version* by John Gardner and John Maier appeared: the last work, Maier notes in his introduction, that Gardner completed before his death in a motorcycle accident in 1982.[8] Gardner, many of whose works were based on classics of the past—for instance, his fictional transpositions of *Grendel* (1971) and *Jason and Medeia* (1973) as well as modernizations of works in Middle English—had been interested in the epic, as we saw in the preceding chapter, ever since *The Sunlight Dialogues*. In 1976 he and John Maier began to collaborate on a version based on a rough translation by Maier and the Assyriologist Richard Henshaw. Unlike most other translations, this one, which closely follows the Standard Version, presents the text in seventy-two units (one for each of the six columns of all twelve tablets) and was warmly received by many reviewers for its freshness, vigor, and poetic language, even though one reviewer, an Assyriologist, took it severely to task for inconsistencies, mistakes, and inept commentary.[9]

The new and widespread popularity of the epic inevitably invited the attention of thinkers and writers, each with his or her particular theoretical agenda. In this chapter we shall examine representative examples of several approaches that seized on Gilgamesh to illustrate their views, ranging from the most abstractly theoretical through the historical and sociopolitical to the intensely personal, and the varied techniques used to achieve their ends.

Gilgamesh Psychoanalyzed

Despite the early interest of Freud and Jung, which we noted in chapter 1, and the conspicuous exception of Joseph Campbell, the Gilgamesh epic was essentially neglected in psychoanalytic studies until the 1980s.

In *The Hero with a Thousand Faces* (1948) Campbell offered a Freudian-Jungian psychoanalytic approach to myth. He devotes only three pages to Gilgamesh as "the greatest tale of the elixir quest" in the prebiblical tradition.[10] Limiting himself to that archetype and, typically for that period, neglecting the themes of friendship and eros, he skips the first half altogether and never mentions Enkidu. Treating the epic simply as Gilgamesh's quest to attain "the watercress of immortality," he discusses only the scenes with Siduri and Utnapishtim, which he briefly recapitulates without commentary. Gilgamesh is thus reduced to simply one among various examples to illustrate what the chapter heading calls "The Ultimate Boon." But Campbell's widely read work was enormously influential in persuading the modern psychiatrically inclined public that "it has always been the prime function of mythology and rite to supply the symbols that carry the human spirit forward, in counteraction to those other constant human fantasies that tend to tie it back" (11). It was the purpose of his book, he proclaimed, "to uncover some of the truths disguised for us under the figures of religion and mythology by bringing together a multitude of not-too-difficult examples and letting the ancient meaning become apparent of itself" (vii). It is in no small measure thanks to Campbell that the Gilgamesh story became such a visible example of the modern quest for identity, as was evident in the poetry and publicizations of Olson and Corso.

During the 1980s two studies were written that can serve paradigmatically as contrasting paradigms of Freudian and Jungian interpretation. In a lengthy essay in *American Imago* entitled "The Epic of Gilgamesh," Tracy Luke and Paul Pruyser explicitly disclaimed Jung's attempt "to absolutize [our psychic inheritance] by fixating its themes and images into archetypes residing as templates in a collective unconscious."[11] Instead, they treat the narrative as "a liturgical drama," using Erik Erikson's developmental stages of human growth as their model. They deny that Gilgamesh is a true mythic hero because he is not the product of a miraculous birth and does not solve any great cosmic problems. Rather, they argue, he is a legendary person who slowly acquires some wisdom and grows "from brutish selfishness and lust to acceptance of his mortality." To prove their point, however, the authors impose their own expectations on the text, even to the extent, occasionally, of distorting it: "If we have appraised his situation accurately, we will be alert to clues about rivalry, incest, and

castration threats." Since the mother motif is central to their argument, it
is important for the authors to find mother-figures everywhere. The harlot
is said to be "an equivalent of Aruru, the divine mother of Enkidu who,
by another name Ninsun, is soon introduced as the mother of Gilgamesh,"
and her mating with him is a *hieros gamos* (a "holy marriage" anticipating
the one that in their exegesis eventually takes place between Gilgamesh
and Ishtar). In Gilgamesh's dream of the star that falls from the sky onto
Gilgamesh, "the star is the absent (murdered) father, come to weigh Gilgamesh down as if the latter carried a load of guilt for his wish to replace
him"; and in the second dream, the mysterious axe has "oedipal-phallic
import as Gilgamesh's fear of castration." In their fight at the wedding-
house door, Enkidu succeeds in preventing a primal crime: the violation
of the goddess-mother by Gilgamesh, and their departure from Ninsun
represents the heroes' "struggle to emancipate themselves from their at-
tachments to this woman." When they kill Humbaba, the guardian of
the sacred mountain abode of Ishtar, "the ominous danger of incest looms
again, hidden in what passes as a noble deed." But the now-mature Gilgamesh refuses the mother's seduction attempts in the person of Ishtar.
Since in the ancient Near East the Bull of Heaven is a symbol of divine
male power, it is also an "imago of the father, out to slay the wayward son,
only to run the risk of being slain by them"—and Oedipus now lurks in
the background (76–84).

At this point the authors make the mistake of attributing the slaying of
the bull, by plunging the sword into his neck, to Enkidu; by their lights, his
slaying of the father-figure must be expiated by his own sacrifice. (The authors add a footnote that "perhaps no story from antiquity declares as un-
equivocally as this epic, Freud's perception that the attempts at resolution
through sacrificial rites were always inadequate.") When Enkidu in his
fury wishes to smash the door with Gilgamesh's axe, "he seeks not the door
but the divine lady within." In their account of the following episodes, the
authors skip the scorpion people and the journey along the nocturnal path
of the sun and move directly to Siduri's house, where his threat to break
down the door is "a ritualized repetition of a forcible entry to a motherly
woman." The punting poles that Gilgamesh cuts for crossing the Waters
of Death are phallic because, when they are used up, Gilgamesh's "phallic
prowess has run out." Utnapishtim's wife is portrayed as "a final female
enticer" because she seeks yet again to lure Gilgamesh with the promise

of eternal youth and potency even after Utnapishtim has revealed the ultimate secret: that death is inevitable (84–91).

When they reach Uruk, Gilgamesh allegedly boasts to Urshanabi, in a statement with absolutely no textual validity, "Here is the Eanna, the temple of Ishtar. I built and care for her house, because she is my protectress." According to the authors' rather confusing conclusion, which makes no further effort to deal with the incest aspect, "As he comes to her now, she will welcome him to her chamber, having herself returned from an underworld journey in preparation for this moment of the king's rearrival." In this Freudian analysis, accordingly, the epic turns out to be an account of the experience that must be lived in preparation for the *hieros gamos,* the sacred marriage of king and goddess, "a liturgical drama in which youthful erotic preoccupations become overtaken by thoughts of death, first leading to fierce narcissistic protest, and then to acceptance in sober resignation that still leaves room for living-on with periodic renewal." The Freudian approach appears to have had little impact on the literary adaptations that followed (91–92).

The more fruitful Jungian approach is exemplified by Rivkah Schärf Kluger's *The Archetypal Significance of Gilgamesh: A Modern Ancient Hero* (1991). The work, as noted earlier, was directly inspired by the author's contact in 1948 with Carl Gustav Jung, almost immediately after which Kluger (1907–87) undertook her careful and extensive research, which is based on the principal translations in German, French, Dutch, and English as well as the most important scholarly studies. In 1962 she presented a seminar on the topic at the C. G. Jung Institut in Zurich and augmented that material in subsequent lectures. Because she was prevented by illness and then her death from completing the work, it was posthumously assembled and edited by her husband on the basis of recordings from her early seminar, her lecture notes, and a 1975 article on "Einige psychologische Aspekte des Gilgamesch-Epos" (in the 1975 Centennial edition of *Analytische Psychologie,* vol. 6, no. 3).[12]

Kluger's book is not only a reasonable Jungian interpretation of the Gilgamesh myth but also a highly readable introduction to the epic itself. In direct contrast to the Freudians, she treats the story as a myth representing "not only eternal archetypal events, but a certain level of the development of human consciousness" (14) and attributes her understanding of myth, archetypes, and the collective unconscious directly to Jung. The mythic hero, who is inevitably partly divine, is "always ahead of the actual level of consciousness of the time, and so the hero is the symbol or carrier of a process of change" that we now know as the process of individuation (23). Accordingly, her interpretation stands, episode by episode, in direct contrast to that of Luke and Pruyser. Enkidu's affair with the hierodule, or temple prostitute, is not, as the Freudians would have it, seduction by a mother-figure but the contamination of his natural existence by contact with the higher eros of the human, leading to his exclusion from his earlier *participation mystique* with animals. Gilgamesh's dream of the falling star, far from being a Freudian symbol for the absent father, is rather a symptom of the inclination to homosexuality that in the author's opinion characterized antiquity as well as the world today (67). (It is worth remembering that Kluger held her seminar in Switzerland around the time when Guido Bachmann was writing his early classic of gay literature.) Similarly, the axe of Gilgamesh's dream is no longer a symbol for castration but rather an anticipation of Enkidu, who helps him "to fulfill the heroic deed of the symbolic killing of the Mother"—that is, "wresting consciousness from the matrix of the unconscious in the process of an expanding development of consciousness" (70–71).

Kluger makes an important distinction between the personal and the archetypal mother: she reads Ninsun's prayer to Shamash as an appeal to the god by the personal mother to help her son overcome the archetypal mother (92). The cedar forest is related to that archetypal realm of the mother, so the killing of Humbaba represents a shift from matriarchal to patriarchal society. (Given the controversial nature of that notion, Kluger avers her preference for the term "era of the mother goddess" [105].) In any case, the myth provides valuable insight into "a transition in a religious development" (105). When Gilgamesh rejects Ishtar as an embodiment of "the whole feminine potential" (113), the deed represents his attempt "to get out of the maternal cycle of nature, into a new spiritual development" (123) and, hence, a decisive turning point in the individuation of the hero and the cultural development of humankind. The heavenly bull, far from being a Freudian imago of the father, is instead "the hypostasis of [Ishtar's] own raging wrath" (133).

Siduri, as a "maiden anima," is one aspect of Ishtar, and Gilgamesh's approach to her is anything but what the Freudians regarded as "a forcible entry to a motherly woman." As *anima*, she seeks to attract him back to the pleasures of life itself. Utnapishtim's account of the flood exposes the secret of the gods: their unpredictability and, ultimately, their own development in self-consciousness, as when Utnapishtim's Ishtar reflects on her guilty responsibility for the flood and the destruction of mankind. From Kluger's mythic point of view, "one could say that with human development, the gods also are transformed"—a development of the God image evident in many religious texts. When Utnapishtim instructs Gilgamesh to bathe and put on fresh garments, he enacts a symbolic rebirth signifying his new consciousness of his own mortality. (The plant of rejuvenation does not bestow immortality; it simply renews youth.) The Gilgamesh epic as a whole, Kluger concludes, "shows in its inner structure a process of transformation in the collective unconscious, an anticipation of the individuation process" and, at the same time, "mirrors a significant era in the history of religion, a time when the Great Goddess Ishtar was defeated by the hero under the aegis of Shamash" (207).

It would be difficult to imagine two more radically opposed interpretations of the myth than the Freudian and the Jungian. Essentially, the one invites us to regard the epic as the story of the hero's movement through fears of incest and castration toward a *hieros gamos,* the union of the hero with the Great Mother. The other, in contrast, sees in it precisely the overcoming of any such union in the shift from matriarchy to patriarchy and the development of human self-awareness. Whether we prefer the one or the other or reject both, Kluger's exegesis is based on a fuller and more accurate reading of the epic than is the more perfunctory and slanted essay by Luke and Pruyser. For our purposes, the presence of these two works from the 1980s signifies the emergence of important new avenues of interpretation in the age of psychoanalysis, beyond the ones already discussed and the emphasis on the modern relevance of the ancient tale.

In the 1980s and 1990s, numerous studies attracted readers in Germany and Switzerland who were interested in the relevance of the epic for purposes of personal development: "Gilgamesh from the Gnostic Viewpoint"; "Gilgamesh: A Religious-Psychological Interpretation"; "The Secret Message of Gilgamesh"; "Gilgamesh: The Search for Meaning"; and "Gilgamesh: The Path to the Self," and so on.[13] In a similar vein, the German sociologist Günter Dux explored "history as a way to human self-awareness" in the epic. According to Dux's "historic-genetic" theory of history, Gilgamesh's experience of love and death can be regarded as exemplary for the attainment of self-awareness in the transition from archaic society to early high culture.[14]

Gilgamesh Deconstructed

Another development that manifested itself in one of the earliest Gilgamesh adaptations of the 1980s was the poorly defined but influential movement, stemming from the work of Jacques Derrida, known as deconstruction. Among its other aims, deconstruction sought to expose the self-contradictions within texts and to dismantle or "deconstruct" the structures with which the preceding structuralism of the 1960s had concerned itself. (Structuralism, emerging from the linguistic theories of Ferdinand de Saussure and gradually spreading to such fields as mythology, anthropology, and literary theory, maintained that the human sciences are based on underlying structures that determine the meaning of all systems.)

The dramatic poem *Lebewohl, Gute Reise* ("Goodbye, Have a Nice Trip," 1980) by Gertrud Leutenegger (b. 1948) may well be regarded as an example of literary deconstruction. The highly regarded Swiss writer turned frequently in her novels and poetic works to such mythological themes as *Nineve* (1977), *Meduse* (1988), *Acheron* (1994), and *Pomona* (2004) to lend sometimes hazy dimensions of symbolic meaning to her works. The title is taken from a song that the Comedian Harmonists, the internationally popular German singing group of the late 1920s and early 1930s, regularly intoned as they danced off the stage—and eventually out of Hitler's Germany. In Leutenegger's work the song is played on a tape recorder by the Great Queen, who among her various hypostases in the poem is not only Gilgamesh's mother and the priestess of Inanna who sends whores to her son and to Enkidu but also the goddess herself.[15]

The dramatic poem in lyrical prose takes place in a timeless dreamworld of lofty mountain tops, empty plazas and the Glass Hotel of Uruk, a large tree clambering with talking monkeys, and vast steppes where Gilgamesh drives a flashy car and smokes cigarettes. As the work begins, ICH ("I"—not unlike Montaigne's "moi" or the objectified "je" of Rimbaud's "Je est un autre"), who turns out to be one of Gilgamesh's discarded lovers, is lying in a coffin on the mountaintop and questioning the Mother, who without responding simply dances to her recorded song, about the mortuary journey she is undertaking. In the disconnected scenes that follow, the whore—the one from the coffin?—is sent out to the wilderness to tame Enkidu: he belongs to the tribe of monkeys, whose conversations suggest that they represent the race of discredited gods as well as mankind at its most primitive level. As the scenes jump from the mountaintop to the steppe to the empty arcades of Uruk, Enkidu is tamed, meets Gilgamesh, and dies. The whore from the opening scene turns up in various other guises—as Inanna, as Siduri, as Utnapishtim's wife, as an aged mummy-like creature who urges Gilgamesh to flee before the earth is destroyed. Gilgamesh's wanderings finally bring him to the mountaintop, where he finds ICH busily distributing pieces of white bread—apparently the bread that Utnapishtim's wife baked for Gilgamesh—around her coffin. As the work ends, she exclaims "Gilgamesh! Gilgamesh lives!" and the ancient drums of Uruk resound loudly across the landscape.

We easily recognize various figures and motifs from the epic, but all have been taken out of any familiar context and assigned wholly new roles and values. The depressing message of this deconstructed epic appears to proclaim the reawakening of the modern consciousness (the ICH on the mountaintop) following the collapse or deconstruction of a former world order (implicit in the title song, which is played in its full text) as well as the eternal recurrence of the same figures and forces (as suggested by the monkeys, the priests, and the many hypostases of the Great Mother). As in Leutenegger's other works, the mythological figures have lost any specific function or meaning but retain their suggestive associations concerning mortality and man's corruption of nature (the devastated city and landscapes).

Gilgamesh Historicized

Twenty-five years after Gianfilippi's initiative, a wave of lengthy historical novels revolving around Gilgamesh swept over the United States and Germany. The conspicuously growing popularity of historical novels during these decades was due in some measure to the desire of readers to escape from an increasingly complex present into the seemingly simpler circumstances of the past. At the same time, the writers often detected in the fictional past a means of dealing with modern concerns in a more objective and readily comprehensible form. As for Gilgamesh in particular, it is evident that the very incompleteness of the epic as it has come down to us almost ineluctably attracts writers to re-view and complete it according to a modern understanding. (A similar temptation helps to explain the concurrent popularity among many scholars of such writers as Friedrich Hölderlin, Franz Kafka, and Walter Benjamin—writers, that is, the fragmentary nature of whose writings allows the critic free and sometimes untrammeled range for the imagination.) It is notably the vacant periods of Gilgamesh's childhood and youth and the years following his return to Uruk that lie open for the novelist—who is also fascinated by the psychology underlying the hero's relationship with Enkidu (hetero- or homosexual?) and Inanna/Ishtar and, above all, his obsession with death and immortality. All of these writers display, to a greater or lesser degree, considerable familiarity with Mesopotamian culture and society as it was known from the available scholarship.

One of the earliest, *Gilgamesh the King* (1984), was written by the enormously prolific American author Robert Silverberg (b. 1935), who turned to the topic after having published more than forty popular science-fiction novels for children and adults. In his "Afterword," the author states that "it is primarily with the historical Gilgamesh" that he has concerned himself and that he has "attempted to interpret the fanciful and fantastic events" of the Akkadian epic as well as the older Sumerian poems "in a realistic way" (318–19).[16] To this end, and relying principally on the translations by Heidel, Speiser, and Kramer, he tells the story in the first person from Gilgamesh's point of view, "as though he were writing his own memoirs."

Silverberg focuses throughout his forty-one chapters on the hero's obsession with death and accounts for it plausibly by having Gilgamesh first encounter death at age six when he attends the funeral ceremony for his father, Lugalbanda. He asks the court harpist if his father will awaken and return from the dead, as did the goddess Inanna in the ancient ballads. When his elderly friend replies that he will awaken but not return, the child begins to consider the meaning of his father's death: If he does not return, where will he journey next? He watches with growing horror as the harpist along with various court officials and even a woman and boy dressed in his mother's and his own royal garb drink a deadly potion and descend into the grave pit. When he learns that they will all die and sleep forever in the ground near his father, he exclaims that "it is a terrible thing to die" (19) and swears that he will never let death seize him too. From this point on, Gilgamesh's obsession with death governs the narrative, even as he goes to school and learns to read and write, then becomes familiar with military arms and building skills, and finally is introduced to sex by a variety of girls and temple priestesses. Despite her powerful eroticism, he is not yet permitted to sleep with the young woman who becomes the high priestess of Inanna, and he is consumed with jealousy when he sees her engaged in the annual Sacred Marriage rites with his father's successor, who has taken the name Dumuzi.

When his life is threatened by Dumuzi, he flees from Uruk and spends the next four years at the court of King Agga of Kish, where he becomes a fabled warrior. When Dumuzi becomes ill, Gilgamesh returns to Uruk and is crowned by the priestess of Inanna. Discovering that she arranged his exile and return for her own scheming purposes, he begins to distrust her.[17] (Here the Sumerian legend of Inanna's descent to the underworld and her betrayal of Dumuzi is inserted.) Nevertheless they both passionately enjoy their repeated couplings during the annual Sacred Marriage rites. Gilgamesh restores Uruk to its glory, cleaning the canals, building the great new walls, and defeating Agga's armies (according to the Sumerian poem on that subject). He also saves the *huluppu* tree that is sacred to Inanna (again according to the Sumerian poem "Bilgames and the Netherworld") by poisoning the snake in its roots and driving out the birds nesting in its branches; in the process he cuts down a huge rotten limb, from which the priestess has fashioned a throne and couch as well as a special drum and drumstick for Gilgamesh. However, the citizens have become aggrieved by the king's heavy demands for their labor by day and his untiring conquest of their women by night.

Only at this point, almost halfway through the novel, is Enkidu introduced and tamed by a temple priestess. When the two men fight, Gilgamesh wins, but their mutual respect causes them to become great friends. The author finds it necessary to stress that there was nothing homosexual about their relationship:

It has been whispered that we were lovers as men and women are. I would not have you believe that. That was not the case at all. I know that that are certain men in whom the gods have mixed manhood and womanhood so that they have no need or liking for women, but I am not one of them, nor was Enkidu. (155)

He explains that "we were one soul in two bodies" (158) and emphasizes their enormous enjoyment of sex with women. The battle with Huwawa is explained as an earthquake and the fence around the forest as an attempt by the Elamites to lay claim to the rich cedar forest. Upon their return, the priestess of Inanna, who has become jealous of Gilgamesh's popularity and influence with the people, visits him with a proposal of a marriage to consolidate their power—and is infuriated by his rejection. During the drought that follows, she releases a great white temple bull into the streets in an effort to frighten the city, but the two friends kill the beast.

At this point, when Gilgamesh is at the height of his glory, he reenacts the twelve-year ritual of Opening and Closing the Gate to the underworld to propitiate Ereshkigal. But his drum accidentally falls into the pit, and Enkidu goes down to retrieve it, after which he falls ill. Gilgamesh has the ill-fated drum burned while soothsayers, physicians, and exorcists try to save Enkidu. Following his friend's death and funeral, Gilgamesh, leaving the city in order to flee the death he fears, goes in search of Ziusudra, who has reputedly escaped that fate and who, as he knows from the familiar tale of the flood, lives on the remote island of Dilmun. After spending the night with the scorpion-man and scorpion-woman, who turn out to be grotesquely disfigured mountain people, he crosses the thorny tableland to a lovely valley and seaport village, where he spends several days sleeping with the tavern keeper Siduri. Dilmun, which he reaches easily by sailing across a perfectly normal sea, is a very earthly paradise—a trading center where Gilgamesh sees people of every color and from every land. Ziusudra lives in a colony of holy men and woman on a smaller island nearby. Spending several days there, Gilgamesh learns the true story of the flood: it was a perfectly natural flood that swept across the steppes and from which the people escaped to higher ground nearby. Ziusudra turns out to be *the* Ziusudra: the name ritually assumed for centuries by the leader of the group. From him Gilgamesh learns the secret of immortality: though no individual is immortal, there is no death for the community or humankind as a whole. As a parting gift he gets a pearl from a plant that he recovers from the sea and then hangs in a small bag around his neck.

He sails back to Uruk, where he learns that the high priestess has declared him dead. When he reaches the city, priestesses encamped outside the walls try unsuccessfully to seduce and poison him. He goes immediately to the temple of Inanna, where he finds the priestess wearing a golden mask. After he kills her, he finds that the mask covers the horribly disfigured face of the woman he once found sexually irresistible. (At the same time, a snake swallows the pearl in the bag torn loose from his neck.) Years later Gilgamesh sets down the account that we have just read and unveils the truth he has learned, "that the escape from death lies not in potions and magic, but in the performance of one's task. That way lies calmness and acceptance" (317). As the story ends, Gilgamesh is confident that he has made a name for himself that will last through the ages and that he will accomplish yet more: "Gilgamesh will not be forgotten. . . . There is no death."

Even after completing his lengthy rationalizing account, Silverberg could not shake off his obsession with the figure of Gilgamesh. Three years later, he wrote the prize-winning science fiction novella *Gilgamesh in the Outback* (1987), which depicts the hero's afterlife, which he spends hunting monsters while continuing to mourn his friend Enkidu.

Gilgamesh Drums for the Greens

A further factor that begins to play a role in historicizations of the epic is the international Green Movement with its emphasis on ecology and environmental protection. One catalyst for the movement was Ernst Bloch's influential philosophical trilogy *The Principle of Hope* (*Das Prinzip Hoffnung*, 1954–59), which is based on the conviction that a ravaged "fallen" nature needs to be redeemed from bourgeois profit-seeking and a merciless technology if a future human utopia is to be achieved: mankind's domination of nature must give way to the humanization of nature. Further important stages were marked by such publications as *The Limits to Growth* (1972), issued by the Club of Rome (established in 1968), and *Global 2000*, submitted in 1982 by the movement of the same name. In Germany the initiative was taken up as a major plank by "Die Grünen" ("The Greens"), a political party that gradually took shape during the 1970s and was officially registered in 1980.

By an odd coincidence, two vast Gilgamesh novels appeared in Germany in 1988, both of which appear to have been influenced not only by the current ecological fervor but also by Günter Grass's *The Tin Drum* (*Die Blechtrommel*, 1959). In both of them, Gilgamesh's drum—the *pukku* of the Akkadian and Sumerian originals—takes on a central role associated with the drum with which Oskar Matzerath in Grass's novel manages, almost magically, to manipulate the Nazi mobs of Hitler's Germany—a role that shows up in none of the non-German treatments of the myth.

Harald Braem's *The Lion of Uruk* (*Der Löwe von Uruk*, 1988), like Silverberg's novel, is a systematic rationalization of the supernatural elements of the epic. At times, moreover, there are clear mythopoeic efforts to hint at the process of myth-formation amid a superstitious people from events that are realistically depicted. Gilgamesh is introduced as an upstanding young man who goes to great lengths to understand the motives of his enemies and displays sophisticated diplomatic skills in dealing with others. Given its focus on Gilgamesh's early pre-epic life and the politicization of religion, the first book of Braem's novel bears a striking resemblance to Silverberg's novel but without the former's emphasis on the theme of death.

Gilgamesh, of unknown parentage and differing conspicuously in appearance from the other boys, has been adopted by Ninsun, the widow of King Lugalbanda, who explains to him the eternal contest between the male and female principles of life, of innovation and preservation, of sun and moon, as represented by the priests of Anu and priestesses of Ishtar. As a temple adept, he carries clay tablets bearing the astronomical observations of the priests from the ziggurat to the cave of the seven wise men, where he is excited by the maps of the world that he sees there and watches the seven sages playing the "game of life" (78), a board game in which the goal is to achieve harmony, not victory.[18] When asked by a friend if he believes in the incorporation of gods in priests and priestesses, he responds: "More important than human doubt, it seems to me, is to maintain law and order, without which no society can survive. If men deny that, then the life together has no meaning and every city, deprived of the favor of destiny, plunges into chaos—even Uruk" (74).

Overhearing conversations between young men and women outside the temple of Ishtar, Gilgamesh learns about sex but also hears rumors about Iluna, priestess of Ishtar, and the political intrigues through which she seeks to win power from King Dumuzi. One day, in his games with other young men, Gilgamesh uproots a rotten and reputedly magical oak tree with a serpent in its root and from its wood makes a drum on which he learns to produce wonderful new sounds. Around this time he himself is introduced to sex in the temple of Ishtar by the lovely temple-harlot Tehiptilla. When Dumuzi suddenly dies, it is rumored that he was poisoned by Iluna, who immediately seizes power.

While Gilgamesh is playing his drum, a delegation comes from the city and chooses him as king—an action that troubles the priestess Iluna because she believes she is entitled to the crown. When Gilgamesh decides as his first act to build a great wall around the city, he consults the seven wise men along with the high priest and architects, all of whom approve, and then uses his rhetorical powers to persuade the people of the wall's benefits. A great celebration commemorates the laying of the foundation stone, which contains a message from the wise men. Then Gilgamesh drums people to work: "It was remarkable: whoever heard the drum, set about his task more firmly in its rhythm, the work seems easier, the sound of the drum seemed to drive away all difficulties" (99).

Gilgamesh enjoys enormous popularity as king; only Ninsum worries because he has no friend, and Tehiptilla, the priestess with whom he often slept, because she loves him and is jealous of the seduction attempts of Iluna, who wants to share his power. Book I ends with verses by the poet Sinnunni, who recognizes the majesty of a king said to be two-thirds god and one-third man but suggests that Gilgamesh's demands on men and women are beginning to arouse the citizens and appeals for a powerful man to come and vie with Gilgamesh and bring peace again. Since nothing in the narrative up to this point has suggested anything but popular satisfaction with Gilgamesh and since there has been absolutely no hint of any improper sexual demands, the poem is the first indication of the poet's creative myth-formation from the materials at his disposal.

At this point the narrative catches up with, and extensively parallels, the epic. The gods listen to Sinnunni and create Enkidu, who knows the laws of nature, not of men. (This turns out to be a further example of mythicization: later it is strongly hinted that Enkidu, born among the blond mountain people of the far North, was lost as a child or abandoned among the animals of the steppe and grew up among them.) He frightens the young hunter, who goes to Uruk and reports to Gilgamesh. Gilgamesh sends him to Iluna, who—unbeknownst to Gilgamesh—chooses his onetime beloved Tehiptilla for the job. They travel to the watering hole, where she seduces Enkidu. After spending the season with friendly shepherds, where Enkidu learns the practices of men, they journey back to Uruk with a traveling circus going to entertain at the Holy Wedding. Iluna schemes to be the bride, but Gilgamesh chooses Tehiptilla, not knowing that she has been sent away. Angrily he spends the symbolic night with Iluna. When Tehiptilla arrives and hears about the wedding, she is dismayed. But Enkidu is offended and challenges Gilgamesh to a fight. Gilgamesh wins, but they become friends—with never (as in Silverberg's work) the slightest hint of a homosexual relationship. Ninsum blesses them as the "left and right halves of the same being" (158).

Immediately Gilgamesh proposes the trip to the distant forest for timber with which to decorate the city gates and to kill Chumbawa. Unwilling to believe the horror stories Enkidu has heard, he seeks the greatness foretold in his dreams. Enkidu worries about the enterprise, but the wise men approve: it fits the plan outlined in their game of life. Meanwhile, Tehiptilla, in protest against Iluna's schemes, leaves the temple and goes to serve Ninsun in her palace. The expedition sails up the Euphrates and marches across the steppe to the fortress of Kadesh, from which they reach Mount Hermon and the enchanted forest. They kill the watchman at the gate to the forest and then seek out Chumbawa—here he is a volcano rather than Silverberg's earthquake—whose premises are guarded by a group of men. When Chumbaba is extinguished by the winds, they fell the tallest cedar, which—in the first hint at the ecological theme that emerges ever more strongly—cries out with pain (that is, with the groans of falling timber) and curses them:

> "You may be right that the face of the earth has changed and is no longer as it once was at the time of the creation. But I am an old, an ancient tree, have seen men and their deeds come and go, and I tell you: Don't take everything that is offered to you, don't blaspheme. Let a bit of the old magic survive. Or do you want to run the risk that heaven will collapse and falls apart when I fall?" (226)

But they are reassured when the forest resounds with the happy sounds of birds and nature.

The city has continued to prosper during their absence, but the scheming Iluna has been interfering in political affairs, making deals with foreign cities and tribes. (In this context we hear rationalizations of her earlier affairs: Tammuz was a poet who loved her but whom she ridiculed so that he fled to the desert; Ischullaru was a gardener whom she turned into a frog: that is, he was so traumatized that he sat glassy-eyed and brooding on the banks of the Euphrates.) Erenda, Gilgamesh's friend and surrogate, warns him against her because she wants him to marry her in a real marriage and not just the symbolic Sacred Wedding—one might even say, the first "power couple" in history. But on Enkidu's advice, Gilgamesh rejects Iluna, whereupon, furious, she reveals her vindictive nature. She prays to Marduk for vengeance by the Bull of Heaven, and he reluctantly agrees but sets it far afield from Uruk. So she sends a temple-priestess to Akka of Kisch to enlist his support in her betrayal of Uruk: he and his army are to drive the bull ahead of them to Uruk. As with loud noises Akka's men steer the bull south—there is no indication that it is anything but an abnormally large and wild beast—it rampages, killing everyone in its path. When Akka's army lays siege to the city, the bull manages to break the walls surrounding the outlying gardens. Meanwhile, Iluna sends a poison gas over city, paralyzing people and making them ill. Enkidu and Gilgamesh offer friendship to Akka and support for his wretched city. He agrees, provided they succeed in killing the bull, which they rapidly dispatch. Akka returns to Kish with master builders to help with irrigation canals and walls. Despite many signs of Iluna's betrayal, fair-minded Gilgamesh still gives her the benefit of the doubt. Iluna, initially ill and furious, has a vision about the death of Enkidu and suddenly becomes repentant and wants to be freed of her sins.

Meanwhile, Enkidu dreams that the gods have decided that he must die for his sacrileges. In his vision, the door made of sacred cedar speaks. The hand with which he struck the tree becomes lame. (It is simply a case of blood poisoning, one doctor diagnoses.) Enkidu curses those who brought him in from the steppe: "It is my destiny, that I fell out of unity into multiplicity. Out there I knew every second what is right. Here, in multiplicity, one must constantly make decisions and must therefore inevitably make mistakes. It is precisely for these mistakes that the gods now punish me" (346). While Enkidu endures weeks of illness, the dying Ninsum sends Tehiptilla for her two adopted sons. She tells Gilgamesh that he has incorporated Enkidu's spirit even though his body is dying. After Enkidu's death, Gilgamesh buries him along with his magical drum.

In another of her lessons on the philosophy of history, Ninsum tells him that, before the flood, men and women lived in harmony:

> Now new times have begun, everything is splintered into ignorance and opposition, harmony is gone. The men want to rule alone, to seize power, and there are women like Iluna who emulate them and think it is the opposite, but it's the same. They all don't know that once upon a time there was Innin [the Urmutter] and with her unity, fulfillment, reconciliation of opposites. (355)

She advises him to seek that harmony with Tehiptilla, and Gilgamesh and Tehiptilla are finally united in their love.

Soon thereafter a scholar from Susa visits Uruk and points out to Gilgamesh, in a lengthy conversation about death and the meaning of life, that his grief stems from his recognition of his own mortality. He tells Gilgamesh about Utnapishtim, also known as Ziusudra, on the island of Tilmun. Inspired by this talk, Gilgamesh secretly leaves on his great journey. Going east, he now sees the steppe with Enkidu's eyes and seems to understand the language of the plants and animals and senses a higher order behind external reality. Making his way to the twin mountain Mashu, Gilgamesh meets the scorpion people with human faces, the guardians of the gate at edge of known world. (Again: in the author's rationalization, Gilgamesh realizes that their strange appearance is an "illusion of the shadows" [405].) Following the tunnel through the mountain, he emerges into a forest of jewels, which blind the eye and harm the body. (Gilgamesh understands that the forest is symbolic: riches cannot satisfy hunger and thirst. The birds that seem to speak are simply his own thoughts.)

He reaches Siduri, a former innkeeper who has left the city for the tranquility of her solitude to commune with the tree in her garden. She tells Gilgamesh that he should seek to enjoy the life he has, and he finds brief respite in her well-ordered hut. But when he awakens, his restlessness sends him to Urschanabi, with whom he sails across the vast ocean and its Sea of Death to reach Tilmun. There they find Ziusudra, who teaches him to breathe, yoga-like, in harmony with nature: "Time and space are the same, Gilgamesh, two folds of the same garment. Reality arises from their interplay" (440). (It is later suggested that this entire episode is a dream and that it has been progressively elaborated in the frequent retellings by the poet Sinnunni [485].) Ziusudra tells Gilgamesh the story of paradise, the first men, their turmoil, and the ensuing flood. Gilgamesh fails the test of sleep, but after he recovers and loses the plant of youthfulness, he has his insight: "Was not my life full, is it not important in every second? The teaching of Ziusudra will give me the strength and the clarity to see everything with watchful eyes" (464). When their boat is sunk in a great storm, the ferryman drowns, but Gilgamesh is rescued after floating for days on a plank, with which he converses.

Back in Uruk, he learns from Tehiptilla, whom he marries, that he has a young toddler son. Sinnunni writes and revises and repeatedly recites the epic—apparently the Standard Edition. Meanwhile Gilgamesh develops an ecological consciousness: "My whole life long I have been involved with trees. If I had to say what was really of significance for my way, then it was the trees" (484)—meaning the magic oak out of which he carved his drum, the cedar forest, Enkidu's exhortations about importance of trees, the false trees in the garden of jewels, the wondrous tree in Siduri's garden, the trees he felled to row Urschnabi's ship, the wooden plank that saved him from shipwreck. "I am happy that I awoke from this dream and that the water of life brought me back into the present, to Uruk. . . . It is senseless to wish to live against nature" (485). He plants trees around Uruk but worries that future generations, for the sake of their trade and ships and houses, will fail to keep the same reverence for nature. But we must not think too much, because life offers us too much to do. "Just don't be too loud in the process or we will fail to hear what the trees have to tell us" (486).

In retrospect we realize that the entire novel has an underlying ecological theme—hardly surprising from the pen of a prolific writer who, beyond his career as a professor of communication and design, has journeyed widely and written about such exotic locales as the Canary Islands and the Balearics. Thus Gilgamesh hears that the scholars in Elam claim that cutting down the forest changes the climate (394). Siduri's tree tells her that human beings regard trees with coldness and hostility (421). Ziusudra informs Gilgamesh that, ever since humankind lost its harmony with the whole, it has been in constant conflict with nature—yet only harms itself, since it is a part of nature (439). Talking to the wooden plank on which he

floats at sea, Gilgamesh promises it and all other trees that he will henceforth strike none of them with a sacrilegious hand (469). And after his
return to Uruk, he exhorts the citizens to border their fields with trees
and to protect them so that everything will thrive in their shade and that
their city will become a fruitful paradise in the midst of the desert (483).
So the novel that began as a systematic rationalization of myth evolves into
a hymn to nature in which the theme of death and immortality is significantly reduced in importance.

The theme of the drum shows up even more prominently in Thomas Mielke's *Gilgamesh: King of Uruk* (*Gilgamesch. König von Uruk,* 1988), which is
based on a careful study of background sources and provides in the appendix a glossary of terms, a chronological table, and a bibliography.[19] While
the author, who has achieved great popular success with historical novels
and works of science fiction, makes no effort to rationalize the supernatural elements, the novel contains a mixture of themes similar to Braem's:
notably, man's break with nature and the turn away from the gods toward
humanity. (In a succeeding novel, *Inanna: The Odyssey of a Goddess* [1990],
Mielke relates the prehistory: the story of Inanna's search for the secret
powers of the gods and her gift of those powers to humankind.)
    The first quarter of the book, like the early chapters of Silverberg and
Braem, is purely fictional invention about Gilgamesh's childhood and
youth. Mielke bases his version on Aelian's account (in *De natura anima-
lium* 12.21) about a Babylonian king who locked up his daughter lest any
son born to her kill him; and on the Akkadian legend of King Sargon,
whose mother bore him in secret, put him in a basket, and floated him
down the river to a gardener who rescued and reared him. According to
the fiction, which is only gradually revealed, his grandfather Enmerkar—
because of an oracle that his grandson would cause his death—locked his
daughter Nin-sun away in order to prevent that fulfillment. However, she
became pregnant (by a god) and, with the assistance of her eunuch Harrap,
secretly sent the child away to Kish, where, like Moses in a basket among
the reeds, he was found and raised by the chief gardener, who taught Gilgamesh the history of his people by reciting to him from the Old Babylonian Book of Kings. Gilgamesh enters the action as a kind of Parsifal
figure—a strong and handsome but essentially naive and ignorant youth of
seventeen—who soon becomes friends with Agga, the son of Mebaragesi,

king of Kish. (The entire novel is rather self-conscious in its repeated suggestions of cultural analogies.)

Unbeknownst to others, Nin-sun and Harrap plot to bring Gilgamesh back to Uruk to take his rightful place as king. To this end, they send a warrior who manages, on a fateful night before the departure of the troops of Kish to overthrow Uruk, to kill one of the head priests "accidentally." A sacrificial person is needed to eradicate the bad omen, and Gilgamesh, an outsider in the city who as a blond does not look like the others, is chosen. Refusing the role, he demands to join the army as a warrior. The fleet sails down the river toward Uruk. But in the encampment one night, Gilgamesh is seduced by a temple-slave from Uruk (secretly sent to ensnare him and bring him to Uruk) and taught the ways of the flesh. She persuades him to go ahead with her to Uruk and, on the way, tells him various origin myths—notably, that the Sumerians were a strange people from the North who came as "Kulturbringer" to Mesopotamia (99).

Gilgamesh and two of his friends are captured by Harrap's guards and hidden away in the tombs beneath the city, where through some mystical process Gilgamesh rapidly matures. When they escape, he shatters the weak mud walls of the city and leads the troops of Kish into Uruk. In the process his grandfather, the king, is accidentally killed by a sword that Gilgamesh strikes out of the hand of an enemy, thus fulfilling the prophecy. Uruk is defeated, and Gilgamesh becomes the new king of the devastated city, acting for the time being as the vassal of the king of Kish, to whom the city must henceforth pay tribute. The coronation ceremony involves several further origin myths: notably about the Great Goddess, who ruled in harmony over Golden Age before men came with their competitiveness and ended matriarchy. Only Inanna rebelled and used her sexual charms to dominate. The statue of Inanna appears to come to life and steps down from her pedestal to crown Gilgamesh.

Gilgamesh begins his reign cautiously. Among other things, he must learn the rules of astrology and priesthood if he is to assume that office. Agga comes secretly from Kish to warn his boyhood friend that he must fortify Uruk with new walls since Kish is eager to demand even more tribute. Gilgamesh learns how to write but also develops a secret new writing system (cuneiform), which he teaches to youngsters. When the goddess Inanna weeps because her chulappa tree has become old and is infested by eagles above and snakes below, Gilgamesh cuts it down and makes from it the *pukku* and *mikku* (drum and stick) with which he can create seven tones, in contrast to the familiar five tones of the flutes. He tells his friends that music is stronger than other means of persuasion:

> Whoever wishes to rule men without the violence of the sword and solely by magical means must take the ancient signs and symbols, the magic of light and the colorful smoke of dreams and use them as oracles. But the strongest of all invisible weapons are rhythm and melody in every prayer, every song, and every movement. Whoever understands that can play with every mortal soul. (242)

Using these means to win over a populace that still regards him as a fatherless outsider, he drums signals to convey his orders: that the entire population must help to build vast and strong new walls. Soon the workers complain about the long hours that keep them away from their homes at night. The high priest warns him that the gods are stronger than any king—even one who has *pukku/mikku* and a great wall. He can't change the movement of the heavens or the waxing and waning of the seasons, but the increasingly arrogant Gilgamesh does not desist from his drumming. A great celebration accompanies the laying of the foundation stone of the wall, built not with mud but with tiles. Gilgamesh, who impresses everyone with his dancing, decides to use seduction of the women as a means of channeling the rage of the men into the wall: "Tyranny was the only possibility of preventing the decline of the defenseless kingdom of Uruk!" (268).

The priests take advantage of Gilgamesh's absence, while he is off sleeping with the city's women, to appeal to the gods from the top of the ziggurat. Aruru creates Enkidu from clay and grass and wool and her own hair, then lies on the figure she has shaped "until the divine breath flowed from her into the clay. She kissed the lips of her creature and breathed her own breath into him" (288). When the hunter reports what he has seen, Gilgamesh sends a temple priestess to capture Enkidu, whom she enchants with a Salome-like veil dance and tells him in words, foreshadowing Genesis, that "the days and nights with me have made you into a knowing human being . . . into one whose eyes I have opened, who from now on will recognize what is good and evil . . . into one who can be like a god or like the most fearsome of all demons" (343). Meanwhile, Gilgamesh has trained a new generation of people, teaching them, among other things, to use the plow ("earth-sword"), to build levees when a flood threatens the foundations of the city, and in the process to bring forth "A new generation of proud and free men who no longer shall grow up in a dull fear of the unknown. Who respect all the gods and secrets of nature, but are not afraid in the presence of any statues, signs and symbols or long empty laws and dark rituals" (340).

While Gilgamesh has not celebrated a Sacred Wedding, he demands the *jus primae noctis* with all brides. The people send a messenger to find Enkidu and Bara and bring them back to the city. Meanwhile, Nansche, the daughter of the carpenter Ugnim, wants to serve as Ischchara, or substitute for Inanna, in Sacred Marriage. When Enkidu tries to prevent the ceremony, he and Gilgamesh fight to a draw—then immediately become friends. Nin-sun is unhappy because their love will bear no children. Circumstances improve in Uruk, but a messenger arrives from Kish to proclaim war. The troops lay siege, but the two friends go forth and their radiance scatters the attackers. They make peace with Agga, who releases the hostaged citizens of Uruk. Only Iranna, still jealous and unhappy, insinuates herself with Gilgamesh, who starts beating *pukku/mikku* again and arouses the people of Uruk into a night of orgies. Enkidu wrests *pukku/mikku* away and hurls them down into underworld through an opening near the gate. Gilgamesh mourns the loss of his instrument, and the land is plunged into sadness. Enkidu, hearing the tale of Inanna's descent into the underworld, decides to go down himself. After three days he escapes and returns with tales of underworld but without pukku/mikku.

Nansche bears the child conceived during her ritual night with Gilgamesh, but the land is still not fertile because no true Sacred Wedding has taken place. Then a sandstorm covers the land, bringing plague and drought. Yet Gilgamesh continues to defy the gods: "We must finally prove that we determine our lives and not the gods! That alone is the adventure for which it is worth living!" (442). He obtains the approval of the priests for his plan to attack Chuwawa and to obtain trees to create a forest around Uruk. But Harrap fears that "the time of the gods is past, and we are seeing how they turn away from us" (445). Gilgamesh and Enkidu cross the desert in three days and see the sea for the first time. They fell the tallest tree of the forest as a challenge to Chuwawa, whom the gods blind with winds and cause to fall. Gilgamesh wants to spare him, but Enkidu demands his death, and they behead "the protective spirit [Schutzgeist] of all trees and all forests" (482). As a result, the trees will no longer be sacred but mere timber.

On their return, Gilgamesh is reminded of his promise to celebrate the Sacred Wedding. He disparages Iranna as a slut but promises to fulfill his obligation. When the goddess comes, however, he rejects her publicly and recounts her treacherous affairs with other men. She complains to the gods, who blame her for stealing the divine properties for mankind but promise the Bull of Heaven for revenge. When the huge bull arrives, Gilgamesh and Enkidu kill it. Then Enkidu falls sick and dies from the burns suffered in the battle with the bull. Gilgamesh mourns for seven days and nights. Whereas he now believes in a single god, the priests still cling to the old polytheism.

The last hundred pages show much less inventiveness and simply fill out details of the traditional story. Deciding to seek immortality, Gilgamesh goes east across the mountains until he comes to the scorpion guardians. Passing through the tunnel of the sun and the forest of jewels, he reaches the hut on the shore where Siduri lives and finds Sursunabu the boatsman there as well. After Gilgamesh destroys the stone oars, he makes 120 new ones from petrified trees. On the island of Dilmun he finds Ziusudra, from whom he hears tales of the primal golden age when gods walked on earth among men. But growing human arrogance and their "desire for decline" ("Lust am Untergang," [566]) causes gods to leave the earth and to plan to destroy mankind. Ziusudra relates the story of the flood and tells him the true secret of life:

> "Life is not-knowing and ever again the decision for one among innumerable possibilities. Nothing in the past is ever concluded and the future can never be wholly foreseen. Doubt and curiosity, trial and error [. . .] that is the bridge between past and future. You are the bridge." (580)

Although Gilgamesh fails the test of sleeplessness and recovers and loses the plant of youthfulness, he learns important lessons: "Perhaps the gods and demons don't come from the heavens but from ourselves. I no longer hear the almighty ones, for I know how I shall live from now on. . . . I no longer need to prove myself! I simply want to use the time that remains to me. Not for myself but all those whom I harmed and wronged" (593, 597).

When he gets back to Uruk, he learns that thirty years have passed and that his son from Nansche is now king. At first people don't recognize him, but he is gradually accepted and happily lives out his life with a few old friends. When he sees his grandson, he realizes that his human posterity is actually the immortality he sought. When he is about to die, he enters the gate to the underworld and (based on the Sumerian poem "The Death of Gilgamesh") makes his way through the seven gates to the throne of Ereshkigal, where he takes his seat on her right, with Enkidu on her left.

Again, the German author, less concerned than Silverberg with the theme of death and immortality, concentrates instead on issues of humankind's development: notably the shift from matriarchy to patriarchy and Gilgamesh's rejection of polytheism in favor of monotheism. As was the case with Braem's novel about the drummer-king, the ecological factor emerges as a dominant theme.

However, the historical novel was not the only fictional mode through which the relevance of Gilgamesh for the present could be exposed.

Gilgamesh Postfigured

Eduardo Garrigues (b. 1944), a Spanish lawyer and since 1973 an active diplomat, was Consul General in Los Angeles when he wrote *West of Babylon* (*Al oeste de Babilonia,* 1987).[20] The author of other novels with exotic settings and using myth, most notably *The Grass Rains* about Kenya, Garrigues read a Spanish translation of Gilgamesh—the translations by Blixen and Peinada had only recently appeared—when he was a student at the Diplomatic School of Spain in Madrid: "I reacted simply to the beauty and force of the poem, which vividly evokes universal feelings of friendship, love, jealousy, and ambition" (vii). Subsequently, while stationed in London, he saw the actual tablets and read George Smith's account of his discoveries. Fascinated, he traveled around New Mexico with the poet Ángel González Muñiz as his guide. Studying the customs and folklore of the native population, he was struck—as was Leonidas Le Cenci Hamilton a century earlier, another lawyer obsessed with the American Southwest—by the similarities between that region and the Near East: adobe architecture, irrigation canals, folkloric dramas. He became acquainted with the Native

American legend of the Twin Warriors, sons of the Sun, who undertook dangerous journeys in their mission to free humankind from such ambivalent monsters as Huwawa/Yeitso, who for all their evil deserve some sympathy. As a conscious postfiguration, the novel stays extremely close to the first half of the epic plot (through the Humbaba episode). Thereafter all similarity ends, as the companions live happily ever after.

The story, each section of which is preceded by lines from the epic, has three basic components: the principal tale of Gil Gómez and his friend Decoy; the many Indian legends that are retold (for instance, the story of the flood and the birth of monsters); and the adventures of the U.S. Army as narrated by Charles Burdette, a dragoon stationed in various frontier garrisons, who allegedly bases his account on diaries he kept in 1850. The three parts, not all of which are relevant in our context, come together only in the final scenes.

Gil Gómez is a *genízaro,* a non-Pueblo Indian captive rescued by Spanish settlers. His mother was Ninsaba, the granddaughter of a great Navajo or Apache chief, but the father remains unknown until late in the story. Burdette serves as an interpreter when Navajo elders complain to the army about Gómez: "Two parts of his body are divine, one part is human. . . . Gil Gómez is like a wild young bull from the mountains, his strength is unmatched, the clatter of his armor has no rival, and at the beat of the drum he rallies his companions" (10). Now the arrogant ruler of the village fortress of Cabézon, he serves the army as a guide and keeps the area calm but ruthlessly abuses the maidens and wives of his people.

Burdette's friend Baltasar, a onetime theology student, makes constant comparisons of their present location and biblical circumstances: he compares the Rio Grande and the Rio Tuerco to the Euphrates and the Tigris; he notes similarities between the Native American tribes and the Chaldeans, Assyrians, and Philistines. Indeed, the army sections of the novel teem with biblical allusions. When the army doesn't help, the tribal leaders complain to Don Anú, the most powerful patron or *cacique* in the region, whose daughter, the lovely Esther (Ishtar), is reputed to be a sorceress of loose morals who abandoned an illegitimate child in the mountains. When neither the U.S. Army nor the Spanish patron can help, they turn to the Apache sorcerer Arorú, who sings charms and molds small figures to "create a warrior as powerful as Gil Gómez, so that his fiery heart will have a rival" (40).

People in the region have all heard the legend of Decoy (corruption of *dikohé,* young Apache warrior), a wild boy from the desert. We learn much later that he is the son of farmers from Missouri who were killed by the Apache chief Humbaba. The twelve-year-old boy is captured but escapes and lives for years among the wild animals: "Young man with a Herculean build, sporting a long beard and hair, dressed in untanned hides, whom they had seen roaming the prairies surrounded by a herd of antelopes and mustangs" (47)—neither white nor Mexican nor Indian. (Baltasar calls him a Samson who needs a Delilah to cut his hair [52].) When the trapper complains, he goes to Gil Gómez, who advises him to hire the prostitute Sam Hat for five silver dollars. The seduction scene stays close to the original: "She opened her bodice, showing off her breasts, and as soon as the strapping lad sensed the smell of the woman's body, he pounced on her" (57). They stay with shepherds, whose flocks he protects, until Decoy's indignation is stirred when he learns of Gil's abuse of *jus primae noctis.* They fight, Decoy wins, and they become close friends or *cuates* (twins or pals).

The people in the region know the legend of the sacred forest, which is protected by Apache warriors and their monstrous leader. Gil and Decoy as well as the U.S. Army decide to go after Humbaba—the ones for glory, the others to avenge his slaughter of troops and settlers. Gil and Decoy visit Ninsaba, who adopts Decoy as her son and tells them where to find Gil's father without naming him. After many ceremonies they are blessed by an old sorcerer. Their trip is betrayed by shepherds to Esther, who is said to have transformed a past lover into a wolf. Fleeing, they find an ancient sorcerer-woman (a scorpion person) in a dark room with spider webs: "Old woman with a small head and thin hair, a very wrinkled face, a fat round body covered with a frayed blanket like a spider web, and long, thin arms" (210). She tells them about the obstacles that lie ahead and gives them protective charms.

They meet the Apache chief Sun Horse, who turns out to be Gil's father and who subjects them to tests that they pass. During the puberty rites for girls of the tribe, they recognize one of the masked dancers as Humbaba, a giant warrior with a buffalo head concealing a scarred face "like a jumble of intestines" (275). Chasing him into the cedar forest, they fight until they believe they have defeated him. Humbaba begs for mercy and curses Decoy, who, under the illusion that he has slain him with his magical flint weapon, then decapitates him. (In fact, it is Burdette who kills Humbaba with his rifle. Chasing army deserters and unbeknownst to the two friends, he has caught up with them and shoots Humbaba from hiding.) Gil and Decoy return by raft and find the remaining soldiers, who help them transport cedar logs and Humbaba's head.

In a "Colophon," Decoy has a dream of Sacred Beings, who, angry at the two brothers for sacrilege, condemn Decoy to death. They fight when Gil wants to sacrifice a stallion to save his friend, but Decoy wins and they both survive and apparently live happily ever after. Burdette starts to return the lost charms given to Decoy by the sorceress and that he has found, "when all of a sudden it dawned on me that perhaps he no longer needed them, since he had triumphed in his expedition and in addition had just taught his robust friend a lesson" (306).

The parallels to the Gilgamesh epic are obvious, perhaps overly so: the quotations for each section, the names (Gil, Decoy, Esther, Ninsaba, Sam Hat, spider woman), and so forth. The action scenes are also analogous but are passed over with surprising rapidity—the seduction by the prostitute, the fight between the two heroes, the battle with Humbaba. The author even includes, allegedly in a contemporary newspaper account of Gil Gómez, a picture identical to the oft-reproduced image of Gilgamesh holding a lion under his arm (from the relief in the palace of the Assyrian king Sargon II at Khorsabad). The narrative moves rapidly and includes a great deal of information for those interested in the history and lore of the Southwest, but the Indian legends are sometimes a distraction. While most of the analogies and parallels can be explained rationally, the legends serve to create the mythical/mystical atmosphere of belief that governs especially Decoy. Oddly, there is no attempted seduction of Gil by Esther: she simply chases them out of her territory. Her seduction is aimed at the army lieutenant who visits her father. In the absence of any obvious thematic connection, the epic serves essentially as a plot device.

Gilgamesh Personalized

It was not only for its theoretical implications and its historical relevance that the epic attracted writers. Some also discovered in Gilgamesh a profoundly personal meaning. Typical for these Gilgameshophiles is the

French essayist Joël Cornuault (b. 1950), who from 1983 to 1996 issued a "review"—actually a series of fifty four-page ruminations occasionally illustrated with engravings by Jean-Marc Scanreigh—under the general heading "Gilgamesh et ses amis" ("Gilgamesh and his friends"). During those same years he published a slender volume entitled *Éloge de Gilgamesh* (1992), a series of brief reflections in the form of a "revery permeated by art and history" (7).[21] The author states at the outset that he has neither the inclination nor the qualifications to undertake a historical study. He hopes, instead, "to reactivate the most ancient myth of humanity and to use it as a spring-board for a personal meditation" (14). As he writes:

> "My" Gilgamesh, "my" Mesopotamia, "my" Chaldeans with the widely opened eyes, to be sure, are the citizens of a poetic country of a sort that never existed. They are myths in which I pick and choose for my own purposes, myths fabricated to serve me as points of reference. (52)

When he goes for a stroll in the geometrically arranged streets of a village in southwestern France, "Gilgamesh was walking at my side," prompting reflections that the white-stoned walls and towers of the village resemble those of ancient Mesopotamia (55): "Sumer has become for me the emblem of several places, things, and personages . . . which, when I dream, provide abundant grain to grind in my meditations" (56). All in all, he confesses, "it is a great pleasure to dream thus about civilizations. The stimulation that this activity exerts within us is considerable" (21). It is unnecessary to take further note of Cornuault's deliberations because, while allegedly stimulated by the epic, which he claims to have read twenty times or more, they have virtually nothing to do with Gilgamesh as such. But his "eulogy" serves as a symptomatic introduction to a group of works in which Gilgamesh has been personalized to an extent not evident in the works considered up to this point.

In 1986 the Québécois poet and novelist Alain Gagnon (b. 1943) published the prose poem *Gilgamesh,* which basically follows the sequence of the epic but makes a number of seemingly meaningless changes along the way. (Gilgamesh tells Siduri, for instance, that he never knew a mother and was born "from the actions of several gods" [50].)[22] The author obviously undertook his work from a powerful sense of identity with the hero—an identity achieved, however, at the expense of the Mesopotamian character of the epic. In his "Avant-propos" he writes: "From the depth of the millennia I have heard your cry, Gilgamesh, my Mesopotamian brother. From Quebec-Land to the fiery banks of the Euphrates, a hand is extended, shriveled by the same griefs and the same hopes." He adds that he has sought "perhaps in vain to repeat to you the words of the angel who does not utter his name: 'Remember, o man, that you are light and that you shall again become light,'" thus anticipating the rather surprising sermonizing turn in the concluding pages, where Shamash tells Gilgamesh that he and the other gods are "only the shadows of your dreams. But there is one god of whom you, human beings, are the dream and the thirst; he alone is able to grant the immortality that makes you tremble with impatience and envy" (50).

The text is rationalized and frequently expanded, especially in the more lubricious passages. After his encounter with the young prostitute, the animals run away because "his sweat was mixed with that of the young woman; he had the scent of her womb ["cyprine"] on his thighs and penis" (17). Huwawa is a "formidable king" whose warriors ravage the countryside (27), and Enkidu dies from injuries sustained when he is thrown from a horse (38). When Gilgamesh leaves the city, rather than slipping away quietly, he delivers a lengthy oration to the citizens, saying that nothing remains for him in the city except grief (43–44). He reaches Siduri without any mention of the scorpion people, the dark passage, or the lovely garden; she tells him that he will never find the immortality he seeks and that the past will always catch up with him (49). It is from Siduri that Gilgamesh first hears of Utnapishtim, whom he reaches without any mention of the Waters of Death and whom he immediately insults, calling him "a fifty-year-old wag [gouailleur], a little too plump and with cheeks reddened by wine" (57). He wonders how such a man succeeded in sharing the destiny of the gods. Utnapishtim repays him in kind by telling him at interminable length (57–71) the story of the flood. When Gilgamesh loses the plant of youth, Shamash reassures him with the Christianizing message already cited above. In sum, Gagnon's *Gilgamesh* is an intensely personal version, which has been altered in numerous ways—some comprehensible but others not so—to reflect his own view of life and the message he wishes to communicate to his son, to whom the work is dedicated.[23]

Gilgamesh Hispanicized

In Spain a remarkable and unique surge of Gilgameshiana was due largely to the efforts of one man, the writer and film producer José Ortega (b. 1958), who, like his countryman Eduardo Garrigues, is a trained lawyer with a strong interest in cultural anthropology.[24] To be sure, it is a weird rendering of the story to which his Spanish audience has been introduced. From 1990 to 2001 Ortega published a trilogy of novels on Gilgamesh under the general title *Khol,* of which only the first, *Gilgamesh y la muerte* ("Gilgamesh and Death," 1995) has any connection with the epic as such. "Khol," we are told, originally designated a race of dragons that could regenerate limbs lost in combat; later it was adopted to designate "the ritual death of the initiate and his rebirth on a higher plane of being"—an apt statement of Gilgamesh's development in the course of the three volumes.[25]

Despite its title, less than half of the first volume has anything to do with the familiar epic of Gilgamesh apart from the names, which are given in their Sumerian forms—Inanna, Huwawa, Ziusudra. Many new characters have been introduced and a wholly new mythological basis for the action provided. Ortega's Lugalbanda is not the king of Uruk but rather one of three gods thrown out of heaven because they had refused to go along with the decision of the other deities to flood the earth and destroy early humankind. Taking earthly form, he mated with the lovely peasant maiden, Ni-Inanna—later revered as the Virgin of the Wind—to produce Gilgamesh. (While Ni-Inanna has no further role, the high priestess of Inanna enjoys a variation of the name traditionally attributed to Gilgamesh's mother: Ninsin.) Subsequently, in the guise of the aged hermit Kei, Lugalbanda appears at crucial points of the story to set his son on the right path.

The account of Enkidu is the familiar one: he is tamed by Ni-Dada, queen of the prostitutes ("la reina de las rameras"), but the action is not portrayed:

> What happened then is a simple story. The methods that experienced women use with timid, frightened adolescents and with insecure men. Ni-Dada knew them all and used them all with exquisite sensibility at that crucial moment. . . . (52)

The customary fight takes place, and the two friends set out immediately on the journey that will lead them to Huwawa, an episode that covers three long chapters. On the way, Kei appears for the first time to give Enkidu two magical protective stones, and they are joined in their endeavor by Enakalli, the son of a neighboring king. It appears for many pages as though Huwawa will overcome the three heroes: he grinds herbs with a stone mortar and thinks greedily about the abundant human meat that will soon be at his disposal from his victims (122). But they finally win when a deer betrays the ogre's secret to Enkidu: Huwawa's heart is hidden in the Sacred Cedar, the largest in the entire forest; and the only way of killing him is to chop down the tree, which he does.

The invitation and rejection of Inanna follow their return to Uruk, whereupon Enkidu—with no battle with a Heavenly Bull—becomes ill and dies. From this point on the novel takes a wholly new course, which is freely invented by the author using various materials from cultural anthropology that he cites, complete with footnotes, along the way (Robert Graves, Kramer, and others, along with passages from the Sumerian songs). As he sets out from Uruk, Gilgamesh soon encounters the hermit Kei, who tells him that he should seek out Ziusudra, the sole survivor of the great deluge, who lives on the mountain Nisir at the northernmost extreme of the world (179). In the course of his search, Gilgamesh, who becomes known as "the Sumerian" ("el sumerio") or the "Sad Warrior" (270: "Guerrero Triste"), is involved at length, and with many complications that are irrelevant here, in the war between the cities of Egione and Magoor. He hears the legend of the White City beyond the Great Sea (203–12), which is ruled by Aradawc, the possessor of the Shining Stone ("Piedra Resplandeciente"). (This episode, which has little relevance for the first volume apart from the fact that Aradawc is later identified as another of the three fallen deities, provides the basis for the third volume of the trilogy.) In the course of these adventures Gilgamesh soars through the air on flying horses and huge vultures, sees crystal towers built by dwarves for the remains of kings, and visits the island of Onud with a boatman named Temme (not Urshanabi), where he finds informants named Nusko and Dorxemme (not Ziusudra).

Finally, again with the assistance of Kei, who reveals his identity and then disintegrates into a puff of wind, Gilgamesh reaches the forbidden Kingdom of the North and finds Ziusudra, who greets him as "the god of death for whose arrival I have been praying night and day" (381). Ziusudra finds his eternal life intolerable: "Truly I tell you that the entire wisdom of the world can be reduced to learning how to die" (384). After further conversation, Gilgamesh, comprehending and accepting his decision, plunges his sword into the entrails of the ancient, who dies with "an expression of radiant hope" (387). In a brief epilogue we learn that Gilgamesh, at last freed of his fear of death, marries Issmir, now Queen of the newly allied cities of Egione and Magoor, and they return joyfully to Uruk, prepared to liberate the city from its past decadence.

Volume 2, *El principe pálido* ("The pallid prince," 1995), takes up the account twenty years later when Gilgamesh, now widowed and having forsaken his dreams of earthly achievement, has assumed Humbaba's role as guardian of the Cedar Forest. Most of the action, based loosely on Mediterranean rumors concerning the birth of a new god—more or less the same lore that fifty years earlier informed Robert Graves's *King Jesus* (1946)—takes place on the Iberian peninsula, where his further adventures lead him and where his life becomes a metaphor for the conversion of earlier religious cults to monotheism. When he dies, promised reunification with Enkidu and his beloved wife Issmir, he disappears like a phantom in a white cloud (as did his father at the end of volume 1). Volume 3, *Piedra resplandeciente* ("The glittering stone," 2001), which is based on the legend related in the first volume, portrays figures from myths of Bronze Age Spain but has nothing further to do with Gilgamesh.

Stating that interest in the epic had hitherto been restricted mainly to the Anglo-Saxon and German cultures (and citing Silverberg and Braem as examples but overlooking the earlier novel by Eduardo Garrigues), advertisements for the trilogy called it, somewhat misleadingly, "the first literary work in Spanish dedicated to the myth of Gilgamesh." (As we have seen, very little of the three volumes actually deals with the epic account.) Then in 2002, for the film company that he had established for the production of documentaries on archaeology, myth, and cultural anthropology—for instance, on the origin of culture ("Genesis") and on myths of the Mediterranean world ("Chronicles of the Enchanted Land")—Ortega released a three-part "dialogue between myth and reality" featuring the interplay between the mythic Mesopotamian past and present-day Spain. In 2007 he released a multi-part TV dramatization entitled *El mito de Gilgamesh,* based on his idiosyncratic literary trilogy.

Gilgameshiana

While the theorists were psychoanalyzing and deconstructing Gilgamesh, while the novelists were historicizing and greening and postfiguring the epic in their huge tomes, and while other writers were personalizing the ancient epic to their own modern purposes, the poets and musicians were not idle. The opening poem in a volume entitled *The Ninth Hour* (*Die Neunte Stunde,* 1979) by the German poet Peter Huchel (1903–81), which traces the course of human development, depicts the critical moment when humankind first achieved consciousness and emerged from its animal stage.[26] Addressing Enkidu directly, he writes:

> Sohn,
> kleiner Sohn Enkidu,
> du verließest deine Mutter, die Gazelle,
> deinen Vater, den Wildesel,
> Um mit der Hure nach Uruk zu gehen.
> Die milchtragenden Ziegen flohen.
> Es verdorrte die Steppe.
>
> (Son,
> little son Enkidu,
> you left your mother, the gazelle,
> your father, the wild ass,
> to go to Uruk with the whore.
> The milk-bearing goats fled.
> The steppe withered.)

Beyond the city gate, Gilgamesh, who walked the border between heaven and earth ("der Grenzgänger zwischen Himmel und Erde"), taught Enkidu to cut through the cord of death. But the civilization-weary poet, looking back from the twentieth century (as did earlier Charles Olson and Louis Zukofsky), urges Enkidu to turn back:

> Was schenkte dir Gilgamesch?
> Das schöne Haupt der Gazelle versank.
> Der Staub schlug deine Knochen. (229)

(What did Gilgamesh give you?
The lovely head of the gazelle sank down,
The dust struck your bones.)

Ten years after Huchel's depressing statement, the American poet Donald Hall ended his "Praise for Death" (1987–90) with a paraphrase of the second part of the epic. In thirty-eight five-line stanzas, the poet surveys the manner in which death has been praised and depicted over the centuries: from the terra cotta armies of the emperor of Qin and Hadrian's statues of Antinous to Henry Adam's memories of his wife Clover and the obituaries of the *Boston Globe*. He remembers the deaths of friends and contemporaries—deaths in battle, in airplane crashes, in old age. Finally he recalls the words of Gilgamesh as he weeps bitterly for Enkidu and wonders, "Should I *praise* master death that commanded my friend?"[27] As he wanders and weeps he despairs that "what happened to my brother will happen to me."

Now, therefore, I climb to the sun's garden, to Utnapishtim
who alone of all men after the flood lives without dying.

The epic continued to exert its appeal for artists and musicians. In 1995 the Deutscher Kunstverlag brought out a new edition of Hartmut Schmökel's 1966 translation accompanied by a folio of seventeen striking full-page illustrations by the German artist August Ohm (b. 1943).[28] The opera *Gilgamesh* (1985) by the Croatian composer Rudolf Brucci (1917–2002) enjoyed a critical and popular success when it was first performed in 1985 in Novi Sad.[29] Based on a scenario by the film-TV-opera director Arsenije Milosevic (1931–2006), the three-act opera recounts more or less the entire story of the epic, from Enkidu's encounter with the temptress to Gilgamesh's interview with Utnapishtim, as a multimedia show with contemporary sets and choreography.[30] The same decade saw the appearance of *Gilgamesh Quartet: For Four Trombones* (1988) by Tera de Marez Oyens and William Coates's *The Secret of Utnapishtim: For Soprano and Archiphone* (1989). In 1981 William Thomas Kidd submitted his score of *The Epic of Gilgamesh: An Opera Cycle* as his thesis to the Virginia Commonwealth University.[31]

In 1992 the strikingly original and popular Italian song-writer Franco Battiato (b. 1941), who composes in every style—experimental, classical, jazz, pop, progressive rock—devoted one of his four operas to *Gilgamesh*. According to Battiato, the myth ought to be read as an illustration that "free choice, which every person has as a divine gift, is used poorly. Through his encounter with Enkidu, Gilgamesh learns submission to and humility before the divine authority."[32] The short (somewhat longer than an hour) two-act work, which the composer calls an "opera lirica," might more appropriately be described as an oratorio accompanied by ballet and pantomime in gorgeous costumes with spectacular lighting effects. It involves only two solo voices (baritone and mezzo-soprano) plus a chorus and two recitativo voices in liturgical passages at the end. (For the most part, the dreamy music is less orchestral than electrophonic plus piano.) In act 1 a narrator (in the composer's own voice) briefly recapitulates the action of the narrative up to the defeat of Humbaba. Then the voices of Utnapishtim and his wife against a choral background tell us in a few lines that Gilgamesh was happy—a happiness acted out as a ballet—until Enkidu dies. Gilgamesh, who has no singing role, goes in search of Utnapishtim in four brief pantomimic journeys. He hears the story of the flood and then dies.

Act two, which begins with a full *Pater noster* in Latin and in which Gilgamesh is not mentioned, takes place in Sicily in the summer of 1240 (the year when the Muslims were driven from the island), where seven sufis come together and recite parables taken variously from the Persian mystic Rumi, the Sufi mystic Ibn Arabi, and Empedocles. The act ends with a "sacred dance" and an *Exultet* in Latin featuring language from the Roman Catholic liturgy. The connection between the two acts is suggested by the sufi maestro's parable (from Rumi) to the effect that the tree is born from the fruit rather than vice versa because it is in hope of the fruit that the gardener plants the tree: the composer's suggestion that the myth of Gilgamesh and his hope of eternity were born in anticipation of the redemption brought by Christ, to whom the final hymn is addressed. Even though its Christianizing tendencies are familiar, Battiato's musically imaginative and impressive work constitutes one of the strangest adaptations of the epic.

The Gilgamania of the 1980s produced several works of considerable aesthetic quality that document the growing familiarity and popularity of the great epic. The poems, poetic dramas, novels, and operas illustrate almost paradigmatically how readily various contemporary themes and interests, ranging from psychoanalysis to ecology, from deconstruction to religion, from historical rationalization to intense personalization, found a satisfactory vehicle in the Sumerian epic. The decade also witnessed, in Carl Sagan's novel *Contact* (1985), the cooptation of the theme to lend an additional dimension to a work that is spacey in several senses. Here a multibillionaire, who has developed among his other vast undertakings an adult amusement park near New York City called "Babylon," complete with an Enlil Gate and ziggurat, is eager to avoid total annihilation by cremation. So he commissions a "flying sarcophagus" that he christens "Gilgamesh"— an auxiliary vehicle attached to his space station, his "chateau in the sky"— in which he sails off into space with the cryogenic equipment that will enable him upon his death to contrive his own resurrection at some point in the remote future.[33]

Michael Ondaatje's prize-winning novel, *In the Skin of a Lion* (1987), which is sometimes mentioned in connection with Gilgamesh, has little in common with the epic save its title, which is explained by the quotation one of the novel's epigraphs: "The joyful will stoop with sorrow, and when you have gone to the earth I will let my hair grow long for your sake, I will wander through the wilderness in the skin of a lion" (from Tablet VIII, lines 90–91).[34] A second Gilgamesh quotation occurs at the end, when the hero lies wounded: "He lay down to sleep, until he was woken from out of a dream. He saw the lions around him glorying in life; then he took his axe in his hand, he drew his sword from his belt, and he fell upon them like an arrow from the string" (Tablet IX, lines 15–18). Otherwise the novel is neither a postfiguration nor even a thematization of the epic: it takes place in Toronto in the 1920s and 1930s among immigrants who work building viaducts and digging tunnels. The grief to which the motto alludes is the lament of the hero, Patrick Lewis, for his dead lover Alice.

Gilgamesh at Millennium's End

In France, meanwhile, after Joseph-Régis Pio's poetic retelling of *L'Épopée de Gilgamesh* (1989), an elegant fictional re-vision, *Le roman de Gilgamesh* (1998), was published by Jacques Cassabois (b. 1947), known primarily for his youth books on such legendary topics as Antigone, Tristan and Isolde, and Sindbad the Sailor. In contrast to the historical novels of the preceding decade by Silverberg, Braem, and Mielke, however, Cassabois makes little effort to create an authentic historical background or to rationalize the supernatural incidents, devoting his attention, instead, to an exploration of the psychological motivation of the figures, including the gods. Following the translation by Jean Bottéro, who provided an appreciative preface for his novel, as well as Bottéro's book on *Mésopotamie, l'écriture, la raison et les dieux* (1987) and Samuel Kramer's *History Begins at Sumer* (1958), Cassabois retells in smoothly readable prose the plot of Tablets I through XI, expanding it in the process and omitting only a few incidents.

The story begins (Part I: "Friendship") with an account of Gilgamesh's early glory and arrogance, which annoys even the gods, who debate methods of discipline: to kill him with a lightning bolt, to make the women so ugly that they will offer no temptation, to garrote him. When Arourou comes up with her suggestion, all the gods descend to earth to watch her create Enkidu: "We have brought [his shape] from Heaven to Earth. It is a star" (31).[35] This statement leads directly to Gilgamesh's dream of the star, which his mother interprets. In the course of his early wanderings Enkidu encounters the as yet unnamed "esprit de la forêt" (38) before he settles down with the gazelles. Gilgamesh's second dream of the axe causes him—without the intercession of a hunter—to send a priestess to capture Enkidu, who is initially attracted by her breasts, which he attempts to suckle, before he enjoys the sexual attractions of the "femme-gazelle" (50). After his "apprentissage" with the shepherds, the priestess leads him to Uruk, where the people exhort him to defy Gilgamesh and to defend the customary old "usage": the sanctity of marriage between man and woman. When Gilgamesh is defeated in their fight and agrees to accept "usage," the people as well as the deities are perplexed and worried by their friendship: "Beware! The wild beasts have formed an alliance" (69). But all turns out well: Gilgamesh—who had "feared the irruption of a furious bull into his life, but found a peaceful ox" (72)—introduces Enkidu to his kingdom and tries to teaches him to govern. But even as the people grow happy, Enkidu's dissatisfaction and boredom increase. When Gilgamesh proposes the journey to the cedar forest, Enkidu describes fearfully the magical powers of Humbaba.

As they cross the steppe, Enkidu rolls happily on the ground, "pays d'Enkidou" ("homeland of Enkidu"; 87), and tries to teach Gilgamesh to savor the raw meat of the animals he kills with his bare hands. The battle with Humbaba leaves it unclear to what extent Humbaba—"a tension of the spirit, a fruit ripened by the invisible" (97)—is a manifestation of nature with winds, rumblings of the earth, and a hurricane or an actual creature with a bull's legs and the head of a lion. Humbaba is killed, but his severed head falls into the river as Enkidu dances ecstatically on the raft. When they get back to Uruk, Gilgamesh sends an expedition to carry out a "systematic exploitation" of the forest.

In a detailed description, Ishtar then makes her proposal in a manner suggesting a predatory nymphomaniac: perfumed, thrusting out her breasts, licking her rouged lips, she grasps his penis, and straddles him with her legs. Furious at his rejection, she demands from the other gods the Heavenly Bull. When the friends kill it, they hurl not only a leg at her but also its testicles and, holding up its entrails, threaten to disembowel her. At this "insulte irréparable" (123), the gods determine Enkidu's death.

Enkidu dreams of the steppe, where instead of suffering and dying in bed he would have fallen like a leaf in winter and returned to earth with the help of the wild beasts, rain, and wind: "He would have taken his place, peaceably, in the cycle of mould" (132). Accepting his own death, he urges Gilgamesh not to see in it any injustice. His death protects his friend. He is buried at the frontier between city and desert, gazing out to the steppe.

In Part II ("Life without end"), after a long period of grief Gilgamesh sets out to find Utnapishti. Marching for months, he meets the scorpion people, passes through the dark canyon where he has visions of the Heavenly Bull and Humbaba and engages in conversations with his protective deity, Shamash, and reaches the bejeweled garden, where "each tree represents a manner of being, a quality raised to its incandescence" (176–77). When he arrives at the seacoast, Siduri, "la Tavernière" (182), tries to persuade him to stay and enjoy life. But after destroying the stone oarsmen he is taken by Urshanabi across to Utnapishti. The ancient sage tells him, to his immense disappointment, that "you already possess what you deserve, and I cannot give you anything more" (199). Rather than trying to develop his human qualities, he has striven instead and in vain to become a miscarriage ("avorton") of the gods (202). He hears the tale of the flood and fails the test of sleep but does obtain and then lose "l'Herbe de Jouvence." But Utnapishti appears to him in a vision and tells him that he gave him the plant of youth "so that you will search and so that you will learn to find it. So that you will find it and learn to love, so that the nostalgia of this love will incite you to search always in your depths" (237). The "voices of the world" then speak to him in chorus and urge him to return to Uruk, to go find confidence within himself, to see the infinity of time, and to understand that life and death are inseparable: "That is the only immortality, Gilgamesh! By living the today of each and every thing, you will live the eternity of all the tomorrows" (239). Having left all fear of death behind, Gilgamesh returns to Uruk: "He had found peace. Today it was a matter of living. So he got up and marched toward the new life" (241).

Thematically Cassabois offers little that is new: the message of his version is the traditional exhortation to find happiness in living one's earthly life, and it includes the familiar ambivalence regarding nature and civilization and the contemporary ecological message. But new connections are made—for instance, between the creation of Enkidu as a star and Gilgamesh's dream. The supernatural apparitions are given a semi-realistic basis. The scenes of heterosexual love are portrayed with relish while a number of passages hint, though ambivalently, at the homosexual relationship between Gilgamesh and Enkidu. Thus the crowd senses that "ils s'aiment" (75: "they like each other" or, more explicitly, "they make love together"). And elsewhere: "Gilgamesh murmured, mouth to mouth with Enkidu, as though trying to breathe his words into him" (140).

The flowering of the 1980s was succeeded in the United States by a decade of considerably less activity, marked principally by such isolated stage performances as *Gilgamesh Conquest* by Ralph Blasting and Mahmood Karimi-Hakak at Towson State University (1991) and Andrew C. Ordover's *Gilgamesh* at the Ohio Theater in New York (1995). In Brenda W. Clough's *How Like a God* (1997), an utterly improbable sci-fi contrivance, "Gilgamesh" enters only toward the end—a Gilgamesh, moreover, fundamentally different from the hero of the epic.[36] Rob Lewis, a computer programmer in a Washington suburb, wakes up one morning to discover that he can read minds and control the actions of others. As this power gets out of hand, takes over his personality, and affects his wife and children, he leaves home and goes to New York City, where he uses his powers to support himself while he reads in the Public Library. There, after working his way though poetry, *The Iliad,* and *The Aeneid,* he stumbles across

Gilgamesh in the Ferry version (later he buys a paperback copy of the Sandars translation):

> Reading Gilgamesh's story was an eerie experience, . . . suddenly finding his own biography in blank verse. My god, this guy is me, he realized. Enormous powers that isolate him from his hometown—that means another person had this problem, even if it was five thousand years ago. Of course it was all wrapped up in the usual epic-myth trappings, goddesses, and angry demons and magical undersea plants that made you immortal if you ate them, but the skeleton of the story was weirdly familiar. Gilgamesh had even been a rapist. (109)

He goes to Maryland to seek out Dr. Edwin Barbarossa at the National Institutes of Health—a man he had once helped and who now becomes his Enkidu as he tries to determine the source of Rob's powers. One day, on a miniature Washington Monument that he encounters in a vision— "voyages in inner space" (188)—he finds a cuneiform inscription that he copies and passes on to Edwin. Meanwhile, with his magical powers he wins thousands of dollars gambling in Atlantic City. Rob finds that the cuneiform inscription spells the name "Aqebin," an archaeological site in Uzbekistan. While Barbarossa is testing his mind with an electroencephalogram, he has another vision and receives a message instructing him to go to Aqebin. They make the trip and discover a cave where they find Gilgamesh, a magnificent apparition who then shrinks into a skeletally thin figure. It appears that he didn't lose the magical plant of immortality after all, as legend reported: "'A story is only a story,' Gilgamesh said." Feeling despite his immortality after five thousand years the need for a companion, he had sent half of his power to Rob, "trashed my life, broke up my family, drove me almost insane, for a *diversion*" (227). Arguing that Edwin may have been Rob's Enkidu, "but not your friend, he is a pawn, a tool" (229), he sends Barbarossa to commit suicide. Rob and Gilgamesh fight, and when the old man collapses, Rob unzips the skin that covers Gilgamesh's body and recovers two beads—"the symbol of his immortality" (237). Leaving Gilgamesh to die now of a normal old age, he rescues the mortally wounded Edwin by giving him the bead of immortality. Then they go back to America, and Rob returns to his family: "He wasn't a god, had never even been close. In the family of humanity he wasn't the dad, but only a younger son. The realization was a tremendous relief, like a titanic rock rolling off his back" (286). As Gilgamesh's power, which had taken over half his personality, recedes, Rob's own natural personality reemerges—a good side evident in the novel through such actions as his helping people in distress and repairing the damaged homeless shelter in Silver Spring, where he lives for a time.

The 1990s could also boast of a growing interest among scholars in various fields and a plethora of first-rate translations into English and other languages: in France (1992 by Jean Bottéro; and 1998 by Jacques Tournay and Aaron Schaffer); in Italy (1992 by Giovanni Pettinato); and in Germany (1994 by Karl Hecker). Robert Temple acknowledges in the introduction to his English translation that it was his frustration with Sandars's prose version that prompted him to undertake his lively verse rendition, *He Who Saw Everything* (1991), which is based on the earlier versions by Heidel, Speiser, Campbell Thompson, and others in English and German. Using complete lines, it bridges parenthetically the various breaks in the text. Danny Thompson confesses in his introduction that his verse rendition, *The Epic of Gilgamesh* (1992), makes use of personal experience—for instance, his background as a comparative classicist and even interviews with streetwalkers from research on teenage prostitution that he carried out for an article for *The New York Times*—but relies principally on the translations by Campbell Thompson, Heidel, Mason, Sandars, and Kovacs and on John Maier, with whom he studied. Like Gardner and Maier, the translator presents the text by tablet and column, and his language is idiomatic and frank. The well-illustrated edition also contains an introduction by the Assyriologist Robert D. Biggs and an appreciation by James G. Keenan. That same year saw David Ferry's "new rendering in English verse," *Gilgamesh* (1992). Ferry, known above all for his translations of Latin classics (Virgil and Horace), presents the text in couplets of five-beat lines and identifies them by tablet and column.[37] Sumaya Shabandar's strikingly illustrated *Epic of Gilgamesh* (1994) is notable as a curio since it is a translation based neither on the original nor on earlier English versions but rather on several Arabic translations. Her version, though set in free-verse lines, reads more like a prose translation than poetry.

The decade, and the century, was crowned by a translation now widely regarded as definitive: *The Epic of Gilgamesh* (1999) by the British Assyriologist Andrew George, which also usefully includes translations of the other Babylonian and Sumerian texts. George, who subsequently (2003) published his now-standard edition with transcriptions of the original text, presents the work in four- and five-line stanzas with running indications of tablet and line as well as of his own bracketed insertions. Readers of the smoothly moving narrative can feel confident that they are being exposed to the text itself with no hidden interpolations or individual shadings to affect the meaning. George's translation was given a dramatic reading in 1999 at the School of Oriental and African Studies, University of London, and again in 2003 at the 49e Rencontre Assyriologique Internationale;[38] and it has been recorded along with readings (in the original) of Tablets II and XI of the Old Babylonian Version.[39]

The period of contemporization that began with the efforts of such theories as Orientalism, psychoanalysis, deconstruction, and ecology to expose sometimes far-fetched new aspects of the ancient epic of Gilgamesh thus ended with a monument of brilliant Assyriological scholarship that laid the groundwork for the reception in the twenty-first century.

5

GILGAMESH IN THE TWENTY-FIRST
CENTURY (2000–2009)

Gilgamesh, who was born and flourished in the mid-third millennium
B.C.E., is alive and well almost five thousand years later at the beginning
of the third millennium of the Common Era. The continuing vitality of
the epic is suggested by its worldwide popularity reaching from England
and France to Australia in books for children, such as Damian Morgan's
Gil's Quest, Geraldine McCaughrean's *Gilgamesh the Hero*, Nicole Leurpendeur's *Das Gilgamesch-Epos*, and Jacques Cassabois's *Le premier roi du
monde—L'épopée de Gilgamesh*, a toned-down adaptation based on his earlier novel.[1] The same years in Germany could boast of a musical for performance by children: *Gilgamesch macht Ärger* ("Gilgamesh makes trouble")
with words by Hans Zimmer and score by Wolfhard Bartel.[2] And in the
Netherlands the well-known actor Frank Groothof published an illustrated *Gilgamesj* with song texts and music by Marjet Huibert.[3]

Artists and musicians continued to find inspiration in the epic. Conspicuously, German artists of the new millennium still outpace all others
in their fascination with Gilgamesh and in the variety and extent of their

treatments. Germany saw exhibitions of drawings and paintings by Reinhard Minkewitz, who depicts various figures from the epic in isolated situations, such as "Ishtar Beats the Drum" (Leipzig, 2006); a series of transparencies by Martin Blessman that, inspired by the fall of the Berlin wall, use the epic to portray the transitory nature of power as well as the search for immortality as a metaphor for the contemporary desire for ever longer lives (Bonn, 2006); and a cycle by Anna Ghadaban, who took isolated images from the story as the basis for abstract gouaches (Kusterdingen, Baden-Württemberg, 2009). In 2005 the Akademie der Wissenschaften und Literatur in Mainz sponsored an exhibit featuring "Das Gilgamesch-Epos" as seen by three generations of artists (specifically Hegenbarth, Baumeister, and Minkewitz). One of the most remarkable enterprises was undertaken in 2005 by Burkhard Pfister (b. 1949), who created a graphic novel (with text by Ursula Broicher) consisting of some 400 drawings organized into twelve individually published "tablets" of about thirty pages each.[4] In 2010–11 the Staatsgalerie Stuttgart presented a special exhibition of Willi Baumeister's "Gilgamesch-Zyklus."

In 2007 the composer Wolfgang Witzenmann premiered his oratorio *Gilgamesch und Christus,* which compares and contrasts the lives of the two figures—a theme going back to Jensen and other scholars and to the Babel and Bible debate at the turn of the previous century. In May 2009, the fiftieth anniversary of Bohuslav Martinů's death was acknowledged in Dresden with a scholarly symposium plus a much-acclaimed performance of the composer's Gilgamesh oratorio at the Sing-Akademie.

The first decade of the new century also produced its share of translations. In the United States, Benjamin Foster, a Yale professor of Near Eastern languages, translated into free verse the first eleven tablets of the Akkadian epic, *The Epic of Gilgamesh,* accompanied by renditions of the Sumerian poems (by Douglas Frayne) and the Hittite version (by Gary Beckman). In keeping with the format of the Norton Critical Editions, the useful volume includes a brief but informative introduction plus three critical essays and a poem by Hillary Major.[5] The American poet Stephen Mitchell, who has published highly regarded translations from several languages (most notably of Rilke), brought out in 2004 his lively "version" of Tablets I–XI, *Gilgamesh: A New English Translation,* undertaken because he "had never been convinced by the language of any translation of it" that he had read.[6] Since he admittedly had no knowledge of Akkadian, he based his own rendition on several earlier versions in English, French, and German and notably on Andrew George's edition, keeping as near as possible to the literal meaning but omitting the formulaic repetitions, filling in the gaps, and elaborating when transitions seemed necessary (65–66). The adaptation uses a loose pentameter line that often, stressing four strong beats, catches the rhythms of the original:

> Surpassing all kings, powerful and tall
> beyond all others, violent, splendid,
> a wild bull of a man, unvanquished leader. (71)

And while his version stays generally close to the line and pace of the original, Mitchell adds vivid touches to enliven the scenes:

> He drew close. Shamhat touched him on the thigh,
> touched his penis, and put him inside her. (78–79)

All in all, it is a informative and jaunty introduction to Gilgamesh for jaded contemporaries expecting something beyond the often less explicit subtleties of earlier versions.

In Germany, meanwhile, the Heidelberg Assyriologist Stefan Maul provided the reading public with *Das Gilgamesch-Epos,* a splendid new translation. His version, based on Andrew George's now-standard edition of the Akkadian text, adds new lines from fragments found more recently. Maul seeks with his language to approximate the rhythms of the Babylonian original, not avoiding the repetitions and stressing, as many modern readers since Rilke have done, as the epic may have been meant to be recited aloud and not read silently (consistent with this view, Maul subsequently produced in four CDs an audiobook with a reading of his translation along with various new textual findings and amplifications):

> Der, der die Tiefe sah, die Grundfeste des Landes,
> der das *Verborgene* kannte, der, dem alles bewußt—
> Gilgamesch, der die Tiefe sah, die Grundfeste des Landes,
> der das *Verborgene* kannte, der, dem alles bewußt—[7]

> (He who saw the depths, the foundations of the land,
> who knew what was *hidden,* he, to whom all was known—

> Gilgamesh, who saw the depths, the foundations of the land,
> who knew what was *hidden,* he, to whom all was known—)

With its knowledgeable introduction, which includes a tablet-by-tablet recapitulation of the action, and especially its extensive and clear notes, Maul's translation fulfilled for the German public the same function as did Andrew George's for readers of English.

In this connection it is worth citing the accessible introduction to the epic in Beck's *Wissen* series by Walther Sallaberger, professor of Assyriology at the University of Munich.[8] In eight readable chapters, the author sketches for a general audience the relevant background of the epic from the Mesopotamian world and the historical Gilgamesh by way of its stages of composition down to its literary shape and more general themes, ending with a quick look at its impact on the Bible and Homer. That a book of this sort appeared in a popular series addressed to a general audience in itself attests to the lively German interest in the epic, as did the TV documentary by Peter Moers and Frank Papenbroock: "The Phantom of Uruk: The Search for King Gilgamesh" ("Das Phantom von Uruk: Fahndung nach König Gilgamesch," 2007), which features on-location shots along with reenactments of various scenes and interviews with such authorities as Andrew George. (Unfortunately, the presence of authorities did not preclude errors, such as dating the rediscovery of Ashurbanipal's library to 1872 and portraying George Smith with the name "Gilgamesh" on his lips.)

Poetic Versions in English and French

Beyond the contributions of Foster and Mitchell, at least four poets in English have been inspired to poetic adaptations that impose their own original poetic inflections on the epic. Derrek Hines, a Canadian writer living permanently in Britain, who pursued ancient Near Eastern studies at the university, specifies that his acclaimed poetic *Gilgamesh* (2002), while based on Andrew George's edition, is "an interpretation . . . but in no sense a translation" of the epic.[9] We need go no further than the opening strophe to grasp the meaning of that statement.

> Here is Gilgamesh, king of Uruk:
> two-thirds divine, a mummy's boy,
> zeppelin ego, cock like a trip-hammer,
> and solid chrome, no-prisoners arrogance. (1)

Hines's slangy and jittery lines transpose the ancient epic into the street-talk of the present. The trapper finds Shamhat "slouched over a back-street bistro table" (4). When she brings Enkidu back to Uruk, "talk dries in the cafés" (12) and paparazzi record the fight with their flashbulbs (13). "The Humbaba Campaign" is presented as the diary of a cynical foot soldier among the accompanying troops:

> Cedar for the temple doors, my ass.
> It's glory's hard-on for those two,
> and no mind for us. Bastards. (19)

In the battle a "new boy stopped a grenade" (23) while "the lieutenant bought it twice" (24). Gilgamesh's sojourn with Shiduri, "the madam who ran a road house there" (52), is recounted anecdotally by Shiduri herself for a man who lights her cigarette in the bar. Ur-shanabi tells Gilgamesh that a boat is not what he needs: "You have the only means to cross the Waters—your soul" (56). Gilgamesh gets drunk, and it is left unclear whether or not the trip to the underworld—mentioned but not described—is nothing more than a dream. In any case, no Utnapishtim appears to tell him about the flood before he returns to Uruk. The poem closes with the monologue of Gilgamesh as, alongside other old men, he waits for death at the zinc tables of a quayside café and reflects on his experiences—"The spirit doesn't exist / because it is greater than existence" (61)—and prays to the Lord to let his servant depart in peace.

Five years later Hines was commissioned to create a theatrical version, *Gilgamesh: The Play* (2007) based on his verse narrative. Given its radical changes, Hines suggests, the two works parallel "the differences between the Sumerian and later Akkadian versions of the epic."[10] While the stage adaptation retains much of the language of the earlier poem, it adds numerous scenes and characters—notably scenes in heaven involving a middle-aged Anu and other senior gods accompanied by "a nervous young god, Zeus" (35).[11] Anu rolls dice to determine whether Gilgamesh or Enkidu shall die in punishment demanded by divine fiat as compensation for their sacrilege (38). At one point, as they gaze down at the activities of humankind, the young Zeus wonders: "Will this go on forever? Will I have a job?" (50), whereupon Anu assures him that the gods "will drift in and out of their lives." Later, as Zeus is "inserting standard illusions into humans" on a conveyor belt, Anu is blackmailed by Ishtar to deny immortality to Gilgamesh, leading him to send a serpent to pinch the magical herb (63–64). In another addition "citizens" are introduced to utter many of the lines spoken by the narrator in the poem. But the essential parallels of plot and tone are evident when, at Shiduri's Roadhouse, a reporter named Buzzon recites from a tabloid a sketch of Gilgamesh's past, summarizing his initial tyranny, his homosexual relationship with Enkidu, the campaign against Humbaba, his rejection of Ishtar, the fight with the Heavenly Bull, Enkidu's death, and Gilgamesh's departure.

> What life this guy's had. Check these headlines: King Is Hard on Pussy. Desert Boy Goes down On King. Army In Cut And Run Scam. Gilgy Disses Ishy. It's All Bull, Claims King. Death Snookers Freak. Booze King Goes Walkabout. (54–55)

The play ends with the words of the dying Gilgamesh, which in their pensive lyricism contrast sharply with the often raucous, racy language of the preceding action.

> In the dusk's quiet, open palm, read
> The lifeline of my past intercepting the future.
> All I have been crowds, stifles.
>
> I have remembered . . .
> Almost too much to be.
>
> Such wealth this was. (70)

Hines's brilliant versions, both the verse narrative and its theatrical analogue, fully justify with their broad spectrum of language and insightful re-visioning of character the comparisons made by various reviewers to such contemporary landmark adaptations as Seamus Heaney's *Beowolf* and Ted Hughes's *Tales from Ovid*.

Edwin Morgan's *The Play of Gilgamesh* (2005) is as ribald in its language as Hines's poem and, from time to time, interpolates songs à la Brecht as a commentary on the proceedings, but it remains strikingly faithful to the plot of the original, albeit with a conspicuous personal emphasis and a biting cynical edge. Morgan (b. 1920), the poet laureate of Scotland and heralded translator of many other works including Racine's *Phaedra* and *Beowulf,* is openly homosexual and calls Gilgamesh "the oldest gay poem in the world," thus locating himself, perhaps unwittingly, in a literary tradition that goes back by way of several German and French works to Hans Henny Jahnn's *River without Shores.*[12]

The dialogue employs rhymed couplets but is slangy and contemporary, as in the opening scene where a court official greets the trapper and hears about the "fearsome creature" robbing his traps:

> How's business then? I've seen you with more skins.
> To be blunt, some of these look bound for the bins.(3)

The action moves swiftly from scene to scene. In the dormitory of the sacred harlots, who envy Shamhat for her new assignment with "six feet of snoring hunk among the heather" (7), we hear "A Little Night-Song of the Sacred Harlots." Gilgamesh pays a visit to the state prison, where, scrutinizing the captives carefully both front and back, he picks out the sturdiest ones, presumably for sexual services. The actual seduction of Enkidu takes place offstage in a small wood. Then, back in Uruk, a court jester dances and comments, in prose with a pronounced Glaswegian accent, on the wedding preparations, followed by a festive chorus of transvestites. After the great fight, the jester comments:

> Aye well, all buddies noo. Whit can come o that, eh? Whit kinna cratur is thon hairy wan? He's no canny if ye ask me. Brought up wae monkeys an plowterin through cowpats? Kin the monkey chynge his spoats? The temple lassie has gien him boxers an a shirt an a whiff o auld spice, but *brithers*? Kin the king an the wolf-boay be brithers? Ah'm no a class activist but there is limits. (18–19)

All becomes clear a few months later. While the attendants sing their "Song of the Little Refreshment," Gilgamesh and Enkidu snort cocaine. As they leave the room, the stage directions explain:

The poem says "hand in hand," as young men still do in Middle Eastern countries, without any necessarily erotic implication. If the director senses a problem with modern audiences, perhaps they could go arm in arm, or perhaps some macho form of hand or wrist contact could be devised. The problem is that there really *is* an unspoken erotic charge between the two men, which was first felt in the wrestling scene and which will become more overt at a later stage in the play. (31)

After a "Song of the Lesbian Blacksmiths," the journey to the Cedar Forest and the fight with Humbaba are quickly represented. Back in Uruk, when Ishtar says that Gilgamesh needs a queen, Shamhat replies: "Some say he *is* the queen" (44). Finally, after the slaying of the heavenly bull, the two friends are alone in the palace, sweating and glistening from dancing and celebrations. And then: "Gilgamesh takes Enkidu by the hand (no doubt about it this time), and they walk slowly to the back of the stage, where a curtain is drawn to reveal a bedroom—with one bed. Gradual blackout as they move towards the bed" (59).

After Enkidu's death, Gilgamesh's "Lament" (unlike the other scenes, a pure poetic monologue in free verse) and a funeral procession with a "Song of the Death of Young Men," Gilgamesh talks to the scorpion man and woman and then, in pantomime, moves through the mountains and the beautiful garden. Siduri sends him to Urshanabi, with whom he sails across a calm sea to Ziusura's shore. As he eats and drinks with them, Gilgamesh remarks on their remarkable preservation:

> You two are the best advertisement for that.
> Is it the air, is it the habitat,
> some divine regimen, or genes, or diet?
> Could Uruk, wealthiest of the cities, buy it? (88)

He hears the story of the flood and then falls asleep but is rewarded with the plant of youth that he finds in the well outside. After the serpent takes the plant, Gilgamesh finally begins to accept his mortality. On his return to Uruk, he tells the people that, for all his wanderings, he has learned only an ordinary lesson: "Whatever good can be done must be done here" (97). He begins his new regime by proclaiming a general amnesty and freeing the prisoners who, as light falls on the statue of Enkidu, emerge from their dungeons in a scene reminiscent of Beethoven's *Fidelio*.

Gilgamesh: A Verse Play (2006) announces on its title page that it is a collaborative effort with concept and dramaturgy by the theater producer Chad Gracia and poetry by the prolific African-American poet Yusuf Komunyakaa. According to Gracia's prefatory note on "The Creation of Gilgamesh," he dreamed for years about staging the epic and persuaded Komunyakaa to write the poetry to give life to his ideas about character development. "Within a few weeks we were hammering out the basic structure of the play over coffee"—a structure modified as they met every other week with a cast who analyzed the text and made suggestions.[13] Twelve months of collaboration resulted in a work that makes a number of not easily justified changes—indeed, it looks rather like a pretentious Hollywood adaptation.

As the play opens, Enkidu, dressed in leaves, is romping with animals when the hunter's teenage son stumbles upon the scene. When the boy reports what he has seen to Gilgamesh, the king threatens to cut out his tongue for lying and imprisons him until the truth is established. At that point an invented character enters, Gestinanna, wife of an imprisoned wine maker, who tries to seduce Gilgamesh and tells him that her son may be his own flesh and blood. As they stand motionless in the semi-darkness, the chorus sings a gospel-like song of "all the old begats" since the first woman was fashioned from a man's rib (14). After the Woman of Red Sashes seduces Enkidu, the couple is frightened away by the sounds of Humbaba nearby. In another wholly invented scene, Ishtar visits Humbaba in the Forbidden Forest, and he expresses his concern that Enkidu is on his way. Ishtar reminds him that Enkidu is only a beast, but Humbaba replies that he dreams of being a man, "and dreams can make lunatics out of men" (20).

When Enkidu has made his way to Uruk and Ninsun has interpreted the dream of the axe for Gilgamesh, the two heroes meet—and talk for four pages, with choral commentary, before they finally fight. When the defeated Gilgamesh says, "You are foolhardy. You are the man I want by my side" (32), they drink wine and discuss the expedition against Humbaba. Meanwhile, the Woman with the Red Sash worships at the altar of Ninsun, praying to be a mother, to sleep in her own bed, and to bake bread. The Elders give their consent to the expedition in the secret hope that perhaps Humbaba will "do the job each of us is too weak to do" (37). In a scene reduced to a silly parody of the stereotypical Jewish mother, Ninsun reproaches Gilgamesh for not loving her—"When is the last time you gave your mother flowers?" (40)—before she prays for the safety of the two heroes.

Ishtar is present at the battle with Humbaba and pleads with him to spare Gilgamesh—"Brandish him till he calls my name, but please do not kill him" (48)—before Enkidu cuts off his arms and Gilgamesh chops him to pieces. As they rest in the Forbidden Forest, Ishtar enters and offers to serve as an intermediary to protect Gilgamesh from the wrath of the gods—if, of course, he will marry her. But Gilgamesh rejects her with surprisingly little rhetoric: "You are an old harlot whose heart belongs to no man" (51). She runs off; the stage goes black; and immediately the Bull of Heaven descends, which they kill. While they lie sleeping afterwards, Ishtar tiptoes in again and, like a voodoo witch, touches Enkidu with a bone. When Enkidu dies there in the forest, Gilgamesh mourns him in a song that consists largely of the words, repeated fifteen times, "And I sit here" (55–56)—"till a maggot drops from Enkidu's nose." (Gracia informs us that "the maggot is a central and recurring character in both the epic and Yusef's work [xi].)

As the second act begins, Gilgamesh is removing the laurel branches with which he had earlier covered Enkidu, but his friend is still dead. When he sets out to find "that timeless man who crossed the desert and rounded the sea," it is not, as in the epic, to find immortality for himself but to "give you back to life, breath and song, to argument and laughter" (57). He chats with the scorpion people and passes through the darkness to the valley of glittering tones. Siduri cleans him, disrobes him, gives him brew to drink, and sings while they dance together and then fall to the ground, where Gilgamesh asks her: "Teach me how to be a king. Teach me how to die a man" (66). As the lights fade, the "sounds of love" are heard. But when Gilgamesh explains that he must go on, she points out the way and he "charges off the stage"—and then, as in a TV soap opera, rushes back to hug and kiss her before he leaves again.

Gilgamesh engages in a long and pointless dialogue with Urshanabi—for instance, "The heart is a selfish forest of twisted vines" (73)—before the boatman sends him across the river (not the sea) with only five (not one hundred and twenty) poles. As Gilgamesh lies sprawled on the ground, in a scene reminiscent of movies about Gulliver or Robinson Crusoe, Utnapishtim appears. When Gilgamesh tells him that "hope brought me here," Utnapishtim responds with a brief account of the flood. In the following conversations it turns out that Utnapishtim's wife is the true philosopher, uttering such cryptic aphorisms as: "You are a question in the heart of lone-liness that we see and live as grace" (82). When he departs and finds the plant of youth, he dances around and yells "I have it! Life. Life. Life." Then he falls asleep, whereupon the serpent enters, eats the plant, and sheds its skin. Gilgamesh falls weeping to his knees.

When he returns to Uruk, transformed, Gilgamesh releases the prison-ers, sends doctors to the sick, and pays the hunter's son a year's wages as the elders try to restrain his enthusiasm. He tells his mother about Siduri, "a beautiful mystery at earth's end" (91), and confesses that it was almost as hard to leave her as to lose Enkidu. As the play ends, he meets the Woman of Red Sashes, asks if he may call her Siduri, and says, recalling his words to Siduri: "Teach me how to be a king. Teach me to die a man," as Cecil B. DeMille–ish "music fills the stage" (94). *Pace* the dust jacket blurbs that it is "the first dramatic adaptation of Gilgamesh," it is neither the first nor dramatic, and with its faux-lyrical prose it trivializes the epic with a happy ending that replaces the grim realism of loss and human mortality with a cheery, feminist-tinged moralism.

In 2009 the English poet Jenny Lewis, who has frequently collaborated with Pegasus Theatre in Oxford with dramatized poems and verse plays, undertook a poetic dramatization entitled *About Gilgamesh* that "looks at the Sumerian epic from the point of view of the incidental characters—the faces in the crowd who, like the Greek chorus, bear witness to the spec-tacle of superpowers behaving badly."[14] These characters include the bar-ber who grooms Enkidu, "my hairiest customer ever," for his new life in Uruk and needs an hour afterwards to sweep up the fur. Another figure, a transgender dancer, explains Gilgamesh's various acts of violence: "He gets away with it because his mother's / a goddess: anyone else would be done for criminal damage / and murder."

While poets have been challenged more often by the dramatic than by the lyric possibilities of the epic, there have continued, at least since Olson and Zukofsky, Bobrowski and Huchel, to be occasional lyrical poems on the subject. Another proud entry in that tradition is American poet Hillary Major's "Gilgamesh Remembers a Dream" (2000).[15] The image that Gil-gamesh is unable to lose in the short poem is that of "that nether plant" that he recovered from the "dark places," which was more tender even than

Enkidu's lips. "The sands we crossed together" have receded into legend, and he cannot recall "the lines of your face":

> but every morning I am stunned
> by the seconds I held eternity
> in helpless arms. (219)

The poem appears to take the homosexuality for granted—as well as the shortness of human memory—but leaves it open to speculation whether the plant of eternal youth—and by extension the entire visit to Utnapishtim—was real or simply a dream.

Gilgameš (2008) by the prolific French poet Anne-Marie Beeckman (b. 1952) comes fittingly at the end of this group because it presents the hero's story as a despondent exercise in futility: it begins with the statement that the longing for adventure and achievement is meaningless because there is nothing to be found in the far distance (9: "Il n'y a rien dans le lointain").[16] Beeckman retells the epic in a series of twenty poems in short lines of free verse: lapidary poems meant to suggest the clay tablets of the original. Each poem is introduced by a brief prose synopsis beginning with the phrase "Where one. . . .": "Where one discovers Gilgamesh, this very young king in very ancient times—He lives in the city of Uruk, in Mesopotamia—He fears nothing—He no longer knows anything—He comes out—For the moment he speaks all alone" (11). The poems themselves consist variously of narrative, monologue (the hunter's complaint to the king), and dialogue (Ishtar and Gilgamesh; Enkidu and the temple prostitute Toute-Joie). Using these forms, the poet recapitulates the principal episodes of the epic down to the hero's encounter with Utnapishtim, in which he sleeps through the sage's account of the flood:

> Je lance des oiseaux.
> Gilgameš dort.
> Un septième jour passe.
> Le pain sèche.
> La colombe revient.
> Le pain mollit.
> Le pain moisit.
> L'hirondelle revient.
> Le pain noircit.

L'eau se retire.
Le corbeau chante,
le pain rassis,
sur les cadavres.
Et j'ai nourri des dieux imbéciles! (75–76)

(I release some birds.
Gilgamesh sleeps.
A seventh day passes.
The bread dries up.
The dove returns.
The bread softens.
The bread grows mouldy.
The swallow returns.
The bread grows black.
The water recedes.
The crow sings,
the bread stale,
over the corpses.
And I have nurtured the stupid gods!)

When Gilgamesh awakens to learn that, in his desire for eternity, he has slept for seven days and nights, he secludes himself in bewilderment. In the concluding section—headed "Where I don't know what to do"—Gilgamesh finds and loses the prickly flower of youth but does not return to Uruk. Instead, he takes stock of his life and realizes, rephrasing the opening line, that it has all been in vain—even his building projects:

Les poutres que j'abats
sont des fétus de paille,
je n'irai pas
jusqu'au lointain. (78)

(The beams that I cut down
are worthless straw,
I shall not go
into the far distance.)

Beeckman's highly personal appropriation of the epic is even bleaker than the Babylonian original because her Gilgamesh is left without even the consolation of simple human achievement: the building of the great walls of Uruk. Her poem appears to be the comment of a disenchanted postmodernist on life in the twenty-first century.

A New Focus

During this same period, a major revision of views regarding the Near East was catalyzed by Samuel Huntington's theory of "the clash of civilizations" as outlined in an influential article in the journal *Foreign Affairs* (Summer 1993) and, three years later, as elaborated more fully in his book *The Clash of Civilizations and the Remaking of World Order* (1996). Twenty years earlier, Edward Said's attention in his *Orientalism* was focused essentially on what he regarded as the Western misinterpretation of Near Eastern culture and history—a focus reflected, as observed earlier, in the literary adaptations, which revisited and sought to understand the epic in light of modern cultural trends: gay, feminist, ecological, and others. Politics had little place in those works.

It was Huntington's hypothesis that the fundamental source of conflict in the post–Cold War world would not be primarily ideological or primarily economic. "The great divisions among humankind and the dominating source of conflict will be cultural"—and he identified the basic cultural root of the conflict as religious.[17] Earlier conflicts within the Western world took place among princes, then among nation states, and finally among ideologies (notably communism, national socialism, and democracy). With the end of the Cold War, Huntington argued, "international politics moves out of its Western phase, and its centerpiece becomes the interaction between the West and non-Western civilizations and among non-Western civilizations" (44). While the differences among these civilizations "do not necessarily mean conflict, and conflict does not necessarily mean violence . . . over the centuries differences among civilizations have generated the most prolonged and the most violent conflicts" (46).

Huntington's thesis is supported indirectly by the conspicuous desecularization of world civilizations toward the end of the twentieth century, as has been noted by theologians.[18] This desecularization, which offsets the widespread process of secularization that began in the West toward the end of the nineteenth century, is evident in the upsurge of faith in Christianity as well as Islam and, in turn, feeds the religious tensions underlying the relations between civilizations.[19]

Huntington's analysis, which shifted the emphasis from culture within the Western world to political clashes among different civilizations and religions, turned out to be depressingly prescient and appeared to be confirmed by the grim events of September 11, 2001, and by subsequent terrorist bombings in cities around the world, from Madrid and London to Bali. The Near East and, in particular, radical Islam with its hostility to the West, moved to the forefront of world consciousness. This new view is reflected in treatments of Gilgamesh, who in animes and video games is often depicted as a monstrous figure. The 26-episode anime *Gilgamesh,* for instance, starts with the assumption that the tomb of Gilgamesh in Uruk is discovered by a young Japanese scientist who hopes to extract from the hero's genetic material the secret to eternal life and, in the process, unleashes a struggle for control among various sinister forces. In the same year as the World Trade Center disaster, G. D. Brettschneider produced a dramatic version of the epic, *Gilgamesch und sein Freund* ("Gilgamesh and His Friend," 2001), in which it is Ishtar who steals the plant of youth (and rejuvenates herself by casting off her garments) and which ends with the announcement that "the great whore-city has fallen," whereupon Gilgamesh collapses and the work ends.

Sometimes, to be sure, the scholars and authors seek to expose positive and universal aspects of that ancient culture before it evolved, among some of its more radical members, into Muslim extremism. As Stephen Mitchell put it in the introduction to his translation of the epic: "In Iraq, when the dust blows, stopping men and tanks, it brings with it memories of an ancient world, much older than Islam or Christianity" (1). Yet Mitchell's own version was composed in keen awareness of the current political and military situation. In the course of his provocative introduction, he suggests that Gilgamesh's campaign against Humbaba is "the original preemptive attack" and that "ancient readers, like many contemporary Americans, would have considered it to be unquestionably heroic" (26). When Gilgamesh tells Enkidu that they must travel to the Cedar Forest where Humbaba lives—"We must kill him and drive out evil from the world" (91)—contemporary Western readers would inevitably think, Mitchell believes, of Saddam Hussein and Osama bin Laden.

This refocused view of the Near East is reflected in the conspicuous emphasis on religion and politics in many adaptations of the century's first decade. I am not implying, of course, that adaptations of the epic inevitably arouse such specific associations as Mitchell suggests—only that authors and readers of this period approach the topic with an enhanced consciousness of its religious and political potential. We have already noted evidence of this new consciousness in art and music: Martin Blessmann's transparencies, using the walls of Uruk as an analogy to the Berlin Wall, and Wolfgang Witzenmann's oratorio comparing Gilgamesh and Jesus.

Gilgamesh as Ritual Drama

The new focus is striking in several recent European variations of the epic, which take up again the aspect that initially caught the attention of George Smith and his readers and of the Bible/Babel scholars in Germany. Specialists from anthropologist Jane Harrison (*Ancient Art and Ritual*, 1913) and Assyriologist Theodor H. Gaster (*Thespis: Ritual, Myth and Drama in the Ancient Near East*, 1950) to the present have long understood the close connection in antiquity between drama and ritual. The British cultural historian Gertrude R. Levy (*The Sword from the Rock*, 1953) expanded that view to suggest that ancient epic generally, from Gilgamesh to the two Homeric poems and the Hindu *Ramayana* and *Mahabharata*, could also be traced back to ritual sources.

In 1990 two Russian Assyriologists published an article purporting to document for the first time in ancient Armenia an actual performance of an Elamite version of the epic of Gilgamesh.[20] Their claim was soon proven to be incorrect: the three tablets turned out to be administrative records dealing with taxes and grain deposits.[21] But the idea caught on and, despite the correction, was passed along, especially among nonspecialists. In particular, interest in the ritualistic aspects of the text was fostered in response to the general belief in the sacred origins of ancient drama and poetry. In the introduction to his translation, *He Who Saw Everything* (1991), Robert Temple referred explicitly to the findings of the Russian scholars and argued: "We may be sure that the *Epic* retained through its long history a sacred status, with the underlying theme of its hero's quest for eternal life."²² Elsewhere he reported on the success with which a stage production of his translation (which included in Tablet X choral passages from the recently discovered Elamite version) was performed by the Royal National Theatre in London.²³ Others, as we have seen, had already put these ideas into practice: for instance, the 1958 performance in the Netherlands and the various operatic versions. (It should be stressed that these sacred dramas have nothing in common with the secularized "liturgical dramas" of the Freudians discussed in chapter 4.)

The earliest work composed specifically as ritual or "sacred" drama was *Gilga.Mesh, or Glory between Power and Destiny (Gilga.Mesh, ou La Gloire entre la Force et le Destin,* 2000) by Patrice Cambronne, retired professor of classical studies at the University of Bordeaux.²⁴ Cambronne is known especially for his studies in late antiquity with a focus on religious phenomena, including such works as the Pléiade translation of St. Augustine's *Confessions* and a two-volume monograph on history, myth, and mystical theology (*Chants d'Exil,* 1998 and 2000). This focus determines his approach to the epic of Gilgamesh.

In his stimulating introduction, Cambronne first presents the epic as "écriture mythique" or "Gilga.Mesh as pictogram," surveying the divine mythology underlying the story and the "anthropogony" of mankind from the period before the flood to its postdeluvial "second" history. Next he turns to the "écriture épique" or "Gilga.Mesh as ideogram" and analyzes the "heroicization" of the historic figure. Third, he investigates the "écriture conceptuelle" of the epic or "Gilga.Mesh as Book of Wisdom," taking up such topics as "the relation to the *self*" (= Enki.du) and "the relation to the *other*" (meaning Shamhat and Siduri) as well as meditations on "the destiny of power" and "the power of destiny." Arguing that these three perfectly legitimate aspects of the epic can be combined and unified under the concept of a "drame sacré," Cambronne organizes his version accordingly.²⁵

Cambronne presents his work as a four-part festival drama in explicit analogy to Richard Wagner's *Ring* tetralogy (75). A "Prologue" ("The Double") deals with Enki.du's birth and his "encounter with the other" (Shamhat) and the friendship of the two heroes: Gilga.mesh's "encounter with the self." The "First Day" depicts "The Destiny of Power": the battles with Humbaba and the Heavenly Bull and the defiance of Ishtar. The "Second Day" or "The Power of Destiny" portrays Enki.du's imprecations and death followed by Gilga.mesh's "initiatory road" to the "revelation" of Uta-Napishtî. The "Epilogue" briefly sketches the scene with the serpent and the return to Uruk. Not surprisingly, this innovative reorganization requires us to re-view the familiar material in a revealing new light.

As pure text, Cambronne's version stays remarkably close to the first eleven tablets of the standard edition, but its uniqueness is evident in various changes. Several narrative passages are spoken by a voice offstage, and we also hear the voices of unseen divinities. Some passages—notably the scenes with Enki.du and Shamhat; the fight, which Enki.du wins; the battle with the Heavenly Bull; the seven loaves of bread; the scene with the snake—are enacted in pantomime. Others—for instance, their eighteen-day march to the Cedar Forest; Gilga.mesh's long walk through the mountain; the voyage across the Waters of Death—are simply indicated in the text. As the curtain falls, the voice from the Prologue proclaims: "This is the story of him who has seen all, known all, wholly penetrated the secrets and mysteries, traversed so many trials, engraved all his labors on the stone of memory" (151). The work effectively exemplifies Cambronne's conception of the epic as a sacred drama combining the three elements outlined in his introduction and conspicuously eliminating the political, ecological, and other aspects motivating many earlier treatments.

The following year saw the publication in Germany of Raoul Schrott's *Gilgamesh. Epos.*[26] The Austrian author (b. 1964) is a trained literary scholar who earned his *licentia docendi* in 1996 at the Institute for Comparative Literature in Innsbruck. Rather than remaining in academics, Schrott chose the career of independent writer and scholar, publishing novels, novellas, and volumes of poetry along with translations of Euripides' *Bacchae* (1999) and Homer's *Iliad* (2008). The latter aroused lively controversy and was criticized by many classicists for the theory advanced there and in an accompanying volume on Homer's home and the historical background behind the Trojan War—*Homers Heimat. Der Kampf um Troia und seine realen Hintergründe* (2008)—that Homer lived as a Greek scribe at the Hittite court in Cilician Karatepe, where he experienced firsthand the Assyrian cultural realm and was inspired to intermingle ancient Greek tales of the Trojan War with local events and narrative traditions. It is easy to sense in that theory the impact of his earlier extensive studies of the Gilgamesh epic, where (19–20) he also raised the question of Babylonian influence on the Greek epics—an issue that, as we have seen, goes back at least to Ungnad's studies in the 1920s and has subsequently been pursued by other scholars.

Schrott's work is relevant in the present connection because, in addition to a straightforward retelling of the standard (Nineveh) version (based on Andrew George's translation) and an informative scholarly apparatus, he included as its *pièce de resistance* a free adaptation of the epic. His more literal translation of the standard version, based primarily on Andrew George's text, was meant to replace what he characterized as the now-antiquated versions of Schott and Schmökel. Without indicating restorations or conjectures, Schrott renders the first eleven tablets in four-line strophes of four-beat lines, which, he believes, best capture the feeling of the original:

> Er, der den ábgrund sáh, die grúndfeste unseres lándes,
> der das méer kánnte und wúßte, was zu wíssen ist,
> Gílgamesh, der den ábgrund sah, die grúndfeste unseres lándes,
> der das méer kánnte und wúßte, was zu wíssen ist.
> (177; accentual marks added)

> (He, who saw the abyss, die foundations of our land,
> who knew the sea and knew what is to be known,
> Gilgamesh, who saw the abyss, the foundations of our land,
> who knew the sea and knew what is to be known.)

In addition to Schrott's introductions to his two versions, the volume's appendix offers informative essays by two Innsbruck professors: the ancient historian and classicist Robert Rollinger on "The Cultural Context of the Epic" and the Assyriologist Manfred Schretter on "The Literary Context of the Epic." Even without Schrott's bold adaptation, the volume would have been received as a valuable addition to German Gilgamesh studies.

However, it is his free adaptation of the epic that makes this edition noteworthy in our context because Schrott treats it as a "theater of ritual" (31). For his purposes Schrott adapts and integrates texts from all three stages of the epic's development: the Sumerian poems, the Old Babylonian version, and the standard text of Nineveh (25), producing a result that with its roughly five thousand extended lines (generally some fifteen syllables) is considerably longer than the epic itself. The Sumerian "Death of Gilgamesh" suggested the idea for a Prologue and Epilogue that, taking place in Irkalla, the City of Death in the underworld, constitute a framework for the whole. In general, the author explains, the older texts are often more vivid than the sometimes less colorful passages of the Ninevetic version: for instance, the Sumerian "Shepherd's Wedding Song," in which the triangular shape of the female pubic area is compared to the shape of the land between the two Babylonian rivers (26) and which provides seductive words for Schrott's Shamhat (60).

Because in his opinion its direct speech is too theatrical for an epic and because the dialogues are too elaborate and repetitive for the theater, he proposes the term "epic oratorium" as the most suitable: a work to be recited ritually by actors and a chorus wearing masks (31). As in Greek tragedy, the sequence of episodes—battle (*agon*), suffering (*pathos*), and lamentation (*threnos*) ending in epiphany and catharsis—parallels the basic scenes of primitive mysteries and religious pantomimes depicting the antagonism of summer and winter or life and death (32). Advancing an argument consistent with the astral-mythological theories of the nineteenth century, Schrott maintains (33–34) that the story may have served as the action for a ritual drama performed on the two days celebrating the Babylonian New Year: when the barley harvest marked the end of winter and the beginning of summer, a date determined by the day on which sun first rose within the constellation Taurus. The association of Enkidu with barley and vegetation along with Gilgamesh's identification with the bull made it logical to tie their story to the ritual mysteries. Finally, that Gilgamesh loses the plant of eternal renewal permits Schrott to share the German predilection noted earlier for ecological themes: "Despite all of the achievements in civilization and genetic technology, man's dependence on nature is unconquerable" (34). (Missing, however, is the drum motif that was so central to the earlier German novels.) The author claims that nothing in his version is newly invented: everything is already present in the corpus of the sources. But he has translated the story into a contemporary idiom, "the *lingua franca* of the Here and Now" (34).

As the prologue begins (41) Ishtar is pounding on the gate of the underworld and demanding rudely to be admitted: "He! mach das tor auf!" Whereupon Namtar, the guard, replies, rather disrespectfully, "You?! What do you want here again already?" It turns out that Ishtar and Ur-shanabi, here identified as the Charonlike ferryman of the dead, are accompanying the deceased Gilgamesh, who—two-thirds divine and one-third mortal—demands to be brought before Ereshkigal and the tribunal of the gods to judge what sort of death he shall have—that of the gods above or of the mortals in the underworld. The action that follows is divided into thirty scenes and then completed by an Epilogue (a structure reminiscent of Bach's *Goldberg Variations,* which has been used prominently as a model by several novelists of the late twentieth century).[27]

In the first scene Ur-shanabi recites the passage that traditionally opens the epic and begins with the words: "Er hat den abgrund gesehen und den grund aller dinge" (47: "He has seen the abyss and the bottom of all things"). But Ereshkigal is not impressed:

> Mein lieber—für den fährmann
> der toten machst du ja große worte—ich wußte gar nicht
> daß du so geschwollen reden kannst—aber wem nützen
> unter einer mauer vergrabne tafeln? (48)

> (My dear fellow, for the ferryman
> of the dead you utter great words—I had no idea
> that you could speak so pompously—but of what use are
> tablets buried beneath a wall?)

She explains that the only thing the dead have in all fullness is time—time for all eternity. The only present they know consists of stories: their own and those of others. In that way they relive their lives and think that they have escaped oblivion. They love nothing better than to be spoken to: their idea of immortality. And if the lords of heaven deign to come down to listen, they too will want nothing more than to take pleasure in the past. So she says that Gilgamesh and those accompanying him should simply relate their own stories. This instruction justifies the form of the entire work, which unlike Cambronne's "sacred drama" and all of the other dramatic or operatic versions heretofore dispenses altogether with a narrative voice and causes the entire action to be recounted by the participants themselves.

Because of this leisurely method of narration, which at the same time does away with most of the repetitive passages of the epic, many of the scenes are considerably expanded: notably the battle with Humbaba (89–97), where all three combatants describe their fight in detail; or Gilgamesh's insulting response to Ishtar (100–102), in which one of the goddess's rejected lovers also appears to speak his part. Elsewhere (116–22) Enkidu relates his dream of the underworld at considerable length, enhanced by the question-and-answer format with Gilgamesh. Ut-napishti steps forward (146–54) to repeat his tale of the flood, saying that in his bleak timelessness all that is left to him is tale-telling, although no one on his island listens to him anymore; so he is pleased to find an audience here in the underworld:

> Erzählen will ich gerne· in meiner ewigkeit ist erzählen
> alles was mir noch blieb—nur daß mir auf meiner insel
> keiner mehr zuhört—hier find ich zumindest noch publikum. (146)

> (I'll gladly tell my tale. In my eternity, tale-telling is
> all that is left to me—only that on my island no one
> listens to me anymore—here at least I find a public.)

When Gilgamesh fails the test of sleep, Ut-napishti exclaims, using an Austrian dialect expression: "But now I've finally had enough of that nitwit ["Deppen"] there—the only place you're going now is home!" (156). In the Epilogue, while the gods are debating the matter, they ponder the technicality of Gilgamesh's division into two-thirds and one-third; if his father was mortal and his mother a goddess, why is the proportion not simply fifty-fifty? Ninsun explains the matter by saying that the child was conceived one night when his father was obsessed in his thoughts with Ishtar (an allusion to the superstitious belief that a child can take on characteristics of the person of whom the mother dreams during intercourse). The gods finally reach a compromise. Because of his mortal part and the gods' earlier promise to Ut-napishti that he would be the only mortal to achieve immortality, Gilgamesh is not entitled to dwell among the gods. But thanks to his immortal achievements, he may enjoy a form of immortality: as king of the underworld, where he may continue for all time to rule, to formulate laws, and to pronounce judgment (Irkalla, they remind him, is a much larger and grander city than Uruk):

> Ein könig über könige
> wolltest du sein: das bist du jetzt—als richter in der unterwelt

Dein wort wird soviel gewicht haben wie das Ereshkigals:
das muß dir genügen. (167)

(A king above kings,
You wished to be: that you now are—as judge in the underworld
Your word will have as much weight as Ereshkigal's:
that must suffice for you.)

On that note, Schrott's remarkable ritual drama ends—a fitting counterpart to Cambronne's French version. Whether or not Cambronne and
Schrott actually intended their versions to be performed, their imaginative dramatic re-visions amply succeed in exemplifying their similar conception of the epic as sacred or ritual drama. We may confidently assume
that both authors, in their scholarly capacity, were familiar with the link-
ing of drama and ritual in earlier scholarship and with the more recent (albeit mistaken) findings of the two Russian scholars.

The same may be said of Gerhard Begrich, theologian and rector of
the Pastoral College of the Evangelical Church of Saxony and a trained
scholar of the Near East who has taught Hebrew and Old Testament at
Berlin's Humboldt University. For that reason, even though it is not dramatic in form, it is appropriate in this context to mention his "re-telling"
of the epic, *Gilgamesh: King and Wanderer* (*Gilgamesch. König und Vagant*,
2003). Out of the conviction that the Gilgamesh epic belongs to world literature in Goethe's sense—that is, that its questions and insights are tied
neither to temporal nor geographical boundaries—Begrich, while con-
sulting other translations, created his new prose version directly from
the Akkadian original on the basis of Campbell Thompson's 1930 edition. In general he follows Tablets I–XI closely, adding occasional phrases
for clarification or shading. For instance, he emphasizes the drum motif
typical of the earlier German novels and in the process downplays Gilgamesh's sexual exploitation of the populace, explaining that lovers
and their brides cannot get together because "he beats his drum loudly
through the whole city—day and night" (19).[28] Elsewhere he adds a modern touch to the prostitute's charms, and one that is not in the original, by
having the hunter advise her to display not only her voluptuous breasts
and womb but also "the length of your legs" (22). But the supernatu-

ral figures are presented without rationalization, exactly as depicted in the epic.

The justification for including Begrich here is not his re-telling but his commentary, which is inserted directly after each tablet, for there his tendency toward spiritual edification is most clearly evident. The prerequisite of all life, we learn from his introduction, is stated in the first sentence of the Bible: "Heaven is the prerequisite for the existence of the earth" (9). And it is heaven that we seek—along with Gilgamesh. Today, he continues, we understand things that were seen and experienced quite differently by earlier generations: "For in the meantime—that is, after Auschwitz, the turning-point of the New Age and the 20th century—we have experienced the 'collapse of reason'" (10). Whenever we have sought to create heaven on earth, hell has resulted; our dreams of heaven have been destroyed. It is with the eyes of persons afflicted in this manner by history that we return to the ancient texts: "We read the Gilgamesh epic not for reasons of cultural education but because we suffer anxiety about the future of the world. Like Gilgamesh, we too seek life—which today, more than ever, means survival" (10). This view determines his commentary and his afterword entitled "Heroes Like Us" (no doubt a tongue-in-cheek allusion to *Helden wie wir* [1995], Thomas Brussig's bestselling satirical novel on the Fall of the Wall in Berlin).

When Enkidu, humanized by the love of a woman, prevents Gilgamesh from entering the bridal chamber, "Enkidu, the son of the steppes, the barbarian from afar, intercedes in the name of humanity against the barbarism of *jus primae noctis* as the right of the king. That amounts to a critique of civilization!" (34). Enkidu's humanization has its price, of course: his alienation from his native roots, from nature, which amounts to alienation from creation itself (43). And this alienation from nature is simply the beginning, followed by the annihilation of the divine world. Ultimately, then, Enkidu, the solitary man ("der unbehauste Mensch," 59)[29], stands alone between heaven and earth. All of Gilgamesh's reason, power, and wealth, even his tears and grief, cannot console Enkidu in the face of death.

As for Gilgamesh, it is his love of Enkidu alone that entitles him to any claim to greatness—the only meaning in a meaningless world. (Begrich stresses in his brief afterword that Gilgamesh's love for Enkidu is like David's for Jonathan or Jesus' for his favorite disciple John: "It is not a matter of homosexuality but of homoeroticism" [89].) As he makes his way in his despair across the steppes and mountains, he reaches the garden of jewels—a garden, Begrich claims with reference to the twelve stones of the Heavenly Jerusalem, that resembles paradise (69). When he tells Utnapishtim about his adventures with Enkidu, he unconsciously speaks always in the plural: "It is Gilgamesh's way from loneliness to relationship, to encounter, to the dialogic nature of dialog. In the 'We' of his speech his realization becomes evident: only in the Thou can the I take shape—and love means the responsibility of an I for a Thou" (70). (The allusion to Martin Buber's theology is unacknowledged but evident.) Why does Utnapishtim relate the story of the flood? "So that Gilgamesh, and we along with him, may understand: we are alive after the flood—and that is divine grace. It is thanks to grace that there is a world instead of nothingness" (90). After the loss of the plant of rejuvenation, Gilgamesh gains his final insight: "I do not create the blessing, the meaning, on my own. All is grace. Life has no meaning but to live. Just as it is, just as it will come: everything must be affirmed" (83). Gilgamesh returns to Uruk because the city according to Revelation is the "place of salvation" ("Heil") and the presence of God (84). Begrich writes of the ending that "not mighty Babylon, but small unknown Jerusalem becomes the city of the great king" (85). But, with a Heideggerian twist, it remains our common hope that man is not simply cast into existence but that it has meaning to live life fully where one has been placed.

Begrich concludes his spiritualized re-telling and commentary with the reminder that the author of the Gilgamesh epic, Sin-leqe-unninni, never lost the ability to think and speak coherently about the world and humankind: "We must regain this ability" (91). He presents the ancient epic, in other words, not as a personal message, as did so many writers of the previous decades, but as a universal model: not only for the life guided by love to meaning lost through alienation from nature and divinity but also as an encouraging example of a narrative still informed by a unified view of man and his world.

Two Fictional Re-Visions

During that same decade, the novelists were not idle. Stephan Grundy's *Gilgamesh* (2000) is a 565-page rationalizing re-vision of the epic based on numerous sources cited in his Afterword and including countless details, including notably many names, from Sumerian culture. Grundy, an American writer with a doctorate from Cambridge in Norse mythology, has published scholarly works on *Teutonic Magic* (1990–93) as well as other mythological/historical novels on such topics as *Rheingold* (1994) and *Attila's Treasure* (1996). He is thus at home with epic narrative generally and its techniques of formulaic repetition and leitmotivic characterization: we hear repeatedly, for instance, of Enkidu's golden curls and muscular body covered with a thick pelt. Also included are various poems and chants from other ancient Sumerian sources, such as Inanna's seduction song (403–4).[30] Although the narrative is wholly realistic, the people it portrays cling fervently to their religion and thus believe the dreams and visions through which many of the supernatural episodes are communicated—notably the events of Tablet XII and of Gilgamesh's voyage to the realm of Utnapishtim. The deities all bear their original Sumerian names. Visions of the deities are rationalized, as when Enkidu first sees a statue of Inanna in a dark hut-shrine and imagines that she speaks to him (160–61) or when people see the Shamhatu dressed as the goddess Inanna, a role that engages her with mystical intensity.

The events are psychologically motivated by the relationship between the temple shepherdess Puabi and Gilgamesh, who grew up and studied together as children and teenagers. When Puabi becomes the Shamhatu— that is, the priestess of Inanna—she is overcome by the presence of the goddess, while Gilgamesh, for his part, is terrified by the legends surrounding the goddess and refuses to undergo the ritual marriage lest he be carried away to the nether world, like Dumuzi and Inanna's other lovers. The narrative tension of the work stems from this relationship between the actual Puabi and Gilgamesh, and between the goddess and the "En" and "Ensi," the role that Gilgamesh as king is supposed to accept. Indeed, Inanna's rage against Gilgamesh is motivated in large measure by Shamhatu's very human anger at her sexual rejection by her onetime friend. She herself is the chief temple priestess, trained in the sexual arts, who not only subdues Enkidu through sex but also entertains numerous worshippers in the official bed. (It is from her that Gilgamesh hears the story of Inanna's descent to the netherworld and the seven gates.)

All the principal episodes of the epic are related in realistic detail—most notably the taming of Enkidu by the Shamhatu, the high priestess who goes into the wilderness to domesticate the wild man. Various characters who are unnamed in the epic and play minor roles emerge more vividly. For instance, it turns out that the hunter, Akaddu, is Gilgamesh's half-brother by an earlier Shamhatu. When Enkidu and Gilgamesh, both of whom have enjoyed many sexual exploits with women, first meet in their contest, it is love at first sight (a homosexual attraction that is not sufficiently anticipated or psychologically motivated). Henceforth they sleep together and love each other sexually while continuing to enjoy women. Enkidu even marries the innocent wife of the man who tried to kill Gilgamesh in order to save her honor. Other figures are invented or enlarged, especially the scribe Shusuen, who is portrayed as the author of the accounts of the various adventures of the two heroes. And several episodes are invented, such as the attempt of an agent of Akka, ruler of Kish, to assassinate Gilgamesh during a hunting expedition. (The plot has a parallel in the temple itself, where an envious priestess's attempt to undermine the Shamhatu leads to various conspiracies.) The ensuing siege of the city by Akka unfolds according to the plot of the Sumerian poem of that name.

The journey to obtain the cedar for the temple gate and the killing of Humbaba are described realistically, although the portrayal of the giant takes on surreal traits: "But it was Huwawa's face that struck dread into Gilgamesh's heart, for it seemed to be a massed tangle of shiny pink bowels, writhing about eyes and mouth like a slimy nest of worms so that Gilgamesh's eyes could fix on no feature, nor his gaze on any place to strike" (361). But the monster turns out to be thoroughly human. The Bull of Heaven that Inanna calls down upon Erech is rationalized into a terrible drought that depletes the country accompanied by a real wild bull that Gilgamesh and Enkidu slay. Enkidu's death is attributed to a wasting fever that he catches during the drought, and his account of the underworld is rationalized as a feverish vision on his deathbed, just as the events of Tablet XII are justified as dreams and visions that Gilgamesh experiences during his wanderings following Enkidu's death. The final episodes—the scorpion guardians, the tavern keeper Siduri, the ferryman Urshanabi, and Utnapishtim himself along with the quest for the life-giving plant—are related in a manner that conflates realism and the supernatural. Are they feverish dreams or not? From the narrative it is unclear, unlike almost all of the earlier episodes of the novel. One must assume that Gilgamesh is simply out of his mind during his wanderings. The novel ends quickly when Gilgamesh returns to Erech and, accepting his destiny, prepares to go to bed with the Shamhatu (564–65).

Like Grundy's novel, Paola Capriola's *Something in the Night (Qualcosa nella notte. Storia di Gilgamesh, signore di Uruk, e dell'uomo selvatico cresciuto tra le gazzelle,* 2003) amounts to a sometimes ambivalent rationalization of the epic. But, like Jacques Cassabois and her countryman Gianfilippi and unlike Grundy, Silverberg, and the German historical novelists, the author makes no effort in her much shorter (200-page) work to recreate the historical atmosphere of ancient Uruk: her version could almost be set in contemporary Afghanistan. Instead, as though convinced that the historicizing effects have already been exhausted by earlier writers, Capriola devotes most of her narrative to the psychological exploration of the familiar events and the depiction of events in a familiar contemporary idiom. Thus Enkidu's origin is never explained and there is no mention of his creation by the gods; we are told only in the subtitle that he is "a wild man who grew up among the gazelles"; the prostitute guides Enkidu "by the hand like a child [bambino]" (28); after a time she decides to give him a name, "as is done with domestic animals" (31).[31] The contest between the two heroes is not so much a fight—there is no mention of the wedding-house door—as a wrestling match in which Enkidu's strength is balanced out to a peaceful draw by Gilgamesh's skill. Most of the supernatural events are rationalized or relegated to dreams and visions. Humbaba turns out to be a voice from the largest tree in the cedar forest; the heavenly bull is simply a large beast that frightens the people and causes them to neglect their fields and crops; Gilgamesh builds his own boat to carry him across the sea to Ziusudra's island. As for Inanna's proposal and rejection: it is left unclear whether she is the high priestess, who has already interpreted dreams for Gilgamesh, or simply a vision. (We know from several first-person dreams included in the otherwise third-person narrative that Gilgamesh is inclined to visions.) All the later events—the crossing of the mountain and the enchanted garden, the days spent in sexual pleasure with Siduri, the journey to Ziusudra's island, Ziusudra himself, and the plant of youthfulness—are recapitulated in a story that Gilgamesh tells a shepherd after months and even years of wandering alone in the desert. Did they really happen or not? In addition, several figures are omitted, such as Gilgamesh's mother, the scorpion people, and the ferryman.

The author's interest is focused primarily on the psychology of the two heroes. Gilgamesh contributes to Enkidu's civilizing by teaching his new friend all that he knows: geography, mythology, and the difference between life and death. But Enkidu, in keeping with the fashionable ecological theme, weakens so noticeably after he leaves his natural habitat that Gilgamesh suggests that he return to the hills to refresh himself, but Enkidu replies that he would no longer be able to be an animal since he has decided to become a man. The turning point comes in the fight with the bull, we realize, when Enkidu and the animal stand face to face:

> They stood there, immobile, the one before the other, while at a distance the king, even more disoriented, observed them. The bull's large brown eyes met those of Enkidu, Enkidu's large brown eyes met those of the bull, and there was a long, warm look of recognition, as though two sons of the same people encountered each other in an alien land. Fear had vanished from Enkidu's spirit, replaced by a profound distress, by a tormenting nostalgia, while he seemed to feel again the consuming and familiar admonition that had echoed around him in the cedar forest. Tears inundated his face, with that brackish taste that he knew so well from when he had left his hills, and still the bull regarded him sadly, so sadly that Enkidu could no longer bear the grief and, sobbing, hurled his sword to the ground. (114–15)

From this moment on, when Gilgamesh plunges his sword into the bull, Enkidu sickens and dies. "My destiny was already written," he later tells Gilgamesh, "from the moment when I forced the bull to bend his head to the ground, or perhaps when I helped you to cut down the cedars in the forest, or from the day on which I left my hills to come and live in the abodes of men. I have always known, Gilgamesh: he who denies his own nature never finds peace" (125). In the days before his death he reverts virtually to his former savage state, rejecting all clothing, lying naked on the floor in a corner, and, having forgotten how to talk, licking Gilgamesh's hand to express his affection.

Gilgamesh, for his part, is troubled by the idea of death from the moment when the priestess interprets an early dream for him in her temple. "Does a life that is not eternal deserve to be lived?" he asks her (34). She offers no consolation: "We mortals have days as brief as a puff of wind: from clay we were drawn and we will return to clay—the same on which the scribes incise with their stiluses the laws and the wedding contracts, the tales of the gods and the deeds of the heroes." Much later, when Inanna makes her proposal to Gilgamesh, she assures him that her beauty will belong to him forever if he becomes her spouse. But Gilgamesh questions the term *forever* (96): "Would I be a god if I should become your spouse?" Looking away, she says that he is divine only to the extent already assigned by destiny. Whereupon he replies: "Sovereignty is my destiny: supremacy over the people, victory in battle, to be light and shadow for other men. But a life that lasts into eternity is not my destiny." He finds no solace from Ziusudra, who tells him that Gilgamesh is the first visitor to his island in centuries and wonders whether the immortality bestowed on him by the deities is a reward or a punishment (181). At the end, therefore, he returns after many years to Uruk, taking satisfaction in his purely human accomplishments. Apart from a few plot twists, Capriola's novel adds no thematic originality to the historical adaptations of earlier decades.

The Politicization of Gilgamesh

Other novelists turned from historical re-visions to thematic and leitmo-tivic adaptations of the ancient epic in which, in several cases, politics or po-litical circumstance provide the background. In Joan London's *Gilgamesh* (2001), a highly readable novel of Australia, Europe, and the Near East *entre deux guerres,* the Babylonian epic is a theme and leitmotif rather than a prefiguring model: the work that inspires both the heroine and, later, her son to travel for adventure.[32] London, an Australian novelist and short-story writer, focuses her attention on Edith Clark, the daughter of an En-glishman who after the First World War emigrated with his wife Ada to Western Australia, where he failed miserably as a farmer. In the mid-1930s and after her father's death, when the teenaged Edith is working as a wait-ress in a nearby vacation hotel, her cousin Leopold, a Near Eastern archae-ologist, comes for a visit with his friend and former driver, the Armenian Aram. On their last night Aram sleeps with Edith and gets her pregnant.

Following the birth of her son Jim, she continues to work and live at home for a year, dreaming always of joining Aram in Armenia and marry-ing him. After a year, having saved and stolen enough money for her fare, she and Jim leave home and sail to England, where she stays for a time with cousin Leopold's mother Irina, a White Russian exile. Then she takes the Orient Express to Istanbul and is befriended by the textile merchant Hagop, who helps her to enter Soviet-controlled Armenia without a visa. In Yerevan she lives for several years in an apartment near Hagop and his wife, a crippled former pianist and singer, while Hagop promises to help her locate Aram. In 1942 Hagop enables her to escape across the border to Iran, where she is met by Leopold, from whom she learns that Hagop was in reality a Soviet agent who had helped to betray and kill Aram, an Armenian nationalist. Leopold takes her to Syria, where she works for a time in an orphanage and then travels with a division of Australian soldiers to Palestine and, from there, back to Australia, where she works in a nursing home and meets Lawrence, with whom a relationship develops as Jim grows up. When a letter arrives years later from Leopold, now back in Baghdad, Jim decides to go there to be with him. As his adventure begins, Edith understands that it is her destiny to remain in Australia.

The Gilgamesh motif first enters when Leopold shows Edith his copy of *The Epic of Gilgamesh,* "a heroic piece of work," which he carries around with him almost like a Bible (41). Indeed, the two friends speak of Gilgamesh virtually as though they had known him. During her pregnancy Edith recalls the story of Gilgamesh and Enkidu, which she associates with Leopold and Aram: "No doubt Gilgamesh and his friend also left behind a child or two in their travels" (54). The name occurs again many pages (and years) later in Yerevan, when Hagop takes her to a restaurant and she wonders "did she hear among the conversations the name *Gilgamesh*" (148). Later and indirectly, in a club (156), she asks Hagop if it is the "underworld," and he replies that she is in heaven. When Leopold takes her to Syria, the name and the story occur again at length as they wonder, "would Gilgamesh have wandered in these parts?" (174). Now she learns that Aram's code name was Gilgamesh—a fact that explains the earlier allusion in Yerevan when Hagop mentioned the name.

When Leopold leaves her in Syria, he gives her his treasured copy of the epic, and the references begin to occur more frequently. Back in Australia, the young Jim occasionally looks at the book and is excited by the myth. As he reads and rereads the story, "he began to understand that everything that happened to Gilgamesh was because he had a friend" (223) and realizes that for his friend Gareth "he must be the wild man from the plains" (243). He identifies his uncle Leopold with Gilgamesh, and the book gradually inspires him to leave home. The final allusion occurs when Leopold writes from Baghdad and asks if Edith still has the book: "It's a consolation sometimes to think that thousands of years ago, men knew about all this. The return. Wasn't he told to go home, eat, drink and be merry? Take the hand of his child? Something like that" (253)—precisely Edith's decision. In Joan London's novel the story of Gilgamesh becomes the structural key, in a world torn by politics and betrayal, to the eternal search for friendship, for adventure, and then for the return home to responsibility—first for Edith and, a generation later, for her son.

The popularity and familiarity of the Gilgamesh theme have meant that it is sometimes invoked in cases where it is not strictly applicable—at least not in any carefully defined sense. One such novel is *1979* (2001) by the cosmopolitan Swiss writer and journalist Christian Kracht (b. 1966). Kracht's earlier works were designated as pop literature because of their concern with trendy consumer culture and the self-centered search of a prosperous "me generation" for identity in a disintegrating society. (In 1999 he published, along with his novels, an "avant-pop-reader" called *Mesopotamia*.) The novel *1979*, which happened to be published during the fateful week of 9/11, depicts the 1979 Iranian Revolution and overthrow of the Shah as witnessed or—more precisely—overlooked by an uncomprehending young European interior designer who cares more about fashion and décor than about politics. He has accompanied his friend Christopher to Teheran—a journey to the east of the sort popularized in those years by American and European hippies—where they participate in the chic parties of the dissolute upper classes: the author's commentary on the debility of decadent Western values in the face of the totalitarian convictions of radical Islam and, later, Maoist doctrine. After Christopher's death in Iran, presumably of AIDS, the narrator goes to Tibet in search of wisdom but is arrested there by Chinese troops and sent to a work camp, where in the course of many months, as his account ends, he is reeducated and learns mindless submission to Marxist authority according to Mao: "Every two weeks there was a voluntary self-critique. I always attended. I was a good prisoner. I always tried to stick to the rules. I have improved myself. I have never eaten human flesh."[33]

The novel coyly displays a few superficial parallels to the epic: it is set in the Middle East (although not Mesopotamia); it is divided into twelve chapters; it features two friends, one of whom dies; the host of the Iranian

garden party has on his wall several (unspecified) paintings by Willi Baumeister, whom we already know as the illustrator of *The Epic of Gilgamesh*;
and the narrator is told by the man he consults after Christopher's death,
the mysterious Romanian Mavrocordato, that he must seek answers on
the sacred mountain Meru (in western Tibet). Otherwise there is no direct mention whatsoever of Gilgamesh or the epic in the text. The two
gay friends bear no resemblance whatsoever, in life or death, to Gilgamesh
and Enkidu. And the "wisdom" achieved at the end could not be further removed from the heroic stoicism and pride in human achievement
of the Babylonian epic. At the same time, the entire action takes place
against a profoundly political background of revolution and ideological
indoctrination.

Not every thematization, of course, has an underlying political theme.
Bring Deeps (2003) by the American novelist Elizabeth Arthur—the title
refers to a channel in the Orkney Islands—is basically a two-character
story revolving around Emrys Havers, like the author an American
teacher-writer, and the British archaeologist Sebastian Ferry. The two
forty-year-olds meet in London, where they sense an instant and powerful lust for each other. Both suffer from troubled emotional pasts from
which they escape into frequent and urgent sex in a series of inventively
varied scenarios, interrupted by Havers's melancholy reflections on death,
as they travel from London to Scotland and north to the Orkney Islands,
where Ferry is excavating a neolithic tomb. Only toward the end, when a
misunderstanding triggers an angry fight in the tense relationship, does
something like an explanatory background and plot emerge. Havers, ir-
rational in her fury, tries to sail back to the main island in a storm; Ferry
manages to rescue her onto a projecting rock but drowns in the attempt.
The first-person narration is Havers's account of their few weeks together.

How does Gilgamesh figure in this brief episode? The two lovers are
initially brought together by Gilgamesh. We learn that Havers spent seven
years translating a version of the epic that she called *Gilgamesh and Enkidu*,
and Ferry writes to express his appreciation for the publication. So they
arrange to meet, and throughout her retrospective account she—but not
Ferry—alludes to scenes from it. Because she has never spent the whole
night in the same bed as a man, for instance, one of her earlier sex partners
jokes that she likes the epic because of the test of sleeplessness (30).[34] When
Ferry asks her if she's a bossy woman, she thinks of Gilgamesh's rejection

of Ishtar (37). As she deplanes at Heathrow through a narrow gateway, she is reminded of Enkidu's curse of the harlot: "May a gateway be your birthing room" (42). When Ferry helps her to understand her dreams, she says that he is "untying" them, as Enkidu did with Gilgamesh's dreams (70). Crossing the rough sea to the Orkneys, she thinks of the epic's Waters of Death (87). The tombs in a Viking church remind her of a line she once translated as "The sleeping and the dead, how like brothers they are" (114–15). On other occasions, when the original does not seem adequate, she recalls lines that she herself invented to fill gaps in the text; at the end, after Ferry's death, the words that she wrote for Enkidu on the road to Humbaba come back to her: "And on that road lies death for one of us. I cannot see which one will die, though" (237).

In a statement written for her publisher's blog, the author reveals that the initial impulse for the novel stemmed from a persistent vision troubling her of a woman tied to a rock in the ocean while the water rises around her. But (apparently avoiding the obvious prefiguration of Andromeda) she found no story to exemplify the vision until she came across John Gardner's translation and realized that "Gilgamesh, upon being separated from Enkidu by death, desperately seeks to bring him back to life—although in the end, he can only do this by writing about him."[35] While the brief fling between the two lovers, like any affair of heterosexual passion, might conceivably remind one by loose analogy of the love of Gilgamesh and Enkidu, the thematic and motivic parallels seem artificial and forced.

But politics reenters with a vengeance in the anonymous novel *Zabibah and the King* (2000), which was generally attributed (without his denial) to Saddam Hussein.[36] Despite the inclination of the Iraqi dictator to identify himself with Gilgamesh as well as other heroes of Assyrian history and lore, the work has nothing to do with Gilgamesh, who is never mentioned in the text. And the action is set not in ancient Assyria but in medieval and already Muslim Iraq. At most one might argue that the king, like Gilgamesh, is initially portrayed as an arrogant young ruler; but even that analogy soon breaks down as his views are moderated by his conversations with the beautiful commoner Zabibah. The novel turns out to be less a fiction than a philoso-political dialogue between the king and Zabibah, who becomes his lover—a relationship that bears a closer resemblance to that of Enkidu and Shamhat than of Gilgamesh and Enkidu. Displaying absolutely no trace of a postfigurative pattern or even thematic motifs, it ultimately amounts simply to a political parable that was allegedly studied by the Central Intelligence Agency for insights into the thoughts and character of Saddam Hussein.

As stated at the outset, then, Gilgamesh is alive and well in the first decade of the twenty-first century: in art, music, and literature from North America by way of Europe to Australia and in forms varying from translations and poetic re-visions to fictional postfigurations and thematic analogies, and in presentations for audiences ranging from awestruck children to jaded postmoderns. All the approaches that arose during the preceding century to interpret the ancient epic, from psychology and feminism to gay rights and ecology, are still in force. But in the desecularized society of the new millennium, religion once again has taken center stage in many world civilizations, while the clash of these civilizations, notably Western and Muslim, has brought the political dimensions of the epic into the foreground to a degree unmatched in earlier adaptations. Not unsurprisingly, then, these developments show up in recent treatments of Gilgamesh. The extensive and broadening popularity of the epic and its hero attests not simply to the universality of the ancient work but also to the powerful identification of contemporary writers and audiences with its many implicit themes.

CONCLUSION

Our representative survey of the reception of the Gilgamesh epic during the past century and a half has revealed an astonishing number and variety of works from many Western countries and in manifold media and genres. (See the chronological list of works in the appendix.) If we compare this phenomenon to the reception of other masterpieces of world literature, it is difficult, if not impossible, to find anything remotely analogous. While Homer's Achilles and Odysseus, Virgil's Aeneas, the figures of Minoan Crete, Ovid's *Metamorphoses,* and the biblical myths have all continued to leave their imprint on our time, nowhere have they had such a varied and pervasive cultural impact as has the Sumerian hero.[1]

The phenomenon may be viewed in one sense as a late episode in the general Western fascination with the Near East that has existed in various forms since antiquity. Cultures identify themselves in part by their uses of the past. The United States has turned repeatedly in its history to Rome in its search for self-definition: from the theory of *translatio imperii* (the shift of empire from East to West) that inspired the Founding Fathers and shaped so many of our institutions, not to mention our federal architecture, but that also triggered millennial fears of a Gibbonian or even Spenglerian decline and fall. Germans of the nineteenth century—see Richard Wagner's Ring cycle—sought their cultural roots in Old Germanic history and mythology. Artists of the early twentieth century—Picasso, Vlaminck, Modigliani, Matisse—turned away from what they regarded as a decadent Europe and looked for inspiration to the primitive arts of Africa. Sir Arthur Evans's discovery of the palace of Minos at Knossos, announced in 1900, captured the imagination of the European public and instigated a wave of artistic and literary works based on Cretan myths.[2] The Egyptomania that obsessed Europeans and Americans from the Napoleonic campaigns down to the discovery of Tutankhamun's tomb in 1922 was exemplified by such works as Verdi's *Aida* (1871) or the obelisk form of the Washington Monument (1884), produced in the twentieth century a wave of fiction and films featuring mummies and Cleopatra, and can still be detected today in the awed faces of the visitors to Berlin's Neues Museum who swarm around the lovely bust of Nefertiti.[3] And as we have repeatedly observed, the turn to Gilgamesh among writers, artists, musicians, and thinkers from the late nineteenth to the early twenty-first centuries reflects successive waves of concern from generation to generation: we recognize aspects of ourselves in the ancient epic hero.

As for the Near East specifically, at least since Herodotus historians have sought to define the West in contradistinction to the ancient East: Greece versus Persia. This contrastive duality continued to occupy thinkers from the time of the Crusades by way of Montesquieu's *Persian Letters* (*Lettres persanes,* 1721) and André Malraux's *The Temptation of the West* (*La tentation de l'Occident,* 1926) down to such contemporaries as Edward Said and Samuel Huntington. That theoretical preoccupation with the East generated a corresponding cultural curiosity.[4] Already in antiquity writers were fascinated by the figure of Semiramis, wife of the Assyrian king Samsi-Adad V (9th century B.C.E.), who was renowned as a warrior queen and notorious for her sexual lust.[5] Later Dante condemned her (along with Dido and Cleopatra) to the second circle of his *Inferno* for her licentiousness (canto 5). Writers from Calderon to Metastasio and Voltaire devoted dramas to her life—works that provided libretti for operatic composers from Gluck to Rossini. The work known in French as *Les Mille et une nuits* and in English as *The Arabian Nights* has enjoyed since its initial collection and translation by Antoine Galland in 1704–16 enormous popularity in every European language and generated numerous translations and retellings—for instance, Richard Burton's unexpurgated translation, *The Arabian Nights' Entertainments; or, the Book of the Thousand Nights and a Night* (1885–88)—as well as such variations as Rimsky-Korsakov's symphonic suite *Scheherazade,* John Barth's novel *Chimera* (1974), and Mary Zimmermann's theatrical adaptation of *The Arabian Nights* (2005).[6] The 1812 translation by the Austrian Orientalist Joseph von Hammer-Purgstall of poems by the fourteenth-century Persian poet Hafiz (Muhammad Hafez-e Sirazi, *Divan*) inspired not only Goethe to his *West-Eastern Divan* (1819) but also volumes of Persian ghasels (*Ghaselen*) by such younger German poets as August von Platen (1821) and Friedrich Rückert (1822). Edward FitzGerald's translation of the Persian *Rubáiyát of Omar Khayyám* (1859) unleashed an international wave of translations and imitations. Following the Mesopotamian archaeological discoveries of the nineteenth century and the decipherment of cuneiform script, Assyriologists began to show up in novels from Harold Frederic's *The Damnation of Theron Ware* (1896) down to Alfred Döblin's *Babylonian Tour* (1934) and Agatha Christie's *Murder in Mesopotamia* (1936).[7] In sum, the public was increasingly well prepared by developments such as these for the reception of Gilgamesh in the decades after 1872, when the Babylonian epic was first presented to the public.

The impact of Gilgamesh specifically may be attributed in no small measure to the fact that the epic burst upon the scene in the late nineteenth century with an urgent immediacy. Unencumbered by the cultural or religious associations that shape and constrain our relationship to the Greek and Roman classics or to the Bible, it encountered an increasingly secularized public that was eager to find surrogates for its lost religious faith.[8] This search manifested itself in a "hunger for myth" that had been promoted, among others, by such figures as Richard Wagner and Friedrich Nietzsche.[9] The universal themes of Gilgamesh—notably the drive for power and glory, the pleasures of sex and friendship, the fear of death, the satisfactions of human achievement—filled that need admirably.

The epic's tantalizingly fragmentary form amounted to an invitation to modern writers and thinkers to fill in the gaps, to provide missing or unstated psychological motivations, and to undergird the action with their own systems of belief. Leaving aside the adaptations for children and juveniles, the TV series and video games, the comic books, murder mysteries, and other more recent forms of popularization, we have encountered Gilgamesh reborn in some eighty works of literature, art, and music. Despite the epic form of the original, the themes of the epic have inspired poets: we noted individual poems by such American and German writers as Charles Olson, Louis Zukofsky, Donald Hall, Hillary Major, Johannes Bobrowski, and Peter Huchel; no doubt there are others. In general, however, the striking scenes of the epic original first suggested narrative and visual treatment. The earliest literary adaptations—Hamilton's *Ishtar and Izdubar* (1884), Pannwitz's *Das namenlose Werk* (1920), and Boyajian's *Gilgamesh: A Dream of the Eternal Quest* (1924)—were poetic narratives while German artists immediately after the First World War—Richard Janthur, Josef Hegenbarth, Rolf Nesch, and others—were early drawn to address themselves to figures and scenes from the epic in their illustrations for Georg Burckhardt's immediately popular translation.

Ever since Hamilton's initiative, the poetic retellings of the epic have continued down to the present: Frank L. Lucas, Bruno Schliephacke, Herbert Mason, Alain Gagnon, Gertrud Leutenegger, David Ferry, Danny Thompson, Derrek Hines, Anne-Marie Beeckman. An equally lively reception took place in fiction, where Gilgamesh began to show up as a prefigurative theme or motif in German novels with a contemporary setting: *The City beyond the River* (1947), *River without Shores* (1949/50), *The Gouffé Case* (1952). Soon the epic tempted authors in several languages to present the material in more or less authentically backgrounded historical novels: in Italy (Gianfilippi, Capriola), the United States (Silverberg, Grundy), Germany (Braem, Mielke), France (Cassabois), and Spain (Ortega). Others were persuaded by the growing familiarity of the theme to use it as a more or less detailed prefiguration of a modern action (Bachmann, Garrigues, Kracht, London, Arthur), as a theme or motif for particular episodes (Bjelke, Gardner, Roth, Lerman, Ondaatje), and in science fiction (Sagan, Clough). At a certain point, inevitably, the very familiarity of the epic cried out for parody, as in Lem's "review" and Morgan's play.

Scenes from the epic have continued to be represented in a variety of contemporary styles as book illustrations or in exhibitions by many artists: Willi Baumeister, Emil Schumacher, Hans-Joachim Walch, Ludmilla Zeman, Sumaya Shabandar, Reinhard Minkewitz, Martin Blessmann, Anna Ghadaban, and others. At the same time, the implicit dramatic possibilities of the epic, appreciated by poets since Rilke, along with the belief by many scholars that it had served in ancient Mesopotamia as the basis for scenic representation, prompted other writers to adapt the plot for performance (Bridson, Garneau, Temple, Morgan, Komunyakaa, Hines, Lewis). Most of these versions, including the dramatic representation in 1958 in the Netherlands, were actually performed or presented as radio plays. The recognition of the liturgical aspects of the work led other scholar/writers to create "sacred" or "ritual" dramas based on the epic (Cambronne, Schrott). The same dramatic potential has challenged composers to present the material in forms ranging from the simple aria (Belden) by way of cantatas/oratorios (Berezowsky, Martinů, Azrié, Uhl) and ballets (Bloch) to full-length operas (Rangström, Schwedeler, Nørgård, Brucci).

From the preceding list it is clear that the universality of the ancient epic has appealed to writers, composers, and artists across the world from North America to Australia and especially in Western Europe from Poland to Italy, from Scandinavia to Spain. (As stated in the preface, this study has consciously omitted the reception in the Near and Far East.) Yet clearly the preponderance of works has been produced by German and Anglo-American writers. And if we discount the three early adaptations by Hamilton, Pannwitz, and Boyajian, the main reception was almost wholly a phenomenon of the late twentieth and early twenty-first century. To understand the reasons both for the geographical and temporal distribution, it is necessary to move beyond the formal characteristics of the reception to its thematic concerns.

As we saw in the introduction and chapter 1, the initial reception was dominated almost entirely by religious issues as the newly discovered document irrupted into a Judeo-Christian Western culture whose assumptions had been shaken by the theories of Darwin and nineteenth-century geological discoveries. Now these ancient tablets were presumptuous enough to challenge even the originality of the biblical narratives. It was the flood account in Tablet XI that first caught George Smith's attention, that he presented in his 1872 address to the Society of Biblical Archaeology, and that he identified in his *Chaldean Account of Genesis* as the item of principal interest in the twelve tablets. That same aspect seized the attention of readers of the London *Daily Telegraph* and *The New York Times*. The epic, still in an incomplete translation, was first introduced to readers of English not as a literary work but in Morris Jastrow's book The *Religion of Babylon and Assyria*. (Hamilton's romanticization of 1884, while it omitted the flood entirely, made a virtually new work of the actual plot of the epic as it was then known.) Meanwhile, the German scholars who prepared the first reliable editions, transliterations, and translations of the epic—notably Peter Jensen with his aggressive depiction of Jesus as an Israelite Gilgamesh and Friedrich Delitzsch, who insisted on the strong Babylonian element in the Bible—almost inevitably became embroiled in the fiery debate over Babel and Bible, which dominated the first decade of the twentieth century.

That these developments took place so conspicuously and publicly in Germany and England, where Kaisers and prime ministers attended the presentations, is due in large measure to the circumstance that the East had during the nineteenth century captured the popular as well as the scholarly imagination in those two countries.[10] In the early 1800s, for instance, while Grotefend was first deciphering Old Persian cuneiform inscriptions and German poets were composing their *divans* and ghasels, German philosophers at the University of Heidelberg, notably Joseph Görres and Friedrich Creuzer, were already discussing the Oriental roots of Western Judeo-Christian culture.[11] At midcentury British adventurers like Layard and Rawlinson were uncovering the ruins at Nineveh and transcribing the inscriptions on the Behistun Rock. During the decades immediately preceding and following the First World War, many thinkers and writers in Germany and England participated in literal or spiritual voyages—called "Journey to the East" by Hermann Hesse and "Sailing to Byzantium" by W. B. Yeats—in search of surrogates for a Western civilization that in their opinion was falling apart, with meaning drifting away in what Matthew Arnold called "a melancholy, long, withdrawing roar."[12]

It was a small group of German-language thinkers and writers—Sigmund Freud, Carl Gustav Jung, Rainer Maria Rilke, Hermann Hesse, Rudolf Pannwitz, Elias Canetti—who first, around the time of the First World War, in letters, reviews, and conversations called more general attention to the epic, which they knew not as Assyriologists or historians of religion but as appreciative readers of the poem as literature and philosophy. They recognized in the ancient literary monument themes of broader human concern: Freud's tentative identification of the two heroes as the individual and his libido; Jung's understanding of Gilgamesh as the individual who loses his dependence on the unconscious (the gods); Rilke's enthusiastic heralding of "the epic of fear-of-death"; Hesse's celebration of the hero who does battle with death; Canetti's empathy with Gilgamesh's grief over the loss of his friend; and Pannwitz's recognition of an ancient Orient embodying a wisdom lost to subsequent Western civilization.

The reception in the United States was assisted by the fact that many of the most important early scholarly works were written by German scholars like Paul Haupt who spent their careers in the United States; by Morris Jastrow, who was trained in Germany but taught in the United States; or by collaborative efforts like William Ellery Leonard's English adaptation of Hermann Ranke's German translation. But despite the continuing interest of such writers and thinkers in the 1930s as Thomas Mann and Will Durant and several splendid new translations in various languages, these preliminary appreciations had little public impact and, indeed, were set back again by the Second World War.

That the initial postwar literarizations again occurred mainly in Germany can be attributed to two circumstances: first, owing to the early Babel/Bible controversy, the publicization efforts of the intellectuals, and the ready availability of several readable translations in inexpensive editions, the reading public was receptive to allusions to the epic; and, second, the writers quickly recognized in the epic a profound sense of loss through death, the grim reality of homecoming, and the impulse to rebuild of the sort that confronted German society in the years immediately following the Second World War. Hence the strong sense of identification that we perceive in those early novels. In England a similar postwar mood, albeit with a Christianizing tint, is evident in Lucas's free verse retelling and Bridson's radio play. Poets in the United States saw the epic in less personal-social and more general cultural-historical terms: in Olson's "transpositions" and Zukofsky's compression, the epic exemplifies the primal and archetypal human nature to which men and women in a decentered modern society need to return; Gregory Corso and his fellow beatniks welcomed in Gilgamesh and Enkidu spiritual prototypes of their own journey in search of meaning. Meanwhile in Europe, Martinů's opera (1958) emphasized the human qualities of love, friendship, and death.

Already in 1948 Bruno Schliephacke had presented Gilgamesh's Uruk as a kinder, gentler socialist society that protects human nature against the ravages of capitalism. In his early fictionalization, Gian Franco Gianfilippi played down the historical aspect in order to stress the modern theme of order and discipline tempered by love and understanding. But as a consequence of the social upheavals of the 1960s, the situation changed noticeably, and many writers began to emphasize the sociopolitical meaning of the epic for the modern world, even as the traditional themes were maintained by others. In Robert Silverberg's novel and Donald Hall's poem, for instance, the theme of death remained central, while Gianfilippi's novel revived and even enhanced the religious aspect of the epic, giving it a monotheistic and even Christianizing twist in his wholly invented second part. It is also probably no accident that the novel's implicit argument against the Babylonian source for the biblical myth of the flood was presented by an author from Catholic Italy.

At the same time, various social agendas became evident in many adaptations of the epic. Thanks to the gay rights movement, the homosexual implications of the epic, at which Jahnn and Jordan had earlier merely hinted, could be raised quite frankly, as Guido Bachmann did in his postfigurative *Gilgamesh*. Bachmann's work was succeeded, in the following decades, by a series of plays and novels in which the homosexual love of Gilgamesh and Enkidu was treated openly by writers in different countries—notably Bjelke, Mielke, Cassabois, Kracht, and Morgan— while the epic itself was heralded in the secondary studies as an early example of gay literature, most notably in *The Columbia Anthology of Gay Literature* (1998).

Meanwhile, feminist writers and critics were scrutinizing the work as ancient evidence for the shift from matriarchy to patriarchy and casting a keen eye on the Sumerian attitudes toward women. The belief in an original gynecocracy or primal matriarchal society had existed for at least a century since Bachofen's pathbreaking work on matriarchy (*Das Mutterrecht,* 1861). It had been supported by such thinkers as Jung and figured peripherally in such early adaptations of Gilgamesh as those by Schliephacke and Jordan. But with the powerful new wave of women's liberation, triggered by Simone de Beauvoir's *Le Deuxième Sexe* (1949) and enhanced in 1963 by Betty Friedan's *The Feminine Mystique,* the theory of matriarchy again gained immediacy and relevance, as witness Rhoda Lerman's novel *Call Me Ishtar* (1973). In the works by Garneau and Mielke as well as the children's books by Bryson and Hodges, as Christine Hopps demonstrated in her study of "mythotextuality," the theme moved into the foreground.

And in Kluger's Jungian analysis of the epic, matriarchy plays a central role as well.

In the 1980s, while Western views of the Near East were being challenged by Edward Said and others and as public interest was intensified by current political events, still another theme emerged: proto-environmentalism. Students of the epic had long been aware of man's alienation from nature in the person of Enkidu, who quite dramatically loses touch with nature as a direct result of the civilizing influence of the temple prostitute. But thanks to the worldwide Green Movement and the efforts of the Club of Rome, the issue of global warming and climate control emerged as one of the most engaging public issues of the period. In consequence, Enkidu's private tragedy developed into a central theme in Anselm Kiefer's photomontage (1981) and the literary adaptations by Leutenegger, Braem, Huchel, Cassabois, Schrott, and Capriola. It was no longer simply the man from the steppes who was alienated from nature; humankind as a whole lost touch with creation as Gilgamesh chopped down forests and killed bulls.

The power of music, which in rudimentary form was already present in the magical power of Gilgamesh's drum, contributed to the frequent adaptation of the epic in a variety of musical works. But it also accounts for the powerful theme of music that we saw in the composer figures in the novels by Jahnn and Bachmann and in the drum motif that plays a central role in the novels by the two German writers, Braem and Mielke.

In retrospect, we see that Gilgamesh constitutes a finely tuned seismograph whose reception registers to a significant degree many of the major intellectual upheavals of the past century. (The adaptations also recorded various peripheral tremors such as deconstruction or the interest of psychoanalysis in the epic.) The great religious controversies of the late nineteenth and early twentieth centuries gave way during and after the First World War to more all-embracing concerns for spiritual values transcending what Oswald Spengler labeled the decline of Western civilization. These general concerns continued, notably in the United States, after the Second World War, but in Germany they were replaced by the more urgent worries about recovery after the death and destruction of the war. As society stabilized in the 1960s, the struggle for recognition and equal rights among previously marginalized or disparaged groups, notably gays and women, began to assert itself. Gradually, larger environmental concerns for the planet Earth itself began to emerge with various manifestations of the Green Movement—concerns directly related to the age-old worry about humankind's alienation from nature. The ease with which the epic of Gilgamesh could be adapted to accommodate these various interests constitutes a striking testimony to the eternal values embedded in the ancient monument.

Since the year 2000, the existing themes and forms have been extended into a significantly greater number and variety of adaptations and popularizations in literature, art, and music than in any preceding decade—a popularization and contemporization symbolized by the many translations and retellings, by the epic's inclusion in the major anthologies of world literature and by such introductions for the general reader as Sallaberger's *Gilgamesch-Epos* or Cornuault's exhortatory *Éloge de Gilgamesh*. With the "ritual dramas" of Cambronne and Schrott, the initial theme of religion has been revived: not in the narrow spirit of the Babel/Bible controversy but in light of a sophisticated historical understanding of the role of ritual and religion in early cultures. This development coincides with the worldwide resurgence not just of religion but, more particularly, of the study of religion.[13] The second main thematic initiative of the decade was the radical politicization of the epic by several writers—in recognition, no doubt, of the international political situation and the political implications of the epic itself.

The enthusiasm for the epic has, if anything, increased, as manifested by the appearance of excellent new translations (Foster, Maul), interesting verse and prose retellings (Mitchell, Hines, Begrich), innovative historical novels (Grundy, Capriola), loosely postfigurative works (Kracht, London, Arthur), and ingenious dramatizing versions (Morgan, Lewis, Hines, Komunyakaa). At the same time the visual and musical treatments have continued apace. Gilgamesh, both as a mythic-historical figure and as a prefiguring archetype, is very much alive and among us at the end of the first decade of this third millennium, and his spirited presence attests to the eternal verities and values of his epic that continue to haunt and motivate us some five thousand years after the hero's birth in ancient Mesopotamia.

CHRONOLOGY [OF WORKS DISCUSSED]

1872   Discovery and decipherment of the tablets
        George Smith, "The Chaldean History of the Flood" (lecture)
1875   George Smith, *Assyrian Discoveries*
        George Smith, *The Chaldean Account of Genesis*
1884   Leonidas Le Cenci Hamilton, *Ishtar and Izdubar* (first
        literarization)
        Paul Haupt, first edition of cuneiform text
1891   Alfred Jeremias, *Izdubar-Nimrod* (first German translation)
1898   Morris Jastrow, *Religion of Babylon and Assyria* (first partial
        translation into English)
1900   Peter Jensen, edition and translation (German)
1902   Friedrich Delitzsch, *Babel und Bibel*
        Chr. Dieckmann, *Das Gilgamis-Epos in seiner Bedeutung für
        Bibel und Babel*
1904   Alfred Jeremias, *Das Alte Testament im Lichte des Alten Orients*
1906   Peter Jensen, *Das Gilgamesch-Epos in der Weltliteratur*

1907   Édouard Dhorme, "Épopée de Gilgamès"
1911   Arthur Ungnad, *Das Gilgamesch-Epos* (translation with
         commentary by Hugo Gressmann)
         Freud-Jung correspondence
1916   Georg Burckhardt, *Gilgamesch* (German prose paraphrase)
         Rainer Maria Rilke's letters on Burckhardt and Ungnad
         Hermann Hesse's review of Burckhardt
1917   Stephen Langdon, *The Epic of Gilgamesh* (partial translation)
1919   Richard Janthur, ten etchings (for Burckhardt re-edition)
1920   Rudolf Pannwitz, *Das namenlose Werk* (poetic retelling)
         Josef Hegenbarth, eleven drawings (for Burckhardt re-edition)
1921   Elias Canetti, encounter with Gilgamesh (as reported in
         autobiography)
1922   Rolf Nesch, portfolio of twenty etchings (based on Burckhardt)
         Hans Steiner, lithographs (for Burckhardt re-edition)
         Józef Wittlin, *Gilgamesz: powieść starobabilońska* (fictional
         retelling)
1923   Arthur Ungnad, *Gilgamesch-Epos und Odyssee*
1924   Zabelle C. Boyajian, *Gilgamesh: A Dream of the Eternal Quest*
         (poetic drama)
         Hermann Häfker, *Gilgamesch* ("German setting" in free verse)
         Hermann Ranke, *Gilgamesch* (German translation)
1926   Erich Ebeling, *Gilgamesch* (scholarly translation)
1927   Wilhelm Wendlandt, *Gilgamesch. Der Kampf mit dem Tode*
         (poetic retelling in 400 sonnets)
1928   R. Campbell Thompson, *The Epic of Gilgamish* (first complete
         English translation)
1934   William Ellery Leonard, *Gilgamesh: Epic of Old Babylonia* (free
         verse adaptation of Ranke's German translation)
         Albert Schott, *Das Gilgamesch-Epos* (German translation)
         Thomas Mann, *Der junge Joseph* (cites epic)
         Alfred Döblin, *Babylonische Wandrung* (thematic/motivic
         analogue)
1935   Will Durant, *Our Oriental Heritage* (recapitulates plot)
1941   Charles Olson, "Tomorrow" (poem)
1943   Willi Baumeister, series of 64 frottages based on epic
         Walter Jonas, "Gilgamesch," depicted in 20 aquatints

1944	Samuel Kramer, "The Epic of Gilgameš and Its Sumerian Sources"
1946	Alexander Heidel, *Gilgamesh Epic and Old Testament Parallels*
1947	Hermann Kasack, *Die Stadt hinter dem Strom* (thematic/ motivic analogue)
	Nicolai Berezowsky, *Gilgamesh* (cantata)
1948	Frank Laurence Lucas, *Gilgamesh: King of Erech* (free verse retelling)
	Bruno P. Schliephacke, *Gilgamesch sucht die Unsterblichkeit* (prose paraphrase)
	Joseph Campbell, *The Hero with a Thousand Faces* (psychoanalytic analysis)
1949	Charles Olson, "La Chute I–III" (poems)
1949/50	Hans Henny Jahnn, *Fluss ohne Ufer* (thematic/motivic analogue, loosely postfigurative)
	Emil Schumacher, series of linocuts based on epic
1950s	Gregory Corso promotes Gilgamesh
1950	Charles Olson, "Bigmans" (poems)
	E. A. Speiser, translation of epic in *Ancient Near Eastern Texts* (*ANET*)
	Samuel Kramer, translation of Sumerian "Deluge" in *ANET*
	Franzis Jordan, *In den Tagen des Tammuz* (poetic retelling)
	Fred Poeppig, *Gilgamesh und Eabani* (free dramatization)
1951	Charles Olson, "The Gate and the Center" (essay)
1952	Theodor H. Gaster, translation of epic in *The Oldest Stories in the World*
	Joachim Maass, *Der Fall Gouffé* (thematic/motivic analogue, loosely postfigurative)
	Ture Rangström, *Gilgamesj* (opera)
1954	Douglas Geoffrey Bridson, *The Quest of Gilgamesh* (radio play)
1955	Samuel Kramer, translation of Sumerian myths in *ANET*
1956	Alfred Uhl, *Gilgamesch. Oratorisches Musikdrama*
1958	Bohuslav Martinů, *The Epic of Gilgamesh* (oratorio)
	Hans-Joachim Walch, woodcuts (for Burckhardt re-edition)
	Performance of "The Epic of Gilgamesh" at Wageningen
1959	Gian Franco Gianfilippi, *Gilgamesh. Romanzo* (historical novel)

1960	Raimund Schwedeler, *Gilgamesch* (opera)
	Nancy Sandars, *The Epic of Gilgamesh* ("translation" based on earlier translations)
	Reading of the epic on Los Angeles radio station KPFK
1961	Johannes Bobrowski, *Sarmatische Zeit* (poems)
	Stanisław Lem, *A Perfect Vacuum* (satire)
1964	Exhibition "Gilgamesch" (Hamburg)
1966	Guido Bachmann, *Gilgamesch* (postfigurative novel)
	Rudolf Pannwitz, *Gilgamesch—Sokrates* (philosophical study)
	Hartmut Schmökel, *Das Gilgamesch-Epos* (translation)
	Anita Feagles, *He Who Saw Everything* (retelling for children)
1967	Vera Schneider, *Gilgamesch* (philosophical study)
	Bernarda Bryson, *Gilgamesh: Man's First Story* (for children)
1968	Augustyn Bloch, *Gilgamesz* (ballet)
1970	Hope Glenn Athearn, "Gilgamesh: A Novel"
	Herbert Mason, *Gilgamesh: A Verse Narrative*
1971	Elizabeth Jamison Hodges, *Song for Gilgamesh* (for juveniles)
1972	John Gardner, *The Sunlight Dialogues* (thematic/motivic analogue)
	Per Nørgård, *Gilgamesh* (opera)
1973	Philip Roth, *The Great American Novel* (thematic/motivic analogue, loosely postfigurative)
	Rhoda Lerman, *Call Me Ishtar* (thematic/motivic analogue)
1974	Henrik Bjelke, *Saturn* (thematic/motivic analogue)
	Michel Garneau, *Gilgamesh* (poetic drama)
1975	Louis Zukofsky, "A-23" (poetic adaptation)
	Gilgamesh—recording by Gilgamesh, British jazz fusion band
1976	George Belden, *Gilgamesh: An Aria for Contralto, Piano, Percussion, and Tape*
1977	James Gunn, *The Road to Science Fiction* (cites Gilgamesh as early example)
	Abed Azrié, *L'Épopée de Gilgamesh* (cantata)
1978	Edgar B. Pusch, *Der kleine Gilgamesch* (for juveniles)
1979	Peter Huchel, *Die neunte Stunde* (poems)
	Abed Azrié, *Épopée de Gilgamesh* (narrative adaptation of cantata)
1980	Gertrud Leutenegger, *Lebewohl, Gute Reise* (dramatic poem)

1981   Anselm Kiefer, "Gilgamesch und Enkidu im Zedernwald"
          (photomontage)
          Victoria Brockhoff/Hermann Lauboeck, *Als die Götter noch mit den Menschen sprachen. Gilgamesch und Enkidu* (for juveniles)
          Tilo Prückner and Roland Teubner, *Gilgamesch und Enkidu* (dramatized version for children)
          William Thomas Kidd, *The Epic of Gilgamesh: An Opera Cycle*
1982   Tracy Luke/Paul Pruyser, "The Epic of Gilgamesh" (Freudian reading)
1984   Robert Silverberg, *Gilgamesh the King* (historical novel)
          John Gardner/John Maier, *Gilgamesh: From the Sîn-Lequi-Unninnî Version* (translation)
          The Tower of Druago (video game)
1985   Rudolf Brucci, *Gilgamesh* (opera)
          Carl Sagan, *Contact* (novel)
1986   Alain Gagnon, *Gilgamesh* (prose poem)
1987   Michael Ondaatje, *In the Skin of a Lion* (loose thematic analogue)
          Eduardo Garrigues, *Al oeste de Babilonia* (postfigurative novel)
          Robert Silverberg, *Gilgamesh in the Outback* (science fiction)
          Marek Żuławski, "Gilgamesh" (series of fourteen graphics)
1988   Harald Braem, *Der Löwe von Uruk* (historical novel)
          Thomas Mielke, *Gilgamesch. König von Uruk* (historical novel)
          Tera de Marez Oyens, *Gilgamesh Quartet: For Four Trombones*
1989   Jim Starlin, "Gilgamesh II" (comic book series)
          Jo Bannister, *Gilgamesh* (murder mystery)
          William Coates, *The Secret of Utnapishtim: For Soprano and Archiphone*
          Joseph-Régis Pio, *L'Épopée de Gilgamesh: Poème*
1990   *Tymewyrm* (science fiction)
          José Ortega, *Gilgamesh y la muerte* (fanciful historical re-vision)
1991   Rivka Schärf Kluger, *The Archetypal Significance of Gilgamesh* (Jungian reading)
          Robert Temple, *He Who Saw Everything* ("translation" based on earlier translations)
          "Darmok" (episode in TV series *Star Trek: The Next Generation*)

Donald Hall, "Praise for Death" (poem)
Ralph Blasting/Mahmood Karimi-Hakak, *Gilgamesh Conquest* (dramatization)

1992   *Highlander* (TV series)
Ludmilla Zeman, *Gilgamesh the King* (first part of trilogy for children)
Danny Thompson, *The Epic of Gilgamesh* (verse rendition)
David Ferry, *Gilgamesh* (verse rendition)
Franco Battiato, *Gilgamesh* (opera)
Joël Cornuault, *Éloge de Gilgamesh* (personal reflections)

1994   Sumaya Shabandar, *The Epic of Gilgamesh* (free-verse translation)

1995   *Xena: Warrior Princess* (TV series)
Andrew C. Ordover, *Gilgamesh* (dramatization)
August Ohn, seventeen illustrations (for Schmökel re-edition)

1997   Brenda W. Clough, *How Like a God* (science fiction)

1998   Jacques Cassabois, *Le roman de Gilgamesh* (historical novel)
The Columbia Anthology of Gay Literature
Irving Finkel, *The Hero King Gilgamesh* (for juveniles)
Arnica Esteerl and Marek Zawadzki, *Gilgamesch von Uruk* (for children)

1999   Andrew George, *The Epic of Gilgamesh* (translation of epic and Sumerian poems)

2000   Patrice Cambronne, *Gilga.Mesh, ou la Gloire entre la Force et le Destin* (ritual drama)
Stephan Grundy, *Gilgamesh* (historical novel)
(Saddam Hussein?), *Zabibah and the King* (novel)
Hillary Major, "Gilgamesh Remembers a Dream" (poem)

2001   Raoul Schrott, *Gilgamesh. Epos* (epic oratorium)
Benjamin Foster, *The Epic of Gilgamesh* (translation)
Joan London, *Gilgamesh* (thematic/motivic analogue)
Christian Kracht, *1979* (thematic/motivic analogue, loosely postfigurative)

2002   Derrek Hines, *Gilgamesh* (verse rendition)

2003   Paola Capriola, *Qualcosa nella notte* (historical novel)
Gerhard Begrich, *Gilgamesch. König und Vagant* (prose "re-telling")

Hans Zimmer and Wolfgang Bartel, *Gilgamesch macht Ärger* (musical for children)
Damian Morgan, *Gil's Quest* (for children)
Geraldine McCaughrean, *Gilgamesh the Hero* (for children)
Elizabeth Arthur, *Bring Deeps* (thematic/motivic analogue)
The Norton Anthology of World Literature (2nd ed.)

2004   Jacques Cassabois, *Le premier roi du monde—L'épopée de Gilgamesh* (for children)
"Gilgamesh" (26-episode anime)
Stephen Mitchell, *Gilgamesh: A New English Version*
The Bedford Anthology of World Literature

2005   Stefan Maul, *Das Gilgamesch-Epos* (translation)
Edwin Morgan, *The Play of Gilgamesh*
Exhibition "Das Gilgamesch-Epos, gesehen von drei Generationen" (Mainz)
Burkhart Pfister, *Gilgamesch* (graphic novel)

2006   Yusuf Komunyakaa/Chad Gracia, *Gilgamesh: A Verse Play*
Reinhard Minkewitz, exhibition of paintings and drawings (Leipzig)
Martin Blessmann, series of transparencies (Bonn)
Frank Groothof, *Gilgamesj* (for children)
Nicole Leurpendeur, *Das Gilgamesch-Epos* (for children)

2007   Wolfgang Witzenmann, *Gilgamesch und Christus* (oratorio)
José Ortega, *El mito de Gilgamesh* (TV dramatization)
Derrek Hines, *Gilgamesh: The Play*
Peter Moers and Frank Papenbroock, "Das Phantom von Uruk: Fahndung nach König Gilgamesch" (TV documentary)

2008   Anne-Marie Beeckman, *Gilgameš* (poetic retelling)
Walther Sallaberger, *Das Gilgamesch-Epos. Mythos, Werk und Tradition* (introduction for general reader)

2009   Anna Ghadaban, exhibition of gouaches (Kusterdingen, Germany)
Jenny Lewis, *About Gilgamesh* (verse drama)

Notes

Introduction

1. J. J. Stamm, "Das Gilgamesch-Epos und seine Vorgeschichte," *Asiatische Studien* 6 (1952): 9–29, here 9. Reprinted in *Das Gilgamesch-Epos,* ed. Karl Oberhuber (Darmstadt: Wissenschaftliche Buchgesellschaft, 1977), 292–311.

2. I refer to the widely regarded authoritative translation of the "Standard Edition" (as it has come to be called): Andrew George, *The Epic of Gilgamesh: The Babylonian Epic Poem and Other Texts in Akkadian and Sumerian* (London: Penguin, 2003).

3. Also known as "droit du seigneur," the term designates the alleged right in many early cultures of the ruler to deflower a virgin on her first night of marriage.

4. The term *Kulturhero* derives from Walther Sallaberger, *Das Gilgamesch-Epos: Mythos, Werk und Tradition* (Munich: Beck, 2008), 49.

5. For a generous selection from the variety of critical approaches, see *Gilgamesh: A Reader,* ed. John Maier (Wauconda, IL: Bolchazy-Carducci, 1997).

6. Jeffrey H. Tigay, *The Evolution of the Gilgamesh Epic* (Philadelphia: University of Pennsylvania Press, 1982). The following paragraphs are based largely on Tigay's work and updated by Andrew George's introduction to his translation. See also the informative general introduction by Sallaberger, *Gilgamesch-Epos,* esp. 60–80.

7. Conveniently compiled from different texts by Thorbild Jacobsen, *The Sumerian King List* (Chicago, University of Chicago Press, 1939).

8. All of these texts are conveniently available in George, *Epic of Gilgamesh*.

9. Raoul Schrott suggests that Enkidu symbolizes an Akkadian nomad in the service of the civilized Sumerian Gilgamesh. Schrott, *Gilgamesh. Epos* (Munich: Hanser, 2001), 12.

10. Schrott suggests that this enhancement of the gods and the almost misogynistic marginalization of the goddesses exemplifies the historical transition from matriarchy to patriarchy. Schrott, *Gilgamesh. Epos,* 14–15.

11. George, *Epic of Gilgamesh,* xxvii; and Sallaberger, *Gilgamesch-Epos,* 122.

12. For a survey of ancient works affected by the Gilgamesh theme, see Jean-Daniel Forest, *L'épopée de Gilgamesh et sa postérité: Introduction au langage symbolique* (Paris: Méditerranée, 2002).

13. See Robert Irwin, *The Arabian Nights: A Companion* (London: Allen Lane, 1994), 74.

14. The entire story of the rediscovery has been told entertainingly in David Damrosch, *The Buried Book: The Loss and Rediscovery of the Great Epic of Gilgamesh* (New York: Henry Holt, 2006), 9–114.

15. George Smith, *Assyrian Discoveries: An Account of Explorations and Discoveries on the Site of Nineveh, during 1873 and 1874* (New York: Scribner, Armstrong, 1975).

16. I cite the American edition, *The Chaldean Account of Genesis, containing the Description of the Creation, the Fall of Man, the Deluge, the Tower of Babel, the Times of the Patriarchs, and Nimrod: Babylonian Fables, and Legends of the Gods; from the Cuneiform Inscriptions* (New York: Scribner, Armstrong, and Co., 1876).

17. Charles C. Gillispie, *Genesis and Geology: A Study in the Relations of Scientific Thought, Natural Theology, and Social Opinion in Great Britain, 1790–1850* (1951; rpt. New York: Harper Torchbooks, 1959).

18. *Das Babylonische Nimrodepos, Keilschrifttext der Bruchstücke der sogenannten Izdubarlegenden mit dem keilinschriftlichen Sintfluthberichte,* nach den Originalen im Britischen Museum, copirt und hrsg. von Dr. Paul Haupt (Leipzig: Hinrichs, 1884).

19. Alfred Jeremias, *Izdubar-Nimrod. Eine altbabylonische Heldensage. Nach den Keilschriftfragmenten dargestellt* (Leipzig: Teubner, 1891).

20. The "contemporary authority" is Max Duncker, *Geschichte des Altertums,* which appeared in several editions from 1852 to 1878–86.

21. Theo. G. Pinches, "Exit Giśṭubar!" *Babylonian and Oriental Record* 4/11 (1890): 264.

22. Morris Jastrow, *The Religion of Babylonia and Assyria* (Boston: Ginn, 1898), 467–517.

23. Karl Oberhuber, "Wege der Gilgamesch-Forschung. Ein Vorwort," in *Gilgamesch-Epos,* ed. Oberhuber, xiii–xxvi, here xiii.

24. Paul Haupt, ed., *Assyrisch-Babylonische Mythen und Epen,* Keilinschriftliche Bibliothek. Sammlung von Assyrischen und Babylonischen Texten in Umschrift und Übersetzung, vol. 6 (Berlin: Reuter and Reichard, 1900), 116–273.

25. Édouard Dhorme, "Épopée de Gilgamès," in his *Choix de textes religieux assyro-babyloniens; transcriptions, traduction, commentaire* (Paris: Lecoffre, 1907), 182–325.

1. The Initial Reception (1884–1935)

1. For brief surveys of the history of the scholarly reception, see Jeffrey H. Tigay, *Evolution of the Gilgamesh Epic* (Philadelphia: University of Pennsylvania Press, 1987), 16; and Karl Oberhuber's introduction in *Das Gilgamesch-Epos,* ed. Karl Oberhuber (Darmstadt: Wissenschaftliche Buchgesellschaft, 1977), xiii–xxvi.

2. For the biographical background, see John R. Maier, "The File on Leonidas Le Cenci Hamilton," *American Literary Realism, 1870–1910* 11 (1978): 92–99.

3. See the "Proemium" to Leonidas Le Cenci Hamilton, *Ishtar and Izdubar, the Epic of Babylon; or The Babylonian Goddess of Love and the Hero and Warrior King* (London: W. H. Allen, 1884), xi–xxiv.

4. I cite Hamilton's poem from the first edition (as above). The work was reprinted—without Hamilton's proemium and appendix, his diacritical marks, or the illustrations—in Epiphanius Wilson, ed., *Babylonian and Assyrian Literature* (New York: Colonial Press, 1901), 3–156.

5. *George Smiths Chaldäische Genesis,* Autorisierte Übersetzung von Hermann Delitzsch, nebst Erläuterungen und fortgesetzten Forschungen von Friedrich Delitzsch (Leipzig: Hinrichs, 1876).

6. Paul Haupt, *Der keilinschriftliche Sintfluthbericht: Eine Episode des babylonischen Nimrodepos mit dem autographirten Keilschrifttext des babylonischen Sintfluthfragmentes* (Leipzig: Hinrichs, 1881); rpt. in Eberhard Schrader, *Die Keilinschriften und das Alte Testament* (Giessen, Germany: Ricker, 1883).

7. Peter Jensen, *Die Kosmologie der Babylonier. Studien und Materialien. Mit einem mythologischen Anhang und 3 Karten* (Strassburg: Trübner, 1890).

8. Friedrich Delitzsch, *Babel und Bibel. Ein Vortrag* (Leipzig: Hinrich, 1902).

9. Friedrich Delitzsch, *Zweiter Vortrag über Babel und Bibel* (Stuttgart: Deutsche Verlags-Anstalt, 1903).

10. *Babel and Bible: Two Lectures Delivered before the Members of the Deutsche Orient-Gesellschaft in the Presence of the German Emperor,* ed. C. H. W. Johns (New York: Putnam, 1903).

11. Friedrich Delitzsch, *Babel und Bibel. Dritter (Schluss-)Vortrag* (Stuttgart: Deutsche Verlags-Anstalt, 1903); and Friedrich Delitzsch, *Babel und Bibel. Ein Rückblick und Ausblick* (Stuttgart: Deutsche Verlags-Anstalt, 1904).

12. Friedrich Delitzsch, *Die große Täuschung* (Stuttgart: Deutsche Verlags-Anstalt). Bill T. Arnold and David B. Weisberg stress the role of what they believe to be Delitzsch's nationalism and anti-Semitism in the formation of his views. Arnold and Weisberg, "A Centennial Review of Friedrich Delitzsch's 'Babel und Bibel' Lectures," *Journal of Biblical Literature* 121 (2002): 441–57.

13. Chr. Dieckmann, *Das Gilgamis-Epos in seiner Bedeutung für Bibel und Babel* (Leipzig: Christoph Steffen, 1902).

14. Alfred Jeremias, *Das Alte Testament im Lichte des Alten Orients. Handbuch zur biblisch-orientalischen Altertumskunde* (Leipzig: Hinrich, 1904).

15. Peter Jensen, *Das Gilgamesch-Epos in der Weltliteratur,* vol. 1: *Die Ursprünge der alttestamentlichen Patriarchen-, Propheten- und Befreier-Sage und der neutestamentlichen Jesus-Sage* (Strassburg: Trübner, 1906).

16. Arthur Ungnad, *Gilgamesch-Epos und Odyssee* (Breslau: Arthur Ungnad Selbstverlag, 1923). For a more recent overview, see M. L. West, *The East Face of Helicon: West Asiatic Elements in Greek Poetry and Myth* (Oxford: Clarendon, 1997), esp. 63–67 (general summary of epic), 336–38, 372–73 (Gilgamesh and Achilles), and 420 (Gilgamesh and Rhadamanthys).

17. Hans Schmidt, "Das Gilgameschepos und die Bibel," *Theologische Rundschau* 6 (1907): 189–208, 229–37.

18. Hermann Gunkel, "Jensens Gilgamesch-Epos in der Weltliteratur," *Deutsche Literaturzeitung* 30 (1909): 901–11. I quote from the reprint in Oberhuber, ed., *Gilgamesch-Epos,* 74–84. The debate aroused less controversy at the time outside Germany: as a representative example, Albert T. Clay, in his *Light on the Old Testament from Babel* (Philadelphia: The Sunday School Times Company, 1907), does not take issue with Delitzsch, is neutral on Jensen, and mentions Gilgamesh only four times briefly in passing.

19. See, for instance, Alexander Heidel, *The Gilgamesh Epic and Old Testament Parallels* (Chicago: University of Chicago Press, 1946), which in contrast to Jensen focuses not on parallel stories but on the more general theme of death as it occurs in both works. Stephanie Dalley mentions neither the Bible/Babel controversy nor Delitzsch, Jensen, and the other German participants in the debate. Dalley, "The Influence of Mesopotamia upon Israel and the Bible," in *The Legacy of Mesopotamia,* ed. Dalley (New York: Oxford University Press, 1998), 57–83.

20. *Das Gilgamesch-Epos.* Neu übersetzt von Arthur Ungnad und gemeinverständlich erklärt von Hugo Gressmann (Göttingen: Vandenhoeck and Ruprecht, 1911). For the comment see Giuseppe Furlani, "L'Epopea di Gilgames come inno all'amicizia," *Belfagor* 1 (1946): 577–89; translated by Rüdiger Schmitt as "Das Gilgamesch-Epos als Hymnus auf die Freundschaft," in *Das Gilgamesch-Epos,* ed. Oberhuber, 219–36, here 220.

21. *The Freud-Jung Letters,* ed. William McGuire, trans. Ralph Manheim and R. F. C. Hull, Bollingen Series XCIV (Princeton: Princeton University Press, 1974), 444–45.

22. Ibid., 448–49.

23. Jung originally used Jensen's translation, *Gilgamesch-Epos* (1900) but subsequently, for the later edition, consulted the translations of Heidel, Schott, Speiser, and Thompson. See C. G. Jung, *Symbols of Transformation,* trans. R. F. C. Hull, 2nd ed., Bollingen Series XX/5 (Princeton: Princeton University Press, 1970), 200n51; trans. from 4th ed. of *Wandlungen und Symbole der Libido* (1952).

24. Jung, *Symbols of Transformation,* 294, 329, 261, 298, 354, 332, 437.

25. For example, in the seventh of his lectures on *Nietzsche's Zarathustra* (November 21, 1934), *Nietzsche's Zarathustra. Notes of the Seminar Given in 1934–39 by C. G. Jung,* ed. James L. Jarrett, 2 vols., Bollingen Series XCIX (Princeton: Princeton University Press, 1988), 246–52; in "Concerning Rebirth" (1940–50), *The Archetypes and the Collective Unconscious,* trans. R.F.C. Hull, 2nd ed., Bollingen Series XX/9 (Princeton: Princeton University Press, 1968), 111–47, here 145; or in "The Philosophical Tree" (1954), *Alchemical Studies.* Trans. R.F.C. Hull, Bollingen Series XX/13 (Princeton: Princeton University Press, 1967), 251–349, here 320–21.

26. See William L. Moran, "Rilke and the Gilgamesh Epic," *Journal of Cuneiform Studies* 32 (1980): 208–10.

27. See Burckhardt's epilogue in *Gilgamesch. Eine Dichtung aus dem alten Orient. Zu einem Ganzen gestaltet* (Wiesbaden: Insel, 1958), 73–75, here 74. This later edition contains twelve new woodcuts by Hans-Joachim Walch.

28. This implication, based on a phrase omitted from some recent editions, should have been suspect from the outset, given that the first translation of the epic appeared in 1891, after the onset of Nietzsche's madness. There is absolutely no evidence in his correspondence or published works of any acquaintance with Gilgamesh. However, on the influence of Burckhardt's words, see, for instance, Wilhelm Wendlandt's introduction to his adaptation *Gilgamesch. Der Kampf mit dem Tode* (Berlin: Brandus, 1927), in which he cites Burckhardt to the effect that "the philosopher Nietzsche exhorted the cultivated persons of the whole world to raise this huge treasure . . . and to make this primal poem arise again newly clad in every possible form of modern culture, whether as drama or opera or as epic poem" (4).

29. Rainer Maria Rilke/Katharina Kippenberg, *Briefwechsel* (Wiesbaden: Insel, 1954), 191–92.

30. Ibid., 198.

31. Rainer Maria Rilke/Helene von Nostitz, *Briefwechsel* (Frankfurt am Main: Insel, 1976), 99.

32. Hermann Hesse, review of Burckhardt's *Gilgamesch* in *Neue Zürcher Zeitung,* November 22, 1916; rpt. in Hesse, *Eine Literaturgeschichte in Rezensionen und Aufsätzen,* ed. Volker Michels (Frankfurt am Main: Suhrkamp, 1975), 15–16.

33. Hermann Hesse, *Gesammelte Schriften* (Frankfurt am Main: Suhrkamp, 1957), vii, 307–43, here 315; also rpt. in *Literaturgeschichte in Rezensionen und Aufsätzen,* 1–14. Kenneth Hughes detects an analogy between Enkidu's civilizing by Shamhut and the humanization of the heroes of Hesse's novels *Siddhartha* (1922) and *Der Steppenwolf* (1927) by women. Hughes, "Hesse's Use of *Gilgamesh*-Motifs in the Humanization of Siddhartha and Harry Haller," *Seminar* 5 (1969): 129–40.

34. Rudolf Pannwitz, *Die Krisis der europäischen Kultur* (Nuremberg: H. Carl, 1947), 180.

35. I base my discussion here on Pannwitz's autobiographical sketch, "Umriß meines Lebens und Lebenswerks," in Udo Rukser, *Über den Denker Rudolf Pannwitz. Mit einer Selbstbiographie von Pannwitz und einer Bibliographie,* Monographien zur philosophischen Forschung, Bd. 64 (Meisenheim am Glan, Germany: Anton Hain, 1970), 143–55.

36. Rudolf Pannwitz, *Das namenlose Werk* (= *Mythen VIII*) (Munich: Hans Carl, 1920).

37. Pannwitz, "Umriß meines Lebens und Lebenswerks," 151.

38. Wilhelm Wendlandt, "Zur Einführung," *Gilgamesch. Der Kampf mit dem Tode. Ein Lebenslied* (Berlin: Brandus, 1927), 3–8, here 5.

39. Elias Canetti, *Die Fackel im Ohr. Lebensgeschichte 1921–1931* (Munich: Hanser, 1993), 51–52.

40. Thomas Mann, *Gesammelte Werke in zwölf Bänden* (Frankfurt am Main: Fischer, 1960), iv, 408.

41. Alfred Döblin, *Babylonische Wandrung oder Hochmut kommt vor dem Fall,* in *Ausgewählte Werke in Einzelbänden,* ed. Walter Muschg (Olten, Switzerland, and Freiburg im Breisgau, Germany: Walter, 1962), 95.

42. Justus Fetscher suggests that Marinetti's novel *Mafarka le Futuriste* (first published in French in 1909) might have been influenced by *Gilgamesch.* Fetscher, "Gilgamesch Mafarka. Reflexionen zum Archaisch-Epischen in Marinettis Roman," in *Körper in Bewegung. Modelle und Impulse der italienischen Avantgarde,* ed. Marijana Erstić, Walburga Hülk, and Gregor Schuhen (Bielefeld, Germany: transcript, 2009), 93–107. The suggestion is unconvincing because there is no evidence that Marinetti was familiar with any of the translations that existed at that time. Moreover, Fetscher himself concedes that the "divergencies" are more notable than any of the vague correspondences. (Mafarka's homoerotic affection and mourning are directed toward his own unheroic brother. The "son" that he creates is a winged creature that flies off into a futuristic heaven.) The plot of Marinetti's pornographic African novel bears no resemblance, thematic or plotwise, to the Babylonian epic, apart from its focus on a titanic and tyrannical hero.

43. *Gilgamesch. Eine Erzählung aus dem alten Orient.* Original-Radierungen von Richard Janthur (Berlin: Fritz Gurlitt, 1919).

44. Hermann Häfker, *Gilgamesch, eine Dichtung aus Babylon,* Kunstwart-Bücherei 13 (Munich: Callwey, 1924). See his appendix "Zum Verständnis des Gilgamesch-Epos" ("On the Understanding of the Gilgamesh Epic"), 78–90, here 89.

45. Hermann Ranke, *Gilgamesch. Das altbabylonische Gilgamesch-Epos* (Hamburg: Friedrichsen, 1924).

46. Erich Ebeling, "Gilgamesch," in *Altorientalisch Texte zum Alten Testament,* ed. Hugo Gressmann (Berlin: DeGruyter, 1926), 150–98.

47. Albert Schott, *Das Gilgamesch-Epos neu übersetzt und mit Anmerkungen versehen* (Leipzig: Reclam, 1934; 4th ed., 1977).

48. Zabelle C. Boyajian, *Gilgamesh: A Dream of the Eternal Quest,* illustrated by the author and with an introduction by E. A. Wallis Budge (London: George W. Jones, 1924).

49. R. Campbell Thompson, *The Epic of Gilgamish* (London: Luzac, 1928). Stephen H. Langdon's *The Epic of Gilgamesh* (Philadelphia: University Museum, 1917), despite its title, offers only the autograph (with photographs), transliteration, and translation of 240 new lines of books I and II from a tablet purchased in 1914 by the Babylonian Section of the University of Pennsylvania's museum.

50. Reginald Campbell Thompson, *The Epic of Gilgamish: Text, Transliteration, and Notes* (Oxford: Clarendon Press, 1930).

51. Leonard in his autobiography *The Locomotive-God* (New York: Century, 1927), 248–49. Leonard also became acquainted at that time with Morris Jastrow.

52. See the jointly signed "introductory note" to William Ellery Leonard, *Gilgamesh: Epic of Old Babylonia. A Rendering in Free Rhythms* (New York: Viking Press, 1934), ix–xi, here x.

53. Will Durant, *Our Oriental Heritage* (New York: Simon and Schuster, 1954), 250–54.

2. Representative Beginnings (1941–1958)

1. Eliot's essay first appeared in *Dial*; rpt. in *Forms of Modern Fiction,* ed. William Van O'Connor (1948; rpt. Bloomington: University of Indiana-Midland, 1959), 122–24. In fact, the technique had already been exploited well before Joyce, notably by early Christian socialist writers who took the pattern of the Gospels for their modern fictions. See Theodore Ziolkowski, *Fictional Transfigurations of Jesus* (Princeton: Princeton University Press, 1972), 52–53.

2. F. L. Lucas, *Gilgamesh: King of Erech,* with twelve engravings by Dorothea Braby (London: Golden Cockerel Press, 1948). Quotation courtesy of Golden Cockerel Press Ltd.

3. D. G. Bridson, *The Quest of Gilgamesh,* with an original lithograph by Michael Ayrton (Cambridge: Rampant Lions Press, 1972)—a limited edition of 125 copies with the author's foreword, notes, and postscript. The original broadcast was positively reviewed in the London *Times,* November 30, 1954, p. 12.

4. On the earlier history of the field, see Benjamin R. Foster, "The Beginnings of Assyriology in the United States," in *Orientalism, Assyriology, and the Bible,* ed. Steven W. Holloway (Sheffield: Sheffield Phoenix Press, 2006), 44–73. Foster stresses the strong German connection.

5. Theodor H. Gaster, *The Oldest Stories in the World. Originally translated and retold, with comments* (New York: Viking, 1952), 21–51.

6. Charles Olson, *Collected Prose,* ed. Donald Allen and Benjamin Friedlander (Berkeley: University of California Press, 1997), 168–73, here 168.

7. See John Maier, "Charles Olson and the Poetic Uses of Mesopotamian Scholarship," *Journal of American Oriental Studies,* 103 (1983): 227–35; rpt. in Maier, ed., *Gilgamesh: A Reader,* 158–69, here 159–60.

8. Charles Olson, *Collected Poems: excluding the Maximus poems,* ed. George F. Butterick (Berkeley: University of California Press, 1987), 9.

9. Kramer, "The Epic of Gilgameš and Its Sumerian Sources: A Study in Literary Evolution," *Journal of American Oriental Studies* 64 (1944): 7–23.

10. Charles Olson and Frances Boldereff, *A Modern Correspondence,* ed. Ralph Maud and Sharon Thesen (Hanover, NH: University Press of New England for Wesleyan University Press, 1999), 34.

11. Ibid., 37.

12. Although Kramer's translation of the Sumerian works did not appear until the 1955 edition of *Ancient Near Eastern Texts,* Speiser of course knew the work of his colleague and, accordingly, translated the terms as "drum" and "drumstick" in his own 1950 account of tablet XII.

13. Maier, "Charles Olson," 163.

14. Olson, *Collected Poems,* 82–83.

15. Maier assumes that Olson was reworking the opening lines of the twelfth tablet in Speiser's translation, but Speiser has none of the key words appropriated by Olson from Kramer's translation in the article, and the "archaic" term *lustiness* and the "stilted 'pulsations'" are taken directly from Kramer. Maier, "Charles Olson," 164–65.

16. Olson, *Collected Poems,* 83–84.

17. Here again Maier assumes that Olson was working with Speiser's translation of the passage (Tablet XII), which he had available in his copy of the second edition of Pritchard's *Ancient Near Eastern Texts,* but Olson's poem covers precisely the lines translated by Kramer in his 1944 article, and the vocabulary in the cited passages is much closer to Kramer than to Speiser. Maier, "Charles Olson," 165.

18. Ibid., 169.

19. Olson, *Collected Poems*, 85.

20. Ibid., 149–54.

21. Maier, "Charles Olson," 175.

22. Kirby Olson, *Gregory Corso: Doubting Thomist* (Carbondale: Southern Illinois University Press, 2002), 75.

23. For a list of his courses, see Internet Archive, available at www.archive.org/search.php?query=creator%3A"Corso"%2C+Gregory, accessed July 19, 2009.

24. Theodore Ziolkowski, *Mythologisierte Gegenwart. Deutsches Erleben seit 1933 in antikem Gewand* (Munich: Fink, 2008), esp. 64–98, 127–60.

25. Bruno P. Schliephacke, *Gilgamesch sucht die Unsterblichkeit. Erzählung aus der Urzeit aller Kultur unter Verwendung keilschriftlicher Urtexte* (Munich: Drei Eichen, 1948).

26. See, for instance, Bruno P. Schliephacke, *Märchen, Seele und Sinnbild. Neue Wege zu altem Wissen* (Münster: Aschendorff, 1974).

27. Hermann Kasack, "Die Stadt hinter dem Strom. Eine Selbstkritik," in his *Mosaiksteine. Beiträge zu Literatur und Kunst* (Frankfurt am Main: Suhrkamp, 1956), 350–54, here 353. In 1942 he published an account of the dream, also included in *Mosaiksteine*.

28. Ibid., 350.

29. Hermann Kasack, *Die Stadt hinter dem Strom* (Frankfurt am Main: Suhrkamp, 1986).

30. Franzis Jordan, *In den Tagen des Tammuz. Altbabylonische Mythen* (Munich: Piper, 1950), 169–93, here 173.

31. That same year Fred Poeppig published the sixty-six-page hectographed typescript of his dramatized version of the epic, which apparently had no broader impact. Poeppig, *Gilgamesch und Eabani: Ein Drama aus dem alten Orient nach dem Gilgamesch-Epos frei gestaltet* (Bern: Troxler, 1950).

32. Joachim Maass, *Der Fall Gouffé* (Munich: Desch, 1961).

33. For an excellent review of Jahnn criticism, see Thomas P. Freeman, *The Case of Hans Henny Jahnn: Criticism and the Literary Outsider* (Rochester, NY: Camden House, 2001).

34. H. H. Jahnn, *The Ship*, trans. Catherine Hutter (New York: Scribner, 1961).

35. On the composition, see Thomas Freeman, *Hans Henny Jahnn. Eine Biographie*, trans. Maria Poelchau (Hamburg: Hoffmann und Campe, 1986), 434–50; and Gianna Zocco, *Sag an, mein Freund, die Ordnung der Unterwelt: Das Gilgamesch-Epos in Hans Henny Jahnns "Fluß ohne Ufer,"* Wiener Beiträge zu Komparatistik und Romantistik, Bd. 17 (Frankfurt am Main: Lang, 2010), 63–69. Zocco provides a survey of Jahnn's dealings with Gilgamesch in the years before the composition of *Fluß ohne Ufer.*

36. I refer by volume and page to the two-volume edition of Jahnn's *Die Niederschrift des Gustav Anias Horn* (Frankfurt am Main: Europäische Verlagsanstalt, 1959).

37. For a full discussion of the parallels, see Freeman, *Hans Henny Jahnn,* 451–68.

38. Hans Henny Jahnn, *Briefe,* 2 vols. (Hamburg: Hoffmann and Campe, 1994), vol. 1, 233.

39. Hans Henny Jahnn, *Perrudja* (Hamburg: Hoffmann and Campe, 1985), 92–93, 573–74; and *Niederschrift des Gustav Anias Horn,* 684–89.

40. *Briefe,* vol. 2, 35 (May 10, 1941).

41. Zocco, *Sag an, mein Freund,* 92–155. Zocco's work was published after my book was in production; her interpretation, more theoretically oriented, deals in greater detail with the structure of the novel and the nature of its "Dialogizität" but emphasizes the role of music somewhat less than I do. As far as Gilgamesh is concerned, it adds no points that require any changes in my text.

42. Hans Wolffheim, *Hans Henny Jahnn. Der Tragiker der Schöpfung* (Frankfurt am Main: Europäische Verlagsanstalt, 1966), 88. Wolffheim is concerned not with Gilgamesch specifically

but with more general mythic elements, including such further examples as Isis and Osiris. Zocco makes the (in my opinion) questionable suggestion that the figure of Ajax von Uchri represents a symbolic return of Tutein and, accordingly, a parallel to Enkidu's return in Tablet XII of the epic. Zocco, *Sag an, mein Freund,* 113–16.

43. See J. M. Sasson, "Musical Settings for Cuneiform Literature: A Discography," which was published as an appendix to Maier, "Charles Olson," 169–74. Sasson does not cite Berezowsky's cantata. I have not heard it myself.

44. Milos Safranek, *Bohuslav Martinů: His Life and Works,* trans. Roberta Finlayson-Samsourova (London: Wingate, 1962), 74–77.

45. Ibid., 304–9.

46. I base my discussion on the recordings of Martinů's work by the Slovak Philharmonic (Naxos, 2002) and the Prague Symphony Orchestra (Supraphon, 2007).

47. Safranek, *Bohuslav Martinů,* 308.

48. See Heinz Spiegelmann, "Baumeisters Illustrationen nahöstlicher Epen. Figurentypen und Erzählstruktur," in *Willi Baumeister. Figuren und Zeichen,* ed. Heinz Spiegelmann, catalogue for the 2005 exhibition at the Bucerius Kunst Forum in Hamburg (Ostfildern, Germany: Hatje Cantz Verlag, 2005), 42–55.

49. See most recently the exhibition catalogue *Willi Baumeister. Gilgamesch,* Freunde der Staatsgalerie Stuttgart—Stuttgarter Galerieverein e.V. (Ostfildern, Germany: Hatje Cantz Verlag, 2010), with text by Corinna Höper.

3. The Popularization of Gilgamesh (1959–1978)

1. *The Epic of Gilgamesh.* An English version with an introduction by N. K. Sandars (London: Penguin, 1960). The translation was reprinted with revisions in 1964 and 1972.

2. *Das Gilgamesch-Epos.* Neu übersetzt und mit Anmerkungen versehen von A. Schott und W. von Soden (Stuttgart: Reclam, 1958).

3. *Das Gilgamesch-Epos.* Eingeführt, rhythmisch übertragen und mit Anmerkungen versehen von Hartmut Schmökel (Stuttgart: Kohlhammer, 1966).

4. I base my account on Franz M. T. Böhl, "Einleitende Bemerkungen der 'Erläuterungen' zum 'Gilgamesch-Epos' " (1958), rpt. in *Das Gilgamesch-Epos,* ed. Karl Oberhuber (Darmstadt: Wissenschaftliche Buchgesellschaft, 1977), 312–24, here 317.

5. Bernarda Bryson, *Gilgamesh: Man's First Story* (New York: Holt, [ca. 1985]). It is worth noting that BookRags offers an online study pack to accompany Bryson's version of the epic.

6. Christine Hopps cites the novels as an example for the positive reinstatement of the Sumerian goddesses. Hopps, "Mythotextuality and the Evolution of Ideologies: The Reuse of the 'Epic of Gilgamesh' in North American Texts" (Diss. Université de Sherbrooke, 2001), 106–18.

7. I have not seen these two German works and know them only from the listing in Jürgen Joachimsthaler, "Die Rezeption des Gilgamesch-Epos in der deutschsprachigen Literatur," *Literatur und Geschichte. Festschrift für Erwin Leibfried,* ed. Sascha Feuchert, Joanna Jablkowska, and Jörg Riecke (Frankfurt am Main: Peter Lang, 2007), 147–61, here 155.

8. This work was published along with other adaptations for children in a series of "Fairy Tales and Myths" by Verlag der Autoren (Frankfurt am Main, 1981).

9. Hope Glenn Athearn, *Gilgamesh: A Novel* (San Francisco: San Francisco State College, 1970). The work appears to exist only as a typescript in the SFSU Library and not to be available in published form.

10. *The Road to Science Fiction,* ed. James Gunn, 2 vols. (New York: New American Library, 1977), 1:5–7.

11. Johannes Bobrowski, *Gesammelte Werke,* ed. Eberhard Haufe, 4 vols. (Stuttgart: Deutsche Verlags-Anstalt, 1987), 1:31.

12. Herbert Mason, *Gilgamesh: A Verse Narrative* (New York: Mentor/New American Library, 1972).

13. This information is based on the author's cover remarks: Michel Garneau, *Gilgamesh: théâtre* (Montréal-Nord: VLB, 1976).

14. Information kindly provided by the author (by email, December 15, 2010), who introduces his show with comments on the Sumerians, the sexagesimal system, and the invention of writing.

15. Hopps suggests that Garneau reinstates the Sumerian goddesses in their original role of authority, but that is, in my view, at most a secondary tendency in a work devoted principally to friendship. Hopps, "Mythotextuality," 81–95.

16. The numbered cantos appeared individually from 1927 on, and the entire cycle was finally published in 1978 as a single 800-page volume by Johns Hopkins University Press (Baltimore). All Louis Zukofsky material copyright Paul Zukofsky; the material may not be reproduced, quoted, or used in any manner whatsoever without the explicit and specific permission of the copyright holder.

17. Charles Bernstein, "Introduction," in Louis Zukofsky, *Selected Poems,* American Poets Project 22 (New York: Library of America, 2006), xiii. This volume also contains the full text of "A-23" (119–51).

18. See the analysis in Mark Scroggins, *Louis Zukofsky and the Poetry of Knowledge* (Tuscaloosa: University of Alabama Press, 1998), 185–225.

19. Scroggins, *Louis Zukofsky,* 228. I cite "A-23" according to the text in the first edition, *"A" 22 & 23* (New York: Grossman, 1975), 33–60.

20. It is not in any sense a "word-for-word translation," as claimed in Joe Moffett, *The Search for Origins in the Twentieth-Century Long Poem: Sumerian, Homeric, Anglo-Saxon* (Morgantown: West Virginia University Press, 2007), 11.

21. See the chapter "Obscurity, Solipsis, and Community in '*A*'-23" in Scroggins, *Louis Zukofsky,* 226–56.

22. I am unable to agree with Scroggins, who believes that "for the most part the reader is hard-pressed to find the principle of continuity in these baffling but sonically exquisite lines" of this poem. Scroggins, *Louis Zukofsky,* 39.

23. I translate from Gian Franco Gianfilippi, *Gilgamesh. Romanzo* (Milan: Gastaldi, 1959). I have been unable to find any information whatsoever about the author.

24. Guido Bachmann, *Gilgamesch* (Wiesbaden: Limes, 1966).

25. Giuseppe Furlani, "L'Epopea di Gilgameš come inno all'amicizia," *Belfagor. Rassegne di varia umanità* 1 (1946): 577–89.

26. David Halperin, *One Hundred Years of Homosexuality and Other Essays on Greek Love* (New York: Routledge, 1990), 76–81. See also Susan Ackerman, *When Heroes Love: The Ambiguity of Eros in the Stories of Gilgamesh and David* (New York: Columbia University Press, 2005); and Jean Fabrice Nardelli, *Homosexuality and Liminality in the Gilgameš and Samuel* (Amsterdam: Hakkert, 2007).

27. I base my account of this chapter on the German translation (under the same English title) by Peter Urban-Halle in *Schreibhefte. Zeitschrift für Literatur* 59 (2002): 157–61.

28. Rudolf Pannwitz, *Gilgamesch—Sokrates. Titanentum und Humanismus* (Stuttgart: Klett, 1966).

29. Vera Schneider, *Gilgamesch* (Zurich: Origo, 1967).

30. *A Perfect Vacuum* has been translated into English by Michael Kandel (New York: Harcourt, 1979). I translate here from the German edition, *Die vollkommene Leere,* trans. Klaus Staemmler (Frankfurt am Main: Insel, 1973).

31. The story is included in the collection: Stanisław Lem, *Imaginary Magnitude,* trans. Marc E. Heine (New York: Harcourt, 1984), here 103.

32. John Gardner, *The Sunlight Dialogues* (New York: Vintage, 1987).

33. See Greg Morris, "A Babylonian in Batavia: Mesopotamian Literature and Lore in *The Sunlight Dialogues*," in *John Gardner: Critical Perspectives*, ed. Robert A. Morace and Kathryn Van Spanceren (Carbondale: Southern Illinois University Press, 1982), 28–45; rpt. in *Gilgamesh: A Reader*, ed. John Maier (Wauconda, IL: Bolchazy-Carducci, 1997), 148–57, here 149.

34. I cannot agree with Morris's central argument that Clumly and the Sunlight Man are analogous to Gilgamesh and Enkidu or with his tentative identification of other figures in the novel with Mesopotamian gods.

35. Hopps discusses the novel as an example of "mythotextual dialogue." Hopps, "Mythotextuality," 209–21.

36. See Frank R. Ardolino, "The Americanization of the Gods: Onomastics, Myth, and History in Roth's *The Great American Novel.*" *Arete* 3/1 (Fall 1985): 37–60.

37. Philip Roth, *The Great American Novel* (New York: Holt, Rinehart, and Winston, 1973), 253–56.

38. For Roth's own explanation of his political intentions in the novel, see Philip Roth, *Reading Myself and Others* (New York: Farrar, Straus and Giroux, 1975), 75–92, esp. 86–91.

39. See Marianthe Colakis, "Gilgamesh and Philip Roth's Gil Gamesh," in *Gilgamesh: A Reader*, ed. Maier, 260–70. I am not persuaded, for instance, by the author's identification of Mike "the Mouth" Masterson with both Enkidu and Utnapisthim or of Gil's death in the Soviet Union as an analogy to Gilgamesh's reign in the underworld. Colakis points more plausibly to a possible parallel between baseball and the *pukku* and *mikku* of the Sumerian myth, which some scholars have interpreted as a ball and mallet and not as a drum and drumstick.

40. Rhoda Lerman, *Call Me Ishtar* (Garden City, NY: Doubleday, 1973).

41. On Lerman, Gardner, Olson, and other American novelists of the 1970s who use Mesopotamian themes, see John R. Maier and Parvin Ghassemi, "Postmodernity and the Ancient Near East," *Alif: Journal of Comparative Poetics* 4 (1984): 77–98.

42. Heide Göttner-Abendroth, *The Dancing Goddess: Principles of a Matriarchal Aesthetics*, trans. Maureen T. Krause (Boston: Beacon, 1991).

43. I base my discussion on the recording by the Swedish Radio Symphony (November 15, 1973) for Dacapo Records (DCCD 9001) with accompanying text. Since no author is mentioned, I assume that the text was created by the composer.

44. On the CD *"America Sings"* by the Society of Composers, Inc. (featuring five American composers), Capstone Records, 1992, CPS-8613.

45. I have not seen the score, which was published by the Seesaw Music Corporation, 1974. I know it only from Maier's bibliography in: *Gilgamesh: A Reader*, ed. Maier, 456.

46. *Épopée de Gilgamesh*. Adaptation du texte, musique et chant: Abed Azrié. Auvidis Ethnic B6800 1977/1994.

47. *L'Épopée de Gilgamesh*. Texte établi d'après les fragments sumériens, babyloniens, assyriens, hittites et hourites. Traduit de l'arabe et adapté par Abed Azrié (Paris: Berg International, 1979). The two Arabic translations are the ones cited by Azrié in his bibliography.

48. Maier and Ghassemi, "Postmodernity and the Ancient Near East," 84.

4. The Contemporization of Gilgamesh (1979–1999)

1. See, for instance, Michael B. Oren, *Power, Faith, and Fantasy: America in the Middle East, 1776 to the Present* (New York: Norton, 2007), 542–44; and Zachary Lockman, *Contending Visions of the Middle East: The History and Politics of Orientalism* (Cambridge: Cambridge University Press, 2010), 182–214.

2. Edward Said, *Orientalism* (New York: Pantheon, 1978), 11–15.

3. Anselm Kiefer, "Gilgamesch und Enkidu im Zedernwald," *Artforum* 19 (June 1981): 67–73. Auction listing available at www.christies.com/LotFinder/lot_details.aspx?intObjectID=303451, accessed December 14, 2010. For reproductions, see *Anselm Kiefer: Bücher 1969–1990*, ed. Götz Adriani (Stuttgart: Editions Cantz, 1990), 256–59.

4. Christine Hopps presents the episode an example of "mythotextual dialogue." Hopps, "Mythotextuality and the Evolution of Ideologies: The Reuse of the 'Epic of Gilgamesh' in North American Texts" (Dissertation, Université de Sherbrooke, 2001), 191–97.

5. Ludmila Zeman, *Gilgamesh the King* (London: Heineman, 1992).

6. Hopps sees in Zeman's omission of goddesses a valorization of males and a christianizing shift toward a single male deity. Hopps, "Mythotextuality," 162–70.

7. Irving L. Finkel, *The Hero King Gilgamesh* (London: British Museum Press, 1998).

8. *Gilgamesh: Translated from the Sîn-Lequi-Unninnî Version* by John Gardner and John Maier (New York: Vintage, 1985), 3–54, here 3–4.

9. William L. Moran, *New York Times Book Review,* November 11, 1984, 13.

10. Joseph Campbell, *The Hero with a Thousand Faces,* Bollingen Series XVII (Princeton: Princeton University Press, 1971), 185–87, here 185.

11. Tracy J. Luke and Paul W. Pruyser, "The Epic of Gilgamesh," *American Imago* 39:2 (Summer 1982): 73–93, here 74.

12. See the editor's preface in: Rivkah Schärf Kluger, *The Archetypal Significance of Gilgamesh: A Modern Ancient Hero,* ed. H. Yehezkel Kluger (Einsiedeln: Daimon, 1991), 11–12.

13. Siegfried Hermerding, *Das Gilgamesch-Epos in gnostischer Sicht* (Berlin: Rocamar, 1988); Andreas Schweizer-Vüllers, *Gilgamesch. Von der Bewußtwerdung des Mannes. Eine religionspsychologische Deutung* (Zurich: Theologischer Verlag, 1991); Werner Papke, *Die geheime Botschaft des Gilgamesch* (Augsburg, Germany: Weltbild, 1993); Andreas Schweizer, *Das Gilgamesch-Epos. Die Suche nach dem Sinn* (Munich: Kosel, 1997); and Horst Obleser, *Gilgamesch. Ein Weg zum Selbst* (Waiblingen, Germany: Stendel, 1998). I have not read these works, which are not easily available and which I know only from their citation in Jürgen Joachimsthaler, "Die Rezeption des Gilgamesch-Epos in der deutschsprachigen Literatur," *Literatur und Geschichte. Festschrift für Erwin Leibfried,* ed. Sascha Feuchert and others (Frankfurt am Main: Peter Lang, 2007), 156n58–59.

14. Günter Dux, *Liebe und Tod im Gilgamesch-Epos: Geschichte als Weg zum Selbstbewußtsein des Menschen* (Vienna: Passagen Verlag, 1992), 46–47.

15. Gertrud Leutenegger, *Lebewohl, Gute Reise* (Frankfurt am Main: Suhrkamp, 1980). The song, printed in full at 13–14, is played in actual performance.

16. Robert Silverberg, *Gilgamesh the King* (New York: Arbor House, 1984).

17. Hopps reads Silverberg as a key example for the devaluation of the goddesses and emphasizes the politicization of religion. Hopps, "Mythotextuality," 151–62.

18. Translated here and below from Harald Braem, *Der Löwe von Uruk* (Munich: Piper, 1988).

19. Thomas Mielke, *Gilgamesch. König von Uruk* (Munich: Schneekluth, 1988).

20. I refer to the introduction and English translation: Eduardo Garrigues, *West of Babylon,* trans. Nasario García (Albuquerque: University of New Mexico Press, 2002).

21. Joël Cornuault, *Éloge de Gilgamesh* (Mussidan: Fédérop, 1992).

22. I give the text in my own translation from: Alain Gagnon, *Gilgamesh* (Chicoutimi, Canada: Éditions JCL, 1986).

23. Hopps argues that Gagnon replaces the Sumerian pantheon with a single male god. Hopps, "Mythotextuality," 171–79.

24. I base this paragraph on Ortega's publicity sites on the Web, videos of his two TV series, and the three volumes of his *Khol.*

25. José Ortega, *Khol, Gilgamesh y la muerte* (Murcia: ERM, 1990), 364.

26. Peter Huchel, *Gesammelte Werke in zwei Bänden,* ed. Axel Vieregg (Frankfurt am Main: Suhrkamp, 1984), 1:229.

27. Donald Hall, *The One Day and Poems, 1947–1990* (Manchester, U.K.: Carcanet, 1991), 229–36, here 235–36.

28. *Gilgamesch-Epos.* Illustrationen von August Ohm; mit einem Vorwort von Hanns Theodor Flemming (Munich: Deutscher Kunstverlag, 1995).

29. I have not read or heard this work, which I know only from reports on the Internet and in reference works.

30. See "Arsenije Milosevic" at wikipedia.com (July 26, 2009).

31. I have not seen or heard these three works, which I know only from their citation in the bibliography in *Gilgamesh: A Reader,* ed. John Maier (Wauconda, IL: Bolchazy-Carducci, 1997).

32. I quote the text and the composer's comments, in my own translation, from the text accompanying the CD recording by the orchestra and chorus of the Teatro dell'Opera di Roma, EMI Classics, EMI Italiana, 1992.

33. Carl Sagan, *Contact* (New York: Simon and Schuster, 1985), 393–99.

34. Michael Ondaatje, *In the Skin of a Lion* (New York: Knopf, 1987). Hopps cites both this work and its sequel, *The English Patient,* as "mythotextual dialogues." Hopps, "Mythotextuality," 221–45.

35. Jacques Cassabois, *Le Roman de Gilgamesh.* Préface de Jean Bottéro (Paris: Albin Michel, 1998).

36. Brenda W. Clough, *How Like a God* (New York: Tor, 1997).

37. Hopps accuses Ferry of turning aggressively against the Sumerian texts and dethroning the goddesses. Hopps, "Mythotextuality," 139–51.

38. See "Gilgamesh at SOAS," available at www.soas.ac.uk/nme/research/gilgamesh/, accessed December 30, 2010.

39. See "The Recordings," available at www.soas.ac.uk/baplar/recordings/, accessed December 30, 2010.

5. Gilgamesh in the Twenty-First Century (2000–2009)

1. Damian Morgan, *Gil's Quest* (Mascot, Australia: Koala Books, 2003); Geraldine McCaughrean, *Gilgamesh the Hero* (Oxford, U.K.: Oxford University Press, 2003); Nicole Leurpendeur, *Das Gilgamesch-Epos* (Baar-Ebenhausen, Germany: AJA Verlag, 2006); and Jacques Cassabois, *Le premier roi du monde—L'épopée de Gilgamesh* (Paris: Hachette Jeunesse, 2004).

2. Hans Zimmer and Wolfgang Bartel, *Gilgamesch macht Ärger. Musical für junge Menschen* (Boppard: Fidula, 2003).

3. Frank Groothof, *Gilgamesj* (Amsterdam: Nieuw Amsterdam, 2006).

4. Now available also as a single volume: Burkhard Pfister, *Gilgamesch,* graphic novel (Halle: Projekte Verlag Cornelius, 2010).

5. *The Epic of Gilgamesh: A New Translation, Analogue, Criticism,* ed. Benjamin R. Foster, Norton Critical Edition (New York: Norton, 2001).

6. Stephen Mitchell, *Gilgamesh. A New English Translation* (New York: Free Press, 2004), 2. Copyright © 2000 by Stephen Mitchell. Reprinted with permission of Free Press, a Division of Simon and Schuster, Inc. All rights reserved.

7. *Das Gilgamesch-Epos.* Neu übersetzt und kommentiert von Stephan M. Maul (Munich: Beck, 2005).

8. Walther Sallaberger, *Das Gilgamesch-Epos. Mythos, Werk und Tradition* (Munich: Beck, 2008).

9. Derrek Hines, *Gilgamesh* (London: Chatto and Windus, 2002), x.

10. Letter of January 17, 2011, from Derrek Hines to Theodore Ziolkowski.

11. Derrek Hines, *Gilgamesh: The Play* (London: Oberon, 2007).

12. Edwin Morgan, *The Play of Gilgamesh* (Manchester: Carcanet, 2005), vii.

13. *Gilgamesh: A Verse Play.* Poetry by Yusuf Komunyakaa, concept and dramaturgy by Chad Gracia (Middletown, CT: Wesleyan University Press, 2006), xi.

14. Jenny Lewis, "From Brain to Breath: Writing Poetry for the Theatre," *World Literature Today* 83 (November/December 2009): 26–28, here 28. The play—*After Gilgamesh* (Cardiff: Mulfran Press, 2011)—, which I have not read, had its premiere performance in March 2011 at the Pegasus Theatre, Oxford. Lewis's article includes two poems from her work.

15. Hillary Major, "Gilgamesh Remembers a Dream," Hollins University *Album,* spring 2000; rpt. in Benjamin R. Foster, ed., *The Epic of Gilgamesh* (New York: Norton, 2001), 219.

16. Anne-Marie Beeckman, *Gilgameš* (Nérac, France: Pierre Mainard, 2008).

17. I cite Huntington's article, "The Clash of Civilizations?" from the reprint in *America and the World: Debating the New Shape of International Politics* (New York: Council on Foreign Relations Press, 2002), 43–70, here 43.

18. See, for example, Harvey Cox, *The Future of Faith* (New York: HarperOne, 2009).

19. See Theodore Ziolkowski, *Modes of Faith: Secular Surrogates for Lost Religious Faith* (Chicago: University of Chicago Press, 2005).

20. I. M. Diakonoff and N. B. Jankowska, "An Elamite Gilgameš Text from Argistihenele, Urartu (Armavir-blur, 8th century B.C.)," *Zeitschrift für Assyriologie* 80 (1990): 102–23.

21. Heidemarie Koch, "Elamisches Gilgameš-Epos oder doch Verwaltungstäfelchen?" *Zeitschrift für Assyriologie und vorderasiastische Archäologie* 83 (1993): 219–36.

22. *He Who Saw Everything: A Verse Translation of the Epic of Gilgamesh,* trans. Robert Temple (London: Rider, 1991), x–xiv, here xiv.

23. See the editor's introduction to the reprint of Temple's introduction in *Gilgamesh: A Reader,* ed. John Maier (Wauconda, IL: Bolchazy-Carducci, 1997), 318–19.

24. Patrice Cambronne, *Gilga.Mesh, ou La Gloire entre la Force et le Destin* (Bordeaux: William Blake, 2000).

25. Cambronne's reconciliation of knowledge of self and other in sacred drama is close to Benjamin Foster's rather Hegelian stages 1, 2, and 5 in the ascent to knowledge: definition of opposites, apparent unity, and (after rejection and disintegration) redefinition of unity. Foster's essay, "Gilgamesh: Sex, Love, and the Ascent of Knowledge," which Cambronne does not appear to know, was first published in *Love and Death in the Ancient Near East,* ed. John H. Marks and Robert M. Good (1987); it is reprinted in *Gilgamesh: A Reader,* ed. Maier, 63–78.

26. Raoul Schrott, *Gilgamesh. Epos* (Munich: Hanser, 2001).

27. Theodore Ziolkowski, "Literary Variations on Bach's Goldberg," *Modern Language Review* 105/3 (2010): 625–40.

28. *Gilgamesch—König und Vagant. Das Epos nacherzählt und kommentiert von Gerhard Begrich* (Stuttgart: Radius, 2003).

29. The term has a particular resonance in German ears, thanks to its occurrence in Goethe's *Faust* (l.3348) and as the title of Hans Erich Holthusen's influential postwar work on modern literature, *Der unbehauste Mensch: Motive und Probleme der modernen Literatur* (Munich: Piper, 1951).

30. Stephan Grundy, *Gilgamesh* (New York: William Morrow, 2000).

31. Paola Capriolo, *Qualcosa nella notte. Storia di Gilgamesh, signore di Uruk, e dell'uomo selvatico cresciuto tra le gazzelle* (Milan: Mondadori, 2003).

32. Joan London, *Gilgamesh* (New York: Grove, 2001).

33. Christian Kracht, *1979* (Cologne: Kiepenheuer and Witsch, 2001), 183.

34. Elizabeth Arthur, *Bring Deeps* (London: Bloomsbury, 2003).

35. Elizabeth Arthur, "Inspiration behind Brings Deep," formerly available at www.bloomsbury.com/Authors/article.aspx?tpid=446&aid=6097, accessed June 25, 2009.

36. Saddam Hussein, *Zabibah and the King,* ed. Robert Lawrence (College Station, TX: Virtualbookworm.com, 2004). On the identification of the novel with Gilgamesh, see David Damrosch, *The Buried Book: The Loss and Rediscovery of the Great Epic of Gilgamesh* (New York: Henry Holt, 2006), 254–69.

Conclusion

1. See, for instance, my studies: *Virgil and the Moderns* (Princeton: Princeton University Press, 1993); *Minos and the Moderns* (New York: Oxford University Press, 2008); *Ovid and the Moderns* (Ithaca, NY: Cornell University Press, 2005); and *Fictional Transfigurations of Jesus* (Princeton: Princeton University Press, 1972). As suggested earlier, only the Cretan Minotaur begins to approximate Gilgamesh as a figure that has invaded popular culture. For an extensive bibliography of scholarly studies of Gilgamesh to 1960, see L. de Meyer, "Introduction bibliographique," in *Gilgameš et sa légende,* ed. Paul Garelli (Paris: C. Klincksieck, 1960), 1–30. De Meyer's collection restricts itself to editions, scholarly articles, and translations. The bibliography in John Maier's *Gilgamesh: A Reader* goes much further and includes popular versions as well as various literary adaptations. Maier, ed., *Gilgamesh: A Reader* (Wauconda, IL: Bolchazy-Carducci, 1997), 357–491.

2. Theodore Ziolkowski, *Minos and the Moderns: Cretan Myth in Twentieth-Century Literature and Art* (New York: Oxford University Press, 2008).

3. Jean-Marcel Humbert, *Egyptomania: Egypt in Western Art, 1730–1930* (Ottawa: National Gallery of Canada, 1994). I am not aware of a treatment of literary or more broadly cultural Egyptomania.

4. Volkert Haas, "Die literarische Rezeption Babylons von der Antike bis zur Gegenwart," in *Babylon: Focus mesopotamischer Geschichte, Wiege früher Gelehrsamkeit, Mythos in der Moderne,* ed. Johannes Renger, 2nd International Colloquium of the Deutschen Orient-Gesellschaft, March 24–26, 1998, in Berlin (Saarbrücken: SDV, 1999), 523–52.

5. Elisabeth Frenzel, *Stoffe der Weltliteratur. Ein Lexikon dichtungsgeschichtlicher Längsschnitte,* 9th ed. (Stuttgart: Kröner, 1998), 719–22.

6. On its influence in Western literature, see Robert Irwin, *The Arabian Nights: A Companion* (London: Allen Lane, 1994), 236–92.

7. Benjamin R. Foster, "Assyriology and English Literature," in *From the Banks of the Euphrates: Studies in Honor of Alice Louise Slotsky,* ed. Micah Ross (Winona Lake, IN: Eisenbrauns, 2008), 51–82.

8. Theodore Ziolkowski, *Modes of Faith: Secular Surrogates for Lost Religious Belief* (Chicago: University of Chicago Press, 2007), 9–26.

9. Ibid., 147–73.

10. Eckart Frahm's "Images of Assyria in Nineteenth- and Twentieth-Century Western Scholarship," in *Orientalism, Assyriology and the Bible,* ed. Steven W. Holloway (Sheffield: Sheffield Phoenix Press, 2006), 74–94, is almost entirely restricted to Germany and Anglo-America. Henrietta McCall's "Rediscovery and Aftermath," in *The Legacy of Mesopotamia,* ed. Stephanie Dalley (New York: Oxford University Press, 1998), 183–213, focuses on the popular reception, principally in England. McCall mentions a few French contributions—notably the paintings of Delacroix (*La mort de Sardanapale,* 1827) and Dégas (*Sémiramis construisant Babylone,* 1860)—but makes the point that the French publications with their exquisite plates—for example, the five-volume *Monument de Ninive* (1849–50)—were, unlike the books in England, prohibitively expensive and inaccessible to the general public.

11. Theodore Ziolkowski, *Heidelberger Romantik: Mythos und Symbol* (Heidelberg: Winter, 2009), 62–66, 181–91.

12. Ziolkowski, *Modes of Faith,* 83–146 ("Pilgrimages to India").

13. Harvey Cox, *The Future of Faith* (New York: HarperCollins, 2009).

INDEX